D0463592

ONE SIGNAL
PUBLISHERS

ATRIA

PANDEMIC, INC.

CHASING *the* CAPITALISTS *and* THIEVES WHO GOT RICH WHILE WE GOT SICK

J. DAVID McSWANE

ONE SIGNAL
PUBLISHERS
———
ATRIA
NEW YORK • LONDON • TORONTO • SYDNEY • NEW DELHI

ONE SIGNAL
PUBLISHERS

ATRIA

An Imprint of Simon & Schuster, Inc.
1230 Avenue of the Americas
New York, NY 10020

Copyright © 2022 by J. David McSwane

All rights reserved, including the right to reproduce this book or portions
thereof in any form whatsoever. For information, address Atria Books Subsidiary
Rights Department, 1230 Avenue of the Americas, New York, NY 10020.

First One Signal Publishers/Atria Books hardcover edition April 2022

ONE SIGNAL PUBLISHERS / ATRIA BOOKS and colophon are
trademarks of Simon & Schuster, Inc.

For information about special discounts for bulk purchases,
please contact Simon & Schuster Special Sales at 1-866-506-1949 or
business@simonandschuster.com.

The Simon & Schuster Speakers Bureau can bring authors to your live event.
For more information, or to book an event, contact the Simon & Schuster
Speakers Bureau at 1-866-248-3049 or visit our website at www.simonspeakers.com.

Interior design by Dana Sloan

Manufactured in the United States of America

1 3 5 7 9 10 8 6 4 2

Library of Congress Control Number: 2022930533

ISBN 978-1-9821-7774-4
ISBN 978-1-9821-7776-8 (ebook)

For those who managed full-time jobs and full-time parenting,
and for the children who endured their parents

CONTENTS

AUTHOR'S NOTE

I KNOW WHAT you're thinking.

Why, after all we suffered, would I read a book about the COVID-19 pan-demic? I already experienced it!

Not like this, you haven't. The story that will unfold in these pages is as outrageous as it is true. What happened to us was unacceptable and heartbreaking, yes, but I do not wish to depress you further. No, anger is more useful than despair.

My goal in writing this book is twofold. First, to make some sense of the larger system churning over our heads and its role in our nation's missteps—that is to say, unfettered capitalism and its byproduct, greed.

Second, for posterity. Some unbelievably stupid and tragic things happened. The story of how America's obsession with capitalism left us for dead while pirates plundered is at once anger-provoking and yet, at times, so twisted that all we can do is laugh. I managed to get a front-row seat to some of it. I pray that this story will serve as a guide to future generations on what exactly they shouldn't do if faced with such a crisis.

The purpose of this book is not to retrace a definitive account of all things COVID, nor is it to remind people of all the disappointments and horror that we by now have drowned out with Netflix, alcohol, and Peloton bikes. I'll spare you the grotesque postmortem and thumb-sucker dissertations on policy, economics, and global trade.

Instead, I invite you on a journey through the shady networks of brokers, scammers, investors, and profiteers who did insane things to get rich while our nation suffered an incalculable loss of life and global standing. They are the inhabitants of a world we encouraged, we created, long before we elected a documented swindler to the Oval Office. This is who we are, though I pray it is not all we can be.

It began on a reporting assignment in April 2020, which involved a mask broker and a private jet. Upon my return, I felt what I'd seen was too bizarre to be molded into the conventions of routine journalism. In fact, so much of what happened, from the White House down to city hall, begged for something more. I set out on an immersive first-person quest of sorts to get it all down. In doing so, I defy some convention. Investigative reporters are not usually invited to crack wise, though these were, as we know, unprecedented times. I have in many instances forgone the antiquated notion of wishy-washy two-sides reporting that fails to hold to account partisan hacks and welcomes false equivalency. I neither belong to nor curry favor with any political party, though neither do I profess to be some robotic arbiter of objectivity. There was one party and one administration handling the arrival of the coronavirus, and its failure to rise to the occasion is definitive and damning. I have treated this legacy with the reverence it deserves. Members of the other party also made mistakes, and I have pointed them out.

I have resisted the notion that capitalism itself is to blame for all of this, though I understand the temptation. President Donald Trump's admitted effort to downplay the virus to prevent a stock market scare is a strong point to consider. We will never know how many lives might have been spared if the president were as concerned with charts of rising American deaths—which he dismissed as "it is what it is"—as he was charts-tracking the S&P 500 Index.

It is impossible to disentangle the callous and inept response of the Trump administration from the broader social, political, and economic forces that also contributed to America's failure. Can we realistically cast blame on our system entirely when it is unfathomable that either Presidents George W. Bush or Barack Obama would have handled the pandemic as poorly as Trump did?

To piece these stories together, I reviewed many thousands of records and interviewed more than one hundred people, mostly on the record. With the exception of one already published example, I do not quote anonymous sources or allow such a source to stake a significant claim. Any background conversations I had served the purpose of bulletproofing a certain context or to help me better understand a complex issue or timeline.

There are scenes and chapters in this book that draw from what I saw and heard and what is in my notes and voice memos. I could not be everywhere, however, so I rely at times on others' reporting at ProPublica, the *New York Times*, the *Washington Post*, STAT News, Kaiser Health News, and many more. I am grateful for the work of these many journalists, and I've cited them often.

If this sort of tale still sounds appealing, strap in. Our journey begins, as with so many disappointments, in Washington, D.C.

PANDEMIC, INC.

CHAPTER **1**

THE PRIVATE JET

ROBERT STEWART JR. STRODE WITH PURPOSE through the exit of the private wing of Dulles International Airport, a glinting Legacy 450 Flexjet whirring ahead of us on the tarmac. He turned to offer a caveat.

"I'm talking with you against the advice of my attorney," he said.

It was the morning of Saturday, April 26, 2020—the year a plague upended our world and I fell into the absurd realm of those trying to profit from the despair. Stewart was sturdy, early thirties, filling out a tailored and shiny gray suit. On his lapel, he wore an American flag pendant emblazoned with the word, in all caps, "VETERAN." I couldn't see his face behind his mask, or through my fog-filled eyeglasses, but his tone registered as a blend of bravado and trepidation.

It felt like foreboding, as if embracing a dare to avoid a truth. I pictured him as a boy, winking from atop the high dive at his friends below, knowing the belly flop he's about to perform will leave him red and stung, yet warm with the perverse validation of having done it. The inquiry that led me to be here was honest, though I can't say altogether naive. I suppose I had dared him, in a way.

I had called just the day before to ask how he intended to fulfill the terms of a $34.5 million contract he'd inexplicably landed with the U.S. Department of Veterans Affairs, which operates the nation's largest network of hospitals, serving 9 million military veterans and their families. The deadline was nearing for him to produce 6 million N95 respirators, the medical-grade masks, which were in scarce supply but crucial to protecting healthcare workers toiling with a contagion about which we knew almost nothing. He said he was about to prove to me and the rest of the world that he was legitimate, and, in fact, he'd soon be boarding a private jet to Chicago to oversee delivery of the masks to a VA warehouse just outside the city.

The stakes were high. He was a brand-new, never-before-hired, out-of-left-field, yet suddenly bona fide federal contractor. The deal had been awarded without the usual competitive bidding, under emergency guidelines that lifted red tape meant to weed out fraud, patronage, and waste. The federal government was desperate, Americans were terrified, and Stewart offered a solution with just a few emails. If he delivered, more federal contracts were sure to come, and he and his company might see generational wealth and a steady stream of business.

I expressed amazement, and some natural skepticism, and asked to tag along on the flight. Eager to prove himself, he agreed.

His was one of the biggest contracts the federal government had awarded in early 2020, when the Trump administration finally opened the financial spigot to address a politically inconvenient pandemic. Every state, local, and federal agency and hospital was locked in fierce competition to buy masks, driving up prices. Extreme demand, scarce supply, and an inept federal government were congealing into a colossal "shit show," as one supply chain expert described it to me.

So there we were, strangers ascending the narrow stairs to a private jet, replete with leather captain's chairs and free snacks and liquor shooters, on a quest to find masks and fortune and maybe even save the world.

His attorney had a late night and didn't check in with Stewart that morning to confirm he'd make the $22,000-a-day private jet that Stewart had booked for this caper. We were lifting off without him. That was fine by me. Lawyers have a way of slowing things down.

Stewart was indeed a military veteran but, I'd later learn, not the decorated Marine he'd claimed to be on paperwork fed to the federal government. He exuded the trappings of a successful federal contractor—the suit, the easy use of arcane contract lingo, the private jet, the limited liability corporation in Falls Church, Virginia, with proximity to the Pentagon and its steady outflows of public money.

He claimed that 6 million 3M N95s were loaded in a Los Angeles warehouse with his name on them. The shipment would be coming into the Chicago area that weekend, he said, and I'd be there to watch it all go down.

But Stewart's aura belied the fact that he clearly had no idea what he was doing. I couldn't begrudge him this. Who among us truly knows what we're doing? In a crisis, no less? We rise to our occasions. This is America. The land of opportunity. A magical place with magical thinkers. Pull up your bootstraps. Take chances. Fake it till you make it. That's why I was there, after all, to see how the hell he managed to get his hands on something almost no one seemed able to get. If he pulled it off, it would be a great American story. If he failed, it would be the type of story I tend to write—an investigation.

The federal government and Congress had failed to shore up the national stockpile. What supplies were in the stockpile were already depleted. In New York, Governor Andrew Cuomo had decried on television the Wild West market that had emerged in the absence of federal preparation and response. He compared fighting against other states and cities for precious masks and ventilators to entering into a bidding war on eBay. In California, Governor Gavin Newsom circumvented the federal mess and signed a huge contract to buy direct from a Chinese company, a move that would earn him some criticism but maybe wasn't altogether the worst idea. In Maryland, the governor was conducting a sort of clandestine mission to get supplies to keep them from being commandeered by the Federal Emergency Management Agency (FEMA). In Texas, well, they were being Texas.

The cable news networks had reported numerous anecdotes of healthcare workers improvising personal protective equipment, sewing their own masks and donning trash bags instead of medical-grade gowns. At the same time, federal law enforcement was beginning to nab price gougers who stocked up on supplies of hand sanitizer and Clorox wipes, or used car salesmen who tried to sell masks that didn't exist to struggling hospitals and government agencies. Then came the counterfeit masks made in China and peddled onshore by homegrown profiteers, which made their way into hospitals and private medical offices.

As the Trump administration made clear, our fates were left to the free market, where fear distorted our sense of reason and left us prey to the predators.

From this chaos rose alluring opportunities for those bold enough to chase the cash. It was a rare and tempting thing—the opportunity to make a killing and at the same time be rewarded with the satisfaction that your work could be credited with saving lives. Many mask brokers, schemers, counterfeiters, and fakes I'd talk to in the coming months would in some way describe themselves as such capitalist saviors. Stewart was one, and as a Black owner of a small veteran-owned firm— a double advantage when bidding on government contracts—he was in a damn fine spot to make something of the mess.

Still, Stewart was an odd recipient for such an important contract. He had been named a key arbiter of a simple device that was the best defense against a virus that killed with horrifying complexity. Yet he had zero experience sourcing medical supplies. None. He was not a mask distributor, nor an importer of record, nor a freight forwarder. He knew little about how to navigate the supply chain, which almost always leads back to China, where American manufacturers had outsourced to keep wages low, prices attractive, and profits high. When I encountered his deal in the federal purchasing data in mid-April, along with dozens of other peculiar deals we'd track down at ProPublica, I wondered what the contracts told us about the federal government's plan to combat COVID-19. It smelled of panic. It seemed inconceivable in any other context, but I wondered: Was the plan to cast money out indiscriminately, like chum into the sea, and just see what bites?

These weren't just any masks to which Stewart claimed to have access. They were the gold-standard N95 respirators manufactured by 3M, the vaunted American company that brought us Scotch tape and the Post-it note. Capable of filtering out 95 percent of particles, the N95 mask, most associated with dusty DIY home repair jobs, had become an unexpected ticket to riches—if you could find a cache of them and sell to the highest bidder. Stewart saw early in this dark chapter of American history, as many other profiteers did, that these once-disposable face coverings had become indispensable. Total seller's market.

N95s used to cost about $1 apiece. But Stewart had gotten the VA to agree to pay almost $6 apiece. At the time, that was about a 350 percent markup. Multiply that margin by a quantity of 6 million and you end up with a fat payday for a guy who'd never been awarded a federal contract, let alone one into the tens of millions. If it worked, he could buy his own private jet, and, I would soon find, he was considering it. This sort of margin was the very definition of price gouging, something that would swiftly result in criminal charges during a localized catastrophe, such as a hurricane. But the moment was too large, too chaotic to know for certain whether this was the result of one man's avarice or out-of-control market conditions. We'd seen nothing like this—a national emergency that simultaneously threatened every community, every business, every American. Whether it was gouging or not, federal and state and local agencies signaled they would be willing to pay.

Once inside the tiny fuselage, Stewart sat on the starboard side facing the cockpit, and I sat on the port side facing him, careful to stay as far from his air as I could manage. I did not yet have a legitimate filtering respirator and had agreed to not hold ProPublica liable for risks I'd accepted with open eyes.

"This is about helping folks," Stewart began to tell me. "About being able to say to my mom and dad, 'Thank you, for all the work you did.' Now we are about to help six million people—well, six million masks."

As the jet rolled up to the runway, I asked him again.

How did you get your hands on 6 million N95 masks?

I did not expect his answer.

His story had changed entirely. He no longer had claim to the masks he said were waiting for him at the port of Los Angeles. He said they'd been sold out from under him the night before. Poof, gone, or so he claimed.

Why are we flying to the VA distribution center outside Chicago, then? I asked. Why didn't he cancel the flight?

"It was kind of a faith thing," he said, shrugging as he clutched an old Bible as if it were a government contractor's sacred talisman.

He said he didn't know how, but he was going to deliver 6 million N95s and meet his deadline, Sunday at midnight. He'd been working the phones all night and had a promising lead on an investor who could secure the masks, for a fee. The deal involved "the attorney general of Alabama," he said, and one way or another he was going to deliver.

Faith had gotten him this far. Besides, look at the jet. Surely this was someone who meant business.

"It comes down to me and my credibility," he said. "Why would anybody pay twenty-two thousand dollars to have a ghost box delivery? It doesn't make any sense."

He was right. It didn't make sense. I gazed out the window as the metal wings grabbed the wind and ascended over my broken country. Our quilted patchwork of land and cities and roads and people floated by, and I thought of the devastation coming for it, of what it meant if this trip went bust. The projections were dire. Any chance of "flattening the curve" had all but diminished. Nature was coming for us with fatal intent.

Nurses and doctors below were terrified as patients diagnosed with COVID-19, the disease caused by SARS CoV-2, came rolling in. We had not yet lost hundreds of thousands of lives, but it was clear we would. Within the VA hospital system, nurses and doctors were being rationed per shift just one surgical mask, those thin blue masks that offer far less protection than an N95. Nurses with whom I exchanged emails and texts were being gaslighted by their superiors, who dismissed legitimate news reports of this dire shortage as "fake news." But the healthcare workers saw it firsthand, and each time they donned the subpar masks, they wondered if any help was on the way, if this might be their final shift.

But help had been outsourced. To Stewart and others. Help was working on a wing and a prayer. And there I was, a passenger aboard a delusion, floating over a nightmare.

The journey that day with Stewart would get yet more weird and disheartening. And his story would launch me off on a wild chase to catalogue the opportunism, greed, and incompetence that frustrated the American response to COVID-19 at every turn. It would take me to

California, Texas, Ohio, Colorado, Chicago, New York, Pennsylvania, and into secret warehouses, stakeouts at industrial strip malls, and, for a moment, into the cannabis industry. Some of the journey might have been funny, if the consequences were not so dire.

As for Stewart, I may never understand why he would do what he was about to do. Maybe it was arrogance. Maybe he sincerely believed he could pull it off. Maybe it was, as he said, an act of faith—a belief that will and a dash of providence might make him an overnight millionaire and a hero to America in its time of need. Such a feat deserves to be observed, to be retold.

I wish I could have told that story, but no, this story is something worse.

What began as journalistic curiosity about supply shortages and a quest to find answers for Americans who were dying or trapped in nursing homes and apartments would morph into a nearly two-year examination of America's underlying conditions. This is the story of the bad guys of the COVID-19 era. It is the story of us. In the eyes and actions of many men I would get to know from April 2020 and into the fall of 2021—it was mostly men—I saw an ugliness that hides beneath our national mask. I saw greed masquerading as entrepreneurial spirit, selfishness as rugged individualism, opportunism as patriotism, recklessness as bravery. I saw hope, as well, and love, but someone else can write that book.

In reviewing thousands of records tracing the COVID-19 era, I found confirmation of what many might have felt: Our obsession with unfettered capitalism hurt us every step of the way.

Long before the pandemic, the national stockpile had been financially hobbled by partisan brinksmanship—prudence supplanted with political expedience. What money was left to prepare for a national emergency—hoarding masks, ventilators, gloves, and more—had been tied up with profit-driven corporations. One company leveraged its monopoly on an anthrax treatment to exact ever-increasing prices on the federal government, depleting a budget that could have been used to buy N95 masks. Ventilators, machines that breathe for patients whose respiratory systems were decimated by the virus, had run out not for a lack of planning, but because of poor oversight of companies that place profit above all else. The small company the government hired to produce the machines had been purchased by a multinational conglomerate, which increased prices and delayed production.

The Trump administration took belated action in spring 2020 and issued the first of nearly $40 billion in contracts for everything from masks to buildings to pharmaceuticals and test kits. The earliest deals were awarded under emergency measures, without bidding. Various federal agencies would claim they vetted thousands of private contractors who emerged to reap the benefits of our devastation. But story after story would prove this was a lie. Records obtained through state public records laws, the federal Freedom of Information Act, and congressional inquiries would show contracts were handed out to anyone with an email address and the pocket change to register a company in their home state. Political connections got many companies to the front of the trough. In this deluge, Trump lieutenants steered contracts to allies and untested companies, wasting money, and, more important, time. Similar deals were cut at the state and local levels.

The supply shortage was not a foregone conclusion. It had been predicted for many years, under both Republican and Democratic administrations. The country was in deep trouble long before the case counts began to rise on the coasts in early 2020, yet there was a tiny window in which a few people tried to lock down supplies for hospitals before the profiteers could get them and hold us hostage.

Subpar and counterfeit masks that claimed the same level of protection as an N95, but were in fact dangerous and ineffective, flooded into this vacuum. The federal government, flat-footed and making up rules on the fly, tried to catch up and catalogue which masks could be used in hospitals and which were garbage. This ad hoc regulation was slow and often ineffective. What barriers did exist were overcome by creative mask brokers who discovered they could repackage poor-performing masks and sell them to hospitals anyway, threatening healthcare workers the American people would at first praise, and later abandon.

Efforts to stop the spread of the virus by closing nonessential businesses were undermined by entrenched capitalist interests and division-stoking politicians and the fringes to which they are captive. In Texas and elsewhere, the sentiment that it was better to keep commerce going, even during the most terrifying months, even if it threatened American lives, was an acceptable trade-off. As with the mad hunt for supplies, the patchwork of states that favored opening their economies too soon versus those that chose science would cancel out any meaningful national response, allowing a pandemic that could have lasted for weeks and months to become an era of intense division and despair.

Our crimes—against morality, civility, and the law—played out in the ubiquity of the twenty-four-hour partisan news cycles, on social media, and in small-time schemes perpetrated by our neighbors. Testing, already delayed by government bungling, was further set back as FEMA hired a company that had formed that very week to deliver testing supplies to all fifty states and territories. The company's founder had a documented history of fraud allegations against him, and the company had no medical expertise or, truly, any expertise at all. Instead of delivering tubes, I would find the company conspired to deliver unusable, contaminated plastic mini soda bottles, thrown together with shovels in a nondescript warehouse. The company got away with more than $10 million. Americans got screwed. Forget the money. This scheme, and many others, wasted time when time was being measured in body bags.

To keep businesses afloat and ensure income for tens of millions of Americans, Congress passed the Paycheck Protection Program. The program would rush nearly $8 billion out the door, much of it into the hands of unsavory actors who used the windfall, not to support employees, but to buy themselves sports cars, jewelry, homes, and yachts. One man took taxpayers for more than $7 million and bought a mansion and a fleet of cars before absconding to Europe. When he was arrested, he said his actions were permissible under the Trump administration and that the transfer of power to President Joe Biden had prompted him to flee. Meanwhile, many businesses and employees that needed that relief waited months for help.

If there is a silver lining, it was the rapid development of vaccines. They were scientific miracles, yes, but also the result of massive investments of taxpayer money and government resources over decades. Their development bestowed obscene riches on a few wealthy people who had made prescient investments to benefit from such chaos. Meanwhile, taxpayers paid for much of their development, most of their production and deployment, and will continue to pay for booster shots and new shields against viral variants in perpetuity, all to the enrichment of shareholders and company executives.

For all their promise and salvation, the vaccines themselves were undermined by the preexisting and profitable machinery of misinformation. Those who had mastered the craft of profiting from medical quackery and lies sprang to action, spreading fear about vaccines while promoting disproven or dubious treatments they packaged and sold to the detriment of the American people.

COVID-19 would render in high definition the contrasts of an inequitable nation. At the same time families waited in miles-long lines for groceries at food banks, the pandemic economy created about 500 new billionaires. Overall, U.S. billionaires saw their wealth surge 62 percent, or $1.8 trillion. In contrast, the relief package Congress passed to keep poor and middle-income Americans from poverty totaled just a little more, about $2.2 trillion.

When the world shut down in early 2020, workers at meatpacking plants were deemed essential. Tyson Foods placed full-page ads in national and regional newspapers, proclaiming, "The food supply chain is breaking. We have a responsibility to feed our country. It is as essential as healthcare. This is a challenge that should not be ignored. Our plants must remain operational so that we can supply food to our families in America. This is a delicate balance because Tyson Foods places team member safety as our top priority."

At the same time, according to court records, a Tyson plant manager in Waterloo, Iowa, organized a "cash buy-in, winner-take-all betting pool for supervisors and managers to wager how many employees would test positive for COVID-19." Whoever won the kitty should spend it on therapy.

Across the country, hundreds of meatpacking plant workers, many of them low-paid immigrants and refugees, died from the virus and more than 50,000 were sickened. The plants kept churning out meat. The Occupational Safety and Health Administration, asleep at the wheel for much of the pandemic, softened rules that allowed the plants to underreport deaths, and the agency was slow to inspect facilities where workers died, if it did at all.

In countless ways, COVID-19 would bring the hypocrisy of our stated American ideals into focus. Unemployment skyrocketed, yet the stock market rallied for those wealthy enough to have skin in the game. Millions of Americans couldn't pay the rent, but purchases of second homes spiked as the wealthy fled cities. The deep-seated fissures in our healthcare and education systems, and physical infrastructure itself, were laid bare as the virus took its outsized toll on poor people and communities of color.

———

For all we didn't know about the virus, it sure knew a hell of a lot about us. Even as I sat in disbelief aboard that private plane in April 2020, the first of many on-the-ground reporting missions during the pandemic, I could not fathom just how bad it would become. Call it arrogance, ignorance, or American elitism—I won't argue. But I hadn't allowed myself to worry until that moment. Cynical as we investigative reporters can be, I still held a sort of blind faith that America, despite our current discourse, was just better prepared. Always. We'd be fine. We would come together, like in World War II.

But with each reporting trip, this faith would diminish. And as the cases and the death counts rose and plateaued and rose again, and the schemes and steady flow of profits continued to reveal themselves, I came nearer and nearer to answering the central question our children and history will ask of us:

How did the most advanced, the wealthiest country in the world, with just 4 percent of the global population, at one point come to account for one in five COVID deaths and nearly a quarter of all cases worldwide?

It was the cost of doing business.

CHAPTER **2**

"HINDSIGHT JUST ISN'T WHAT IT USED TO BE"

AS WITH ALL MONUMENTAL FUCKUPS, it was no one's fault. Or at least there was no one eager to own their share of the blame.

Former Republican congressman Denny Rehberg and I had been dancing around the question for an hour. It was the only question that mattered.

"Knowing what you know now . . ." I began.

We had talked about the Strategic National Stockpile and his role in cutting its funding, about the Tea Party budget battles a decade before the pandemic, about that time he played drums alongside Skunk Baxter of the Doobie Brothers for a fundraiser at the Hard Rock Cafe. We covered the Obama administration, cattle ranching in the Rockies, the Affordable Care Act, about how he used his wealth to bring Popeyes chicken to his home state. Some of the questions I asked the retired representative from Montana were tough, others not so much. He had answered with the self-assurance of someone who'd spent his life in the public eye, in state government and in Congress, as a villain in unflattering headlines, and a hero in others.

But it was the obvious hypothetical that threw him.

"What would you do," I asked, "if you had to do it all over again?"

"If we only, uh, had stuff to do all over again," he said. "What would we do differently? Yeah. That's an interesting, interesting question. It's been probably debated in a lot of different arenas."

Our arena was specific. I was asking if he regretted his part in Congress's cuts to funding for the Strategic National Stockpile, whose depleted stores of emergency equipment a decade later proved a devastating barrier to protecting healthcare workers from a contagion and which spawned a madcap national hunt for medical supplies.

"Hindsight just isn't what it used to be," he continued, an awkward chuckle piping through the phone.

Let's refresh our memories.

It was 2011, in Washington, D.C., amid a partisan war that hadn't yet gone nuclear. After winning control of the House amid the Tea Party wave, Republicans had united to combat anything then President Barack Obama tried to do. Atop the kill list was the Affordable Care Act, Obama's defining legislation, passed the year before when the Democrats controlled Congress. The ACA, or Obamacare, sought to bring healthcare benefits to millions of Americans through an expansion of federal health insurance programs and a subsidized private exchange.

Even though Obamacare was projected to lower the nation's overall healthcare costs and decrease the national deficit, Republicans opposed it, citing a philosophical devotion to small government and minimal taxes.

They resolved to use the power of the purse to thwart the Obama administration, especially at the agency that would administer the expensive and unwieldy program: the U.S. Department of Health and Human Services (HHS). With control of just one chamber, Republicans couldn't directly dismantle Obamacare. They could, however, hold the entire government hostage.

Led by House Speaker John Boehner and Senate minority leader Mitch McConnell, Republicans tipped the scale by leveraging the debt ceiling. In years prior, raising the debt ceiling—a limit on the amount of debt the U.S. Treasury can take on—was perfunctory. It occurred typically without debate to allow the Treasury to keep borrowing and paying the country's obligations. But in 2011, Republicans created a standoff, saying if Democrats didn't agree to spending reductions equal to an increase in the debt ceiling, they'd refuse to raise it. Refusing to raise the government's ability to pay its bills would force a government shutdown and place the country itself on the path to defaulting on its debt, likely decimating the broader economy and job markets. It was a significant threat not just to Democrats but to the nation.

This standoff forced Obama and congressional Democrats to agree to a compromise, the 2011 Budget Control Act. It allowed a temporary increase of the debt ceiling and formed a bipartisan "super committee" to find ways to drive down spending. If that super committee failed to agree to major cuts, the bill would trigger automatic across-the-board cuts at just about every government agency, known as "sequestration." This ticking time bomb was conceived to force some sort of compromise, because no one in their right mind wanted sequestration. This assumed right minds prevailed in Washington.

The Republicans' top target, HHS, is a sprawling umbrella agency presiding over not just social welfare programs and Obamacare but less-contested functions such as the Centers for Disease Control and Prevention, the National Institutes of Health, and the Food and Drug Administration. And nestled deep down in this budget, where discretionary spending for countless government functions are delineated, are many programs that most Americans don't know about, don't care about, and if all goes well, don't need to learn about.

Among them: the Strategic National Stockpile. Originally housed under the CDC, it was at first a limited repository for vaccines and drugs that either needed to be hoarded away as insurance or because manufacturers would stop making them without continued government investment. It was born of science fiction, inspired at least in part by former president Bill Clinton's reading of a Richard Preston novel in the late 1990s about a terrifying virus that vexed scientists. Clinton had sought the counsel of real-life scientists, who advised it was a good idea to prepare for outbreaks of a novel virus or biological attack. Nature has all sort of untold terrors lying in wait.

The stockpile's earliest work involved building an inventory of "push packs" ahead of the Y2K scare, supplies that could be dispatched anywhere in the country in twelve hours to respond to a crisis somehow wrought by a bunch of ones and zeros. The stockpile played a small role in the response to the September 11, 2001, terrorist attacks and the subsequent anthrax letter attacks, events that sent its funding upward amid rising fears of biological terrorism.

The stockpile's role would expand under Presidents George W. Bush and Obama, both of whom recognized the need to prepare for an inevitable pandemic, where supply chains can disintegrate, and basic equipment like masks and gloves become precious commodities. Its mission was creeping and, in the early days, so too was the stockpile's funding, thanks to bipartisan support for the notion that it would be ideal to mitigate deaths in the event of a contagion.

By 2011, oversight of the national stockpile fell to a House subcommittee, controlled by Rehberg, which marked up spending bills and reported them to the full House Appropriations Committee. Such committees are the first stop where legislative dreams can live or die. It's in these hearings where the president's lofty budgets crash into political reality—and personalities.

Rehberg is a Republican of a bygone era. This is not to say he wasn't as right-leaning as, say, Ted Cruz plays on Fox News when he isn't absconding to Cancun. This is to say it was just easier to tell what Rehberg actually believed.

From Billings, Montana, Rehberg is your archetypal rural conservative, mustachioed and often wearing flannel or an earth-toned blazer, concerned foremost with matters of the wallet and home rule. A fifth-generation rancher, he'd earned his GOP bona fides the western way, with a story of bootstrapping wealth and on-the-ground politicking. After working as a staffer in the Montana state senate and a stint working for a congressman in D.C., Rehberg returned to ranching, at one point overseeing 500 cattle and 600 goats. In the mid-1980s, Rehberg was elected and served in the state legislature. By the early 1990s, he had been appointed and later elected Montana's lieutenant governor, where he argued inside all fifty-six Montana counties that local governance was the best governance. It seemed obvious then that Rehberg's political ethos left little room for expensive, federally controlled programs with no obvious benefit to him or his constituents.

For instance, in January 1994, when he was still lieutenant governor, Rehberg told a group of county commissioners during a discussion about healthcare: "The problem with AIDS is, you get it, you die. So why are we spending any money on people that get it, when we can't even take care of the people who we can fix because we don't have enough money? Yet society has made the determination that we are going to spend money on AIDS."

He later said his comment was taken out of context, but the quote struck at his rationale of how budgets work. Something's got to lose. As well, I suppose it said something about his thinking on public health responses to epidemics.

In 2000, Rehberg won Montana's sole seat in the U.S. House of Representatives. Over six terms, he supported and introduced the era's popular conservative measures such as cuts to CDC funding for HIV/AIDS programs in favor of abstinence-only education and reforms that environmentalist groups said catered to oil and gas industry at the expense of public lands. He also targeted Pell Grants, which help poor students pay for a college education, and the free school lunch program, which enables poor children to eat. That they were popular and very visible programs didn't, in Rehberg's view, preclude them from being scrutinized.

Nothing was off the table. Everything could be on the chopping block.

By 2011, Rehberg's committee focused in on the Obama administration's budget request for HHS. The administration asked for $892 billion for the entire HHS enterprise, and tucked in there was a request for about $655 million for the national stockpile. That was about $59 million more than the previous year, an increase the Obama administration said would help replenish supplies and pharmaceuticals that had expired or been doled out to states in response to the H1N1 "swine flu" epidemic of 2009.

Relative to the administration's total request for HHS, the stockpile accounted for just .073 percent of spending. Chump change.

As Republicans forced Democrats to negotiate deep spending cuts, Rehberg authored legislation that set the floor for funding the stockpile at $522.5 million, about $132 million less than Obama requested and about a 12 percent cut overall; this promised to strain the stockpile's ability to, well, stockpile.

The Senate offered more, and in a compromise bill between the two chambers Congress approved just $534 million, about a 10 percent cut from the prior year. It was the first substantial cut to the stockpile since its funding stabilized after September 11, and its funding wouldn't recover until the coronavirus claimed its first victims in the United States in early 2020.

This marked the beginning of a ratchet effect. The next year, the two parties failed to come to a budget compromise, and mandatory "sequestration" cuts forced the Obama administration to decide where to spread the pain. At the CDC, it was 5 percent across the board.

As part of a wide array of cuts, in 2012, the administration proposed deeper cuts to the stockpile, a decrease of $48 million.

A year after he pushed to lower the stockpile's funding, Rehberg now questioned the decreased funding.

"Disaster preparedness is something that has been very important to me," Rehberg said during a budget hearing he led in March 2012. "And I noticed that the president's budget proposes a reduction in the Strategic National Stockpile by 9 percent or $48 million in the fiscal year 2013. I just would like to have you explain how such a large reduction can possibly not impact the national preparedness posture."

Kathleen Sebelius, Obama's HHS secretary, responded but didn't quite answer: "The budget request will allow the Centers for Disease Control and Prevention to replace the high-priority expiring countermeasures, such as smallpox and antibiotics for the treatments of anthrax."

In other words, facing forced austerity and brinkmanship, the federal government chose to focus what funding it maintained on expensive medical treatments for a potential but unlikely biological attack, not for restocking front-line defenses to an inevitable viral pandemic—supplies such as respirators and masks, ventilators, and testing supplies. In the years to come, that philosophy would send hundreds of millions of dollars that could have gone to pandemic preparedness instead to one pharmaceutical company that increased prices on its anthrax cocktail as it edged out competitors and held the stockpile captive to its demands.

The next year, facing another manufactured budget crisis aimed at the ACA, the Obama administration proposed an additional $38 million in cuts to the stockpile, though it acknowledged, "Reduction could result in fewer people receiving treatment during an influenza pandemic."

And thus, nominal savings were achieved at an extraordinary cost.

Republicans may point to 2012, when Democrats began defunding the stockpile. Democrats may point to the hostage negotiation that set it off the year before. Americans should point to all of the above. For in this way, the shameful and enduring failure to prepare for COVID-19 is among the most consequential bipartisan accomplishments of the twenty-first century.

———

I was beginning to annoy Rehberg, as is my nature.

"You're asking the same question six different ways," Rehberg said.

"We're sort of trained to do that," I responded. "The reason it matters is, setting politics aside, there's a narrative either way on who owns the onus of trimming the stockpile. Was it the Obama administration? Was it this Tea Party wave and an appropriations act that was, you know, just one of many? Or was it a little bit of both? I'm genuinely interested."

"If we could have predicted this situation, we might have made a different decision," Rehberg said, relenting, only to add a qualifier: "But based upon the decision at the time, I took the recommendation of the Obama administration. Yeah, so maybe—maybe they missed it. Maybe they didn't see COVID coming."

In fact, it was predicted, voluminously and repeatedly, with clarity and understanding from both parties.

Starting in 2003, the Government Accountability Office had warned that the nation and states need to study supply chains and stockpile pandemic response gear.

In 2005, President George W. Bush read about the 1918 so-called Spanish flu, and it scared the hell out of him. His administration soon drafted a seventeen-page playbook dubbed the "National Strategy for Pandemic Influenza" and called for $7.1 billion in emergency spending. A key piece of that strategy included ensuring that the national stockpile and state stockpiles had caches of personal protective equipment such as masks and gloves.

The next year, in May 2006, the nonpartisan Congressional Budget Office released an assessment of the potential costs of a national pandemic. Many of the conclusions were drawn from an outbreak of an earlier mysterious coronavirus, first observed in China, in the early 2000s. This coronavirus caused severe acute respiratory syndrome and was thus named SARS-CoV-1. It had at this point been contained after killing nearly 800 people worldwide, a fraction of the millions that would perish years later to its viral relative, SARS-CoV-2, which causes COVID-19.

That report foretold that hospitals' cost-saving practice of forgoing large inventories of supplies for on-demand supply shipments— a so-called just in time strategy—would create a nightmarish scramble for supplies.

The urgent need to stock up and prepare was again brought to the fore in 2009, when the Obama administration worked to contain the H1N1 swine flu epidemic, which killed an estimated 12,000 Americans. The administration had doled out to states and hospitals about 75 percent of its entire supply of N95 respirators and about a quarter of its less effective face masks to help stop the virus.

Its inventory would not recover. What remained was left to expire and rot in federal warehouses.

Following H1N1—by all accounts nature's warning shot—the CDC commissioned a study that outlined in stark terms just how screwed we'd be if we didn't replenish emergency response supplies. The study made sweeping observations about likely breakdowns between local, state, and federal agencies.

It now reads like prophecy.

"Delays and conflicts in federal guidance on respiratory protection (N95) led to confusion . . ." scientists wrote a decade before COVID-19.

"States experienced significant challenges with the N95 supply chain. . . ."

"There should be a central repository of N95s which is replenished for future events. . . ."

Yet, the very next year, beginning in Rehberg's committee, lawmakers from both parties, with this information in their hands, politics on their minds, their eyes open wide to the consequences, allowed our first line of defense to wither.

CHAPTER **3**

"WE'RE IN DEEP SHIT"

THERE IS AN AXIOM IN AMERICAN JOURNALISM that goes something like this: There is always a guy.

Whatever the assignment, however arcane the subject, there is always one person who has devoted obsessive amounts of time to understanding it, to collecting evidence and data and sharing it with anyone who will listen. To the casual observer, these people may seem too odd to be taken seriously. Their years of being ignored may have made them a bit too gruff or obscene for the average bureaucrat to bear. But that doesn't make them wrong.

When it comes to masks, Mike Bowen is the guy.

Tall and sturdy despite his years, with soft green eyes that betray his Texas-tough persona, Bowen walked confidently through the side-entrance glass doors of Prestige Ameritech, a crumbling factory and warehouse outside Dallas. He passed the counter where security used to be, down a long tiled hallway with an atrium overhead, scattered light popping through grime-frosted glass. He turned right past a trash can that collects rain when it comes and marched along the next unlit hallway, atop loose, wrinkled, and stained blue and pink carpet from the

1980s. To his left stood the dusty glass showcase Prestige Ameritech staged in 2010 for a ribbon-cutting ceremony with Governor Rick Perry, who'd come to show off Texas's bustling job market and the rare resurrection of an American factory. The masks and respirators inside the case, propped up and folded next to their branded boxes, had not been touched since Perry's visit a decade earlier.

Bowen, sixty-two, had worked in this factory, the largest remaining domestic manufacturer of medical masks, since the carpet in its sales office was new and arguably fashionable. The office, along with the vast and better-maintained manufacturing warehouse behind it, had changed hands several times over the years. But Bowen somehow stuck to the place and the dream dying within it.

First, it belonged to Tecnol Medical Products, which Bowen recalls supplied about nine out of every ten surgical masks in the United States. In 1997, medical supply giant Kimberly-Clark acquired Tecnol, its facilities, and hundreds of employees. Bowen stayed on as an executive. But the company soon downsized and closed the plant. Bowen found other work. That was until 2005, when a former Tecnol colleague and soon-to-be business partner invited Bowen aboard a new company with plans to buy back the mothballed plant at a discount.

Together, the two resolved to resurrect domestic mask manufacturing, which had been offshored due to globalization and cheaper labor and production costs in China and Mexico. Hospitals and their market-dominant buying groups wanted to pay the lowest price possible, and big companies including 3M, Honeywell, Cardinal Health, and Medline looked to foreign materials and production in a race to the bottom. Bowen believed that the company could buck the trend and attract dedicated American customers with a simple and—so he thought—unassailable argument: Domestic mask production is vital to national security.

It was idealistic, if not altogether naive. And the years since had not been kind.

On January 22, 2020, in the dim and empty wing that was once the accounting department, Bowen arrived at his office and dropped his backpack on a large oak desk, where reports and old letters and surgical masks and trinkets coalesced into entropy, a reflection of the memories, anger, and concerns bopping around his head.

Buried in stacks and files around him, Bowen kept every warning he'd ever fired off—to Congress, to three presidential administrations, to newspapers, to officials overseeing the national stockpile, and to an array of other agencies that would soon blast from obscurity into the American consciousness.

In 2007, he wrote to veteran Texas congresswoman Kay Granger: "[V]irtually all of the U.S. medical face mask companies have gone offshore, leaving the U.S. dependent upon foreign governments who, in a pandemic, will retain face masks for their own populations, leaving Americans unprotected."

In June 2010, he wrote several letters to President Barack Obama's White House: "In a 1918 type pandemic it is likely that the US won't have surgical masks unless you encourage the rebuilding of the US mask making industry. . . ." Also, "[U]nless the US mask supply is brought back under American control, Americans may die needlessly in future pandemics."

In October 2013, he wrote to Senator Patrick Leahy of Vermont: "If there is a severe pandemic, due to the fact that it is imported and foreign controlled, the US mask supply could be cut off."

And in a letter dated February 2017, Bowen took a shot at speaking then-president Donald Trump's language: "90% of the United States protective mask supply is currently FOREIGN MADE!"

At industry conferences and in phone calls and emails with federal officials, for thirteen years, Bowen had made the case. But by 2019, all but one office in the federal emergency response apparatus had tuned him out. That agency was the Biomedical Advanced Research and Development Authority—BARDA.

Immensely important yet chronically overlooked, with about a billion and a half dollars a year, BARDA funds research and development of vaccines and other medical countermeasures in anticipation of epidemics and nuclear or biological attacks. It's a sister agency of the Strategic National Stockpile, under HHS, but BARDA's money and work are tied up with the biomedical industry and in scientific pursuit—not in buying masks.

If Bowen's only motivation was to sell his products, he'd endeared himself to the wrong agency, and he knew as much. But Bowen appreciated that someone was listening and didn't think he was nuts. Due in part to his persistence, BARDA leaders came to share his concerns, and for his self-effacing candor, they came to even like the mask fanatic down in Texas. For years, they'd quietly encouraged Bowen to keep up the pressure because nothing was being done within HHS. He became, in essence, an unofficial spokesman, and an outspoken one at that.

Through years of emails, texts, and phone calls, Bowen had established a rapport with BARDA's longest-serving director, Robin Robinson. When Robinson left that post after the 2016 election, that relationship fell to his successor, an accomplished immunologist named Dr. Rick Bright.

Having run the agency's influenza program since 2011, Bright was more than familiar with Bowen. And though the two wouldn't find occasion to meet in person, over the next three years Bowen and Bright became something approaching friends, bonded by a common fear.

In the early weeks of January 2020, Bowen glued himself to the virus that had found its way into humans at a giant market in Wuhan, China.

As with previous outbreaks or bad flu seasons, Bowen watched for clues to see if the company should speed up production. What little we knew, in part because the virus was new, and in part because China was concealing its true wrath, was concerning: The virus appeared to spread and attack efficiently, ravaging the respiratory systems of its victims.

But it was what he saw in his company's own sales data that scared the hell out of him.

In the second and third weeks of January, Prestige Ameritech had noticed a dramatic uptick in small purchases of N95s from a seldom-used corner of its website. The company's bread and butter was whole-sale production for large buyers of cheap surgical masks, but the company decided to dabble in by-the-case sales after multiple inquiries from patients who'd been treated at MD Anderson Cancer Center in Houston. The site was not a moneymaker, taking in just $1,900 in 2019. And because it was a tiny part of the business, Bowen's daughter, a member of the sales team, set up her phone to ding each time a purchase had come through; this ensured smaller shipments were handled promptly outside of the routine business. By the second week of 2020, the dings were picking up, and by the third, they were incessant. Curious, Bowen and his daughter pulled up the purchase data and noticed that many of the surnames on the orders seemed to be Asian. Some customers had come back multiple times to order, and the orders were growing in quantity. Bowen suspected the orders were coming from Chinese Americans who were sending masks to family in China and Hong Kong. In three decades in the mask business, he'd seen nothing like it.

It was time to write to Bright.

Later that day, January 22, Bowen fired off an email that, had the Trump administration acted upon it, might have saved innumerable American lives.

"Rick, We still have four like-new N95 manufacturing lines . . ." Bowen began.

"To activate them, we'd need more people, raw materials, emergency [approval] and large, non-cancelable orders. Reactivating these machines would be very difficult and very expensive but could be achieved in a dire situation and with government help."

He closed: "Rick, I hope that your and my predictions about the foreign made US mask supply don't come true."

Fifteen hundred miles away in Washington, D.C., Bright was fighting hard and losing badly.

He had been pleading with senior HHS officials to obtain genetic sequencing information from the Chinese CDC and a specimen of the virus from infected people. If both were disseminated through the country's large patchwork of public and private laboratories, the United States could swiftly develop a diagnostic test, key to containing spread, and begin work on a potential vaccine. Following updates from the scientific community and media reports in early January, he could see that

COVID-19 was highly contagious, likely more fatal than the average flu, and that the country needed to prepare for imminent spread beyond China. He'd requested funding, more people, more urgency, but senior officials at HHS were downplaying the virus both in private and in public.

He was among the world's leading experts in vaccines, therapeutics, and testing, but within his own chain of command had come to be viewed as a nuisance. His relationship with his boss, Assistant Secretary for Preparedness and Response Robert Kadlec, "the ASPR," had been strained since 2017, when the two had clashed over how lucrative BARDA contracts were being steered to politically connected firms outside of traditional contract vetting.

Bright viewed their standing as not great, nor altogether acrimonious, but simply tolerable. So Bright was stunned to find himself in 2020 being sidelined by Kadlec and other HHS leaders from key meetings and discussions about a threat over which BARDA had direct purview and expertise.

Kadlec, and the resources he commanded as ASPR, were focused on repatriating and quarantining U.S. citizens coming back from China, part of the fantastical hope that the virus wouldn't penetrate U.S. borders. Bright questioned the strategy.

The virus was already hopping the globe, in fact, with the first confirmed case outside of China arriving January 12 in Thailand. The World Health Organization was already advising other nations to prepare.

Bright had nudged Kadlec the next week, on January 18, to assemble cross-agency, senior-level meetings called the Disaster Leadership Group. Those meetings would bring leaders and key people from BARDA, HHS, CDC, the Defense Department, and the National Institutes of Health together, to get on the same page and free up and direct resources. Such meetings had been beneficial during past outbreaks, including response to the Ebola and Zika virus scares in 2014 and 2015. But Kadlec wanted to slow-play it, writing to Bright in an email that he was "not sure if that is a time-sensitive urgency."

Among several good reasons to hold the meeting, cash needed to be moved around. Bright controlled BARDA, but its hands were tied, its money already dedicated to work with the private sector. It wasn't yet clear who would be doing what, or who was paying for it, though it was clear to Bright that someone should be doing something and there should be a boatload more funding to do it.

Another key priority: making sure the country had ample stocks of N95 respirators, surgical masks, cotton swabs, nitrile gloves—all materials that were susceptible to a potential supply chain disruption. If hospitals were overrun, Bright understood, the increased use of these items to treat patients—"the burn rate"—would far exceed the supply chain's ability to restock shelves. Cheap personal protective equipment was the single best defense. Without it, healthcare providers would be exposed to a contagion the U.S. government knew little about, and Americans would die.

Supply chain issues fell to ASPR's Critical Infrastructure and Protection division, which, Bright was astonished to find, hadn't mobilized in any significant way.

It was in this bureaucratic tangle that Bright received Bowen's January 22 email from Texas.

Bright read it and thought maybe such an update from the front line, from the mask guy, could at least speed up the supply angle. Hoping to guilt his colleagues into doing their jobs, Bright did what any civilized office dweller would do: He CC'd a bunch of people.

"Mike. Thank you for reaching out to me about this important resource and plan . . ." Bright wrote to Bowen and an audience of other key HHS officials.

"I am connecting you all directly in hope of expediting a conversation . . ." he continued. "Thank you for all that you are doing. Your leadership in this area remains an important resource for our nation and public health. . . ."

A few hours passed, and just minutes before the end of the workday, Laura Wolf, director of Critical Infrastructure and Protection, responded to Bowen's email, writing, "I don't believe we as an [sic] government are anywhere near answering those questions."

"I'm dealing with a sick kiddo and that may spill over into tomorrow," Wolf wrote.

Bright's passive-aggressive email seemed to have worked, though not with the immediacy he had hoped. Wolf pushed the discussion until two days later, Friday, January 24. After speaking with Wolf, Bowen followed up Friday evening with an exhaustive breakdown of his read on potential mask shortages and of what his facility could do if the United States made formal commitments to purchase masks off machines— elegantly simple but expensive machines that needed engineers to be fired up.

"It took me all day to write this," Bowen wrote to Bright and Wolf. "My phone rang off the wall with mask requests. Last week nobody wanted to hear me. This week, I'm quite popular."

Bowen had plenty of business coming from private buyers, he explained. Too much business. He was simply trying to spur the government to buy masks, if not from him, then from one of the many competitors he had shared with Bright. Prestige Ameritech could activate new assembly lines for N95s, but it would only make financial sense if the U.S. government committed to buying off those lines through the crisis and beyond. The last time Bowen had fired up new production lines, hiring hundreds of workers, was during the 2009 H1N1 swine flu epidemic. After the virus disappeared, so did the government investment. His business partner, Dan Reese, was forced to wind down the machines and lay off 150 employees. It brought the men to tears. The company narrowly avoided bankruptcy.

The next day, Saturday, Bowen sent another warning to Bright and Wolf, forwarding an email he'd received from a government official in Hong Kong. The official wanted to buy more than 10 million N95s—an astronomical outlier of an order. As the federal government sat on its hands, other countries were scrambling to secure what supplies the country had from right under its nose, and it was driving Bowen batshit.

The next day, Sunday, Bowen wrote to Bright and Wolf that he feared China would soon cut off mask exports—choking off as much as 90 percent of masks that make their way to doctors' offices and hospitals.

"The US mask supply is at imminent risk," he wrote at 10:15 p.m.

An hour later, just to Bright, he wrote: "Rick, I think we're in deep shit. The world."

At four in the morning, now Monday, Bright asked, "Mike. Have you ramped up production to full capacity?"

At 6:31 a.m., Bowen replied: "We are planning. We have to be cautious. It's dangerous. The hard landing after H1N1 nearly put us out of business."

News outlets were catching up to the looming mask shortage, thanks in part to Bowen and others who were reaching out to reporters. Home improvement and drug stores were beginning to see people making a run on supplies.

Attempting to get ahead of panic buying, HHS told the news site Axios that the risk to the public was low, and that the Strategic National Stockpile "holds millions of face masks as well as N95 respirators that could be used if needed in responding to a public health emergency. . . ."

But as would repeatedly play out over the course of 2020, what the Trump administration told the public did not reflect the panic within.

A couple of miles away, at the White House, Peter Navarro, a top adviser to the president, was doing his part to light a fire under the administration at a critical time. Brusque and confident, Navarro was an economist and a self-proclaimed expert on China known most for his influence over and support of Trump's trade wars. Unlike most other Trump lieutenants, Navarro was immediately concerned about the outbreak in China, a country he distrusted so much he wrote a whole book about it.

On January 29, Navarro dispersed a cogent and fearful memo to the White House, warning that the coronavirus could take half a million American lives and cost the country trillions of dollars.

"The lack of immune protection or an existing cure or vaccine would leave Americans defenseless in the case of a full-blown coronavirus outbreak on U.S. soil," Navarro wrote.

That same day, Trump announced a White House task force to prepare for outbreaks in the United States. That Friday, January 31, the White House announced it would bar entry of foreign nationals who'd visited China, a move pushed by Navarro.

Navarro was not yet aware of what was happening with Bright at

HHS and Bowen at Prestige Ameritech, but the three were on a collision course to becoming uneasy allies, for a time.

The force that would bring them together? None other than Steve Bannon. Because of course Steve Bannon.

By the first days of February, Bowen realized that his friend Bright didn't have the sway needed to escalate the nation's preparation effort. So he turned to the press, securing an interview with the *New York Times*, some broadcast interviews, and a write-up at Wired.com.

As word of his travails spread, Bowen got a call from a producer at *War Room*, the podcast hosted by Bannon, a former top adviser to Trump who still held clout in the administration, despite leaving the White House in a delightful tizzy and saying on his way out that the president was "like an eleven-year-old child." In addition to having led the once-fringe right-wing website Breitbart, Bannon had run the successful Trump campaign and its hollow promise to keep and rebuild vestigial American manufacturing. Bowen's story, and his company's near-religious defiance of market forces in the name of American patriotism, was a natural fit and a legitimate news story.

Bowen was intrigued but had reservations. A lifelong Republican, he had voted for Trump in 2016. But while observing the man's many indecencies over three years as president, Bowen had come to regret the vote and, in fact, had begun to consume less Fox News and more MSNBC. Still, he knew Bannon had powerful friends and harbored a like-minded disdain for cheap Chinese manufacturing.

"Well, okay," Bowen told Bannon's producer. "But I fucking hate Donald Trump. Is that a problem?"

"Well, can you just not say that on the air?" the producer asked on the phone.

"Yeah, I just want you to know who you're talking to here. I am not a Donald Trump supporter."

Somewhere in his discussions with the producer and Bannon's co-host, Bowen was asked what could be done. He said the CDC and the White House needed to immediately invest in new mask machines and place large orders with every manufacturer it could find. They needed to listen to Rick Bright at BARDA.

The podcast wouldn't air for more than a week, but Bannon's team promised to use its connections to get word to the White House, specifically to Navarro. On the evening of February 5, Bowen sent an email to Bright with the subject "Prepare for a call from the White House."

Rick,
I'm pretty sure that my mask supply message will be heard by President Trump this week. I'm getting a ton of press and I'm passing out your email address and saying that you're the guy who knows that I'm telling the truth. . . . I'm handing you the power to fix the US mask supply. Please don't let American(s) down.

No pressure, Bright thought.

Kadlec, who did not respond to my requests for an interview or comment, had finally called for regular Disaster Leadership Group meetings, though Bright found that the group illustrated more disaster than leadership.

During such a meeting, on February 7, Bright presented to HHS and CDC officials data that Bowen had sent about his company's spike in sales—a jump Bowen estimated showed demand was about 200 times the existing supply of masks in the country. What would the country do, Bright asked, if this trend continued and there wasn't more supply coming in?

His colleagues, including Wolf, the Critical Infrastructure Protection director with whom Bowen had spoken, didn't buy it. There was enough supply for now, Bright was told.

Bright knew it was bullshit. Earlier that morning, he stopped by the Home Depot in Northeast Washington, D.C. Inside, he found two Asian women staring up in anticipation as a worker pulled the last case of 3M respirators from the overhead bins. "Don't you understand?" one woman said to him. "We need all of these for our family. There's a virus in China." As the worker dropped the last of the N95s to the floor, Bright lunged in and snatched a box. It was uncharacteristic, but he knew that might be the last box of masks in the entire city.

Bright took a picture of the Home Depot tableau and told his colleagues what he had witnessed.

That's when he was told that HHS would simply ask the CDC to issue guidance that people who don't need masks—well, they shouldn't buy them. Bright was furious. This was not a solution. While it is true that medical-grade masks should be reserved for healthcare workers, it was well established that masks help prevent disease spread through air, a fact the public would learn sooner or later.

"That's not what happened in 2009, in 2010," Bright remembers saying. "People panicked; they hoarded the supplies of masks and respirators. The same with Tamiflu and other drugs—anything they could get their hands on. So it won't work to just change the CDC guidance."

Well, that's the only methodology HHS and the CDC were considering, Bright was told. He began to believe his colleagues were not just negligent, but downright "lazy."

He looked to his colleagues and said, "You have got to be kidding me. I can't believe that you can sit there and say that with a straight face."

He left in disbelief and called Bowen.

"Mike, they're not listening to me."

Bowen "twisted off" into a profanity-laden lament.

Later that same day, Navarro's assistant called the HHS switchboard and asked for some guy named Rick Bright, whom no one at the White House had ever heard of. The assistant got through to Bright's desk line and told him that he was being summoned to the White House to discuss the coronavirus. Bright was astonished that his pen pal down in Texas had managed to get the attention of the Trump White House. Behind the scenes, HHS officials were nervous that their own fly in the ointment was now taking his case to the most powerful office in the world. They tried to stall the meeting, but after an insistent call from Navarro himself to Kadlec, Bright was cleared to go to the White House the next day, a Saturday.

Just before 2 p.m., Bright arrived at the White House in a pressed suit. When Bright entered his office, Navarro, wearing jogging shorts and a T-shirt, jumped right in.

"Why are you all dressed up?" Navarro asked.

"Well, I'm coming to a meeting in the White House," Bright responded.

"First question," Navarro said.

Bright nodded.

"Is this real?" Navarro said.

"Yes, I'm afraid it is," Bright responded.

"Second, what do we need to do about it?" Navarro asked.

"There are a lot of things we need to do right now," Bright said.

Before he could elaborate, Navarro slapped a book on the table. It was *Three Seconds Until Midnight,* a book whose primary author was Steven Hatfill, a controversial virologist and associate of Bannon's who, in the early 2000s, gained fame for being wrongly suspected by the FBI as the perpetrator behind the anthrax letter attacks. Drawing from the 1918 influenza pandemic, Hatfill's book was published in the fall of 2019 and warned that the United States was unprepared for the next pandemic.

"Have you read this book?" asked Navarro.

Bright said he hadn't, noticing Navarro had several copies on his desk.

"Go home. Read this book," Bright remembers Navarro telling him. "And come back and see me tomorrow. Come back with five points—the most important things you think we should do."

Navarro gave Bright a twenty-page white paper, also written by Hatfill, that distilled some of the book's larger points and purported to break down everything the United States needed to do to address a pandemic.

As Bright left the room, Navarro boomed, "And don't dress up!"

Bright returned to Navarro's office the next day, Sunday, dressed down. This time Navarro had another guest in attendance—Hatfill, the author of the book. For his prescience, Navarro in the coming weeks would enlist Hatfill's counsel and insert him directly into the middle of the White House's response efforts. Navarro's affinity would give Hatfill, and some of his more controversial ideas and whims, outsized influence over the White House response.

Bright had perused the materials the night before but believed the book lacked substance.

"Did you read the book?" Navarro asked.

"No, I glanced at it," Bright responded, Hatfill in the corner of his eye. "I wasn't impressed with it."

Navarro, whose "no bullshit" mantra was the stuff of legend in the

West Wing, smirked. Bright interpreted this as one straight shooter rec- ognizing another, and in this moment felt genuine relief that someone with true power understood the urgency the situation required.

Bright was eager to jump into the key steps he'd drafted up the night before. He started with the mask supply and an imminent short- age that would contribute to untold infections and deaths. Bright said the United States needed to immediately place large orders for masks with various manufacturers and needed to halt the export of PPE out- side the U.S.—and yesterday. Navarro was curious to know how Bright knew so much about masks and supply chains.

"Who do you talk to about this?" Navarro asked Bright.

"I talk to the CEOs and heads of these mask companies," Bright said.

"Who do you know in the mask companies?" Navarro asked.

"I know Mike Bowen," Bright responded. "I can get him on speak- erphone right now."

Navarro agreed, and Bright dialed Bowen.

"I'm standing here in Peter Navarro's office," Bright said. "So you need to watch your language. Tell me once again—what needs to be done? Tell me about these idle pieces of equipment and what it would take to get them up and running."

Bowen explained the finer details of the N95 machines he had sit- ting in the warehouse, which the company had purchased after a com- petitor went out of business. He couldn't fire them up without a guarantee from the government that they'd purchase off those lines. It was too expensive and complicated, and those masks would need emer- gency clearance from NIOSH, the National Institute for Occupational Safety and Health, which certifies masks claiming to filter out 95 percent of particles. That could take months. As a stopgap, Bowen explained that his business partner and fabricator was building additional ma- chines to produce masks for which the company already had NIOSH approval—itself a complicated process. With both lines of effort, and buy-in from the government, the company could spit out 10 million masks a month.

After the call, Bright and Navarro worked together to draft a memo

to the White House Coronavirus Task Force, then overseen by HSS secretary Alex Azar. It called for three immediate steps.

1. Halt the export of N95 masks and ramp up U.S. production.
2. Secure all existing doses of and materials needed to brew
   remdesivir, a therapeutic scientists believed could help infected
   patients recover.
3. Fund and launch a Manhattan Project–style effort to develop a
   vaccine.

For the first time in weeks, Bright felt optimistic that the country
could get ahead of the virus. He left Navarro's office, went home, and
worked through most of the night. At 4:26 a.m. on February 10, he
texted Bowen.

"Thank you."

"I'm up if you need me," Bowen replied. He was preparing for interviews with the *China Morning Post* and the BBC. "I'm (about) to create a
shit storm. Get ready."

"You've been very generous," Bright responded. "I can't thank you
enough. I might need more info today but I'll let you know. Try to rest
some, too. This could be a marathon. I think we are running up a steep
hill right now. Pace."

CHAPTER **4**

INTO A GUNFIGHT WITH A BOX OF TISSUES

JUST HOURS AFTER BOWEN AND BRIGHT'S twilight text exchange, President Trump, in the afterglow of being acquitted in his first impeachment trial, spoke to a rally of supporters in New Hampshire. He downplayed the virus, comparing it to the seasonal flu, a dangerous and false refrain he and his lieutenants surfaced again and again, saying, "The virus, they're working hard. Looks like by April, you know, in theory, when it gets a little warmer, it miraculously goes away."

The day after, Tuesday, February 11, the World Health Organization coined the name for the disease caused by SARS-CoV-2: COVID-19.

While Bowen and Bright saw the moment clearly, the inertia of the federal government under Trump steered the nation toward disaster. The weeks and months that followed were like a fever dream, a bad acid trip on a careening bus with no one at the wheel, a wicked soundtrack of newsreels overhead, Trump shouting into the fear centers of our brains. Except it wasn't a hallucination. It was just the news. Our national response to an existential threat.

And all 330 million Americans were along for the ride.

Moments after our "invisible enemy" was named, the nation's foremost disease expert, speaking at a public forum in Aspen, Colorado, sought to elucidate the virus. He said the risk was "relatively low" to most Americans but hedged.

"Is there a risk that this is going to turn into a global pandemic?" said Dr. Anthony Fauci. "Absolutely, yes."

For more than thirty-five years, Fauci had served as director of the National Institute of Allergy and Infectious Diseases, under the National Institutes of Health, advising six presidents on everything from HIV/AIDS to Ebola to the disease that had been named just moments before. Fauci knew better than anyone the precarious intersection of public health and politics and public perception. As far as anyone knew, there were only thirteen confirmed cases in the United States.

So, what if he told the public in this early stage that the virus could bring us to our knees, and then nothing happened?

"Your credibility is gone," Fauci said of the hypothetical.

The next day, the CDC issued guidance that the general public didn't need and shouldn't buy masks, noting "the virus is not spreading in the community." But in fact, it was. Though the first reported U.S. death would come at the end of February in Seattle, coroners would later find that two people in the San Francisco Bay area, who had no recent travel history, had died of the disease in the first and second weeks of February. Later examinations would find it was killing Americans in January. There was very little testing, no vaccine, not enough supplies. It was no longer a question of if the country could contain the virus, but how badly the virus would overrun us. It was the doomed strategy Bright had warned against.

Meanwhile, HHS leaders continued to stall, telling Navarro and the White House in a February 14 briefing "there are no known immediate problems with supply chains."

Officials at HHS weren't content to just ignore the tsunami before their eyes; they took the additional step of throwing our life rafts to the country that had generated it. Throughout January and February and into early March, the federal government urged mask manufacturers to export hundreds of millions of dollars' worth of PPE to China at the same time it ignored calls from within to do the opposite. HHS officials, including Kadlec, steered supplies to China as late as February 21, according to emails ProPublica obtained through the Freedom of Information Act.

In Italy, just weeks after a Chinese couple infected with the virus were discovered in Rome, the virus was showing off its ability to spread. The country had closed off travel from China, yet what started as small clusters of infections had ballooned into nearly eighty confirmed cases in just days.

On February 23, just after 9 a.m. on the South Lawn of the White House, Trump delivered to reporters a quote that would be his administration's epitaph: "We have it very much under control."

Trump revealed in a tweet the next day what many news reports would later confirm: His concerns for the virus were indelibly tied to its effect on Wall Street and, by extension, his prospects for the 2020 election.

"The Coronavirus is very much under control in the USA," the president tweeted. "We are in contact with everyone and all relevant countries. CDC & World Health have been working hard and very smart. Stock Market starting to look very good to me!" In private, Trump would later tell journalist Bob Woodward that he intentionally downplayed the virus's threat to avoid a panic.

The administration's upbeat messaging was cooled the next day by comments from Dr. Nancy Messonnier, the director of the National Center for Immunization and Respiratory Diseases, housed under the CDC. She warned that many Americans would become sick and that "disruption to everyday life may be severe."

"We expect we will see community spread in this country," she said.

On warnings from a top CDC official that schools might close and businesses might move to remote work, the Dow Jones Industrial Average slid 879 points and the S&P 500 dropped 3 percent. In four trading days, U.S. stocks on the whole lost some $2.1 trillion in value. It was now official: The virus was the biggest economic and political challenge Trump would ever face.

The next day, February 26, Trump announced he was replacing HHS secretary Azar with Vice President Mike Pence as the head of the

White House Coronavirus Task Force. To some, the move conveyed that locking the virus down was a top priority for the administration; to others, it signaled that politics was guiding the way. The national supply strategy was at this point a glorified public relations campaign. HHS and the CDC attempted to use media coverage and its platforms to urge civilians not to buy or hoard masks. As Bright predicted, the message produced the opposite effect.

Panic buying was in full swing. And price gouging followed. By February 27, a ten-pack of the gold-standard 3M N95 respirators that sold on Amazon.com for about $18 was going for $100.

HHS secretary Azar told the House Ways and Means Committee on February 27 that COVID-19 "will look and feel to the American people more like a severe flu season in terms of the interventions and approaches you will see."

But both Trump and his cabinet knew better.

As March neared, the evidence that HHS had botched the messaging and wasted critical weeks was mounting. On February 29, Washington State announced the first known death from COVID-19 in the United States, though it was not truly the first. Officials there were seeing community spread, including in nursing homes, and signs of larger outbreaks to come.

That day, Washington State health officials requested 200,000 N95s, 200,000 surgical masks, 5,000 face shields, 64,000 pairs of gloves, and 60,000 disposable gowns from the stockpile. Based on what HHS said were Washington State's "actual needs," the federal government instead released 100,000 N95s, 100,000 surgical masks, 2,565 face shields, 32,000 pairs of gloves, and 30,000 disposable gowns—conveniently, likely arbitrarily, half the amount of each item requested. Officials overseeing the stockpile were already safeguarding precious inventory and were, in essence, winging it.

Pence, now overseeing the White House Coronavirus Task Force, said in a press conference that day that the federal government was working with 3M to speed up production of N95s by tens of millions more a month. As Bowen knew, that was no easy task. Much of the company's mask supply came from China, and even if U.S. production ramped up as it had during World War II, the materials needed to make masks were now dependent on suppliers in Asia and Mexico.

On that eventful last night of February 2020, Kadlec read through a scientific analysis published by Chinese scientists titled: "The epidemiological characteristics of an outbreak of 2019 novel coronavirus diseases in China." It provided some of the first scientifically rigorous conclusions and was a harbinger of the devastation to come.

The study examined more than 72,000 COVID-19 cases to track the virus's toll on humans and its spread across mainland China in just one month. The early data found an overall case fatality rate of more than 2 percent, though it was much higher for patients with preexisting conditions like heart disease and diabetes. For people over the age of eighty, the fatality rate was near 15 percent. The data was early, and estimates would change, but the baseline trend was horrific. In comparison, infectious disease experts estimate that seasonal flu's overall mortality rate is typically less than .1 percent. This was nothing like the flu.

However dismissive he'd been of Bright, Kadlec now seemed to grasp the urgency. Just past 10 p.m. on Saturday, February 29, in an email to several top HHS officials including Bright, Kadlec wrote: "Having reviewed this I feel we are going into a gunfight with a box of Kleenex tissues."

On March 3, Kadlec and other high-ranking officials took questions from the Senate Committee on Health, Education, Labor & Pensions, often referred to as the HELP committee.

As of that morning, there were more than 100 confirmed COVID-19 cases in the United States. The devastation overseas was much worse, causing supply chain disruptions and widespread economic concerns.

Speaking as the ranking member for the minority, Democratic senator Patty Murray of Washington State, where nine people and counting had died of the disease, provided a stark assessment. In her state, cases were climbing, people who wanted to get tested could not, and those who could were waiting weeks for results. As of that morning, the Life Care Center nursing home in Kirkland, a Seattle suburb, was the epicenter of the U.S. outbreak with seven patients dead and another fifty residents and staff showing symptoms.

"While I am profoundly grateful for the work public health officials are doing," Murray said, "I am very frustrated at the steps the president has taken, from repeatedly contradicting experts' advice to downplaying the seriousness of this threat, and to appointing a politician to lead the response," referring to Pence.

In their questions, Democrats expressed frustration with Trump's leadership and worry that the administration's persistent attacks on the Affordable Care Act might affect the delivery of health services to populations most vulnerable, such as nursing home patients and people in low-wage "essential" jobs. Republican senators, in turn, emphasized calm and reiterated that the risk to the public was, as the scientists had said, still relatively low.

But two of the Republicans asking questions that day had already put their money where their mouths weren't.

One was Richard Burr, a Republican from North Carolina. Burr was something of a pandemic expert, having helped pass the seminal Pandemic and All-Hazards Preparedness Act, signed into law in 2006 by then-president George W. Bush. The act made sweeping changes to the HHS bureaucracy, with a mind toward national security. It was also that legislation that created both BARDA and ASPR. Burr had helped create both Bright's and Kadlec's jobs. The guy knew his stuff, and he reminded his colleagues as much as he asked a few mild questions about funding and the lag in testing.

Burr also happened to be chairman of the Senate Intelligence Committee, a powerful post which afforded him access to classified information about national security. Long before the public knew much at all about the virus, his committee had received daily briefings on its attributes and its advance toward the United States. From this perch, he had made public assurances that the pandemic response apparatus he'd helped build was ready.

But Burr had sold off as much as $1.7 million of his stock portfolio in mid-February, just after senators received a classified briefing on the coronavirus and just before the market began to collapse on February 24. Those holdings would have lost about 30 percent of their value by the time Robert Faturechi, a ProPublica colleague of mine, broke the story in late March. An investigation by the Securities and Exchange Commission would later reveal that Burr's brother-in-law also sold off stocks, just minutes after the two talked by phone.

On February 27, just five days before the hearing, Burr shared grave concerns with a VIP group during a luncheon at the Capitol Hill Club. According to a secret recording obtained by NPR, Burr told that group: "There's one thing that I can tell you about this: It is much more aggressive in its transmission than anything that we have seen in recent history. . . . It is probably more akin to the 1918 pandemic."

About an hour after Burr spoke at the March 3 HELP committee, its newest Republican member, Senator Kelly Loeffler of Georgia, asked softball questions about how HHS would work hand in glove with the private sector to develop drugs and vaccines. She and her husband, who also happened to be chairman of the New York Stock Exchange, sold off more than $1.8 million in holdings just before the market slide pummeled most Americans' 401(k)s.

Financial records show other senators traded and cashed in stock at curious times. Republican senator James Inhofe of Oklahoma sold off hundreds of thousands of dollars in stock, avoiding steep losses. Dianne Feinstein, a Democrat of California, sold between $1.5 million and $6 million in those crucial weeks. Senator David Perdue of Georgia timed his trades impeccably, selling between $1 and $5 million he held in a financial technology company just before the market dipped and buying much of that stock back at a deep discount weeks later, in March. All the legislators would deny wrongdoing, some blaming money managers and pre-planned trades. The Justice Department investigated these transactions to see if members of Congress were benefiting from knowledge the public did not yet have, but no charges were brought before the case was closed.

Toward the end of the hearing, questions from Senator Mitt Romney, Republican of Utah, provided the news hook.

"Given the fact that our medical professionals need masks, gowns, gloves, and so forth," Romney began, ". . . [i]f we were to have a full-blown pandemic—and I hope we don't—but if we have one, what percentage of what we would need for our medical professionals is in the Strategic National Stockpile?"

"Ten percent of what we need, right now," Kadlec told the senator.

"It strikes me that we should have substantially more than ten percent than what would be needed for a substantial pandemic," Romney responded. "I can't believe we don't have that in stock."

Ten percent of what we needed. For a pandemic that many experts believed was now inevitable. It was startling enough for headlines. But it was also wrong in the worst way.

The day after the hearing, Kadlec corrected his comments. The country had closer to just 12 million N95s and 30 million of the far less protective surgical masks. So, in fact, the United States had on hand *just 1 percent* of what we needed for the coming onslaught.

A day after the hearing, the Commerce Department stopped helping U.S. companies sell masks to China. Two days later, officials from Massachusetts wrote to Kadlec and requested 750,000 N95 masks, 750,000 surgical masks, 750,000 gloves, 750,000 surgical gowns, and more. On March 6, according to HHS emails, Honeywell began a bid to secure an eighteen-month contract to produce 100 million N95 respirators, a timeline and a quantity that sounded big but was a small fraction of what would be needed in the months ahead.

On March 9, many weeks after Bright and Bowen and others had sounded the alarm on the looming mask shortage, Kadlec's office sought a meeting with the CEO of 3M to get more masks flowing into the stockpile, according to emails obtained through the Freedom of Information Act.

On March 11, the WHO made it official: COVID-19 was a global pandemic.

That same day, responding to an outbreak in New Orleans, officials in Louisiana requested tens of thousands of respirators, masks, face shields, and gowns. Oregon requested 400,000 N95s and 600,000 surgical masks. And the requests kept coming. Officials in North Carolina, seeing little help from the federal government, reached out to the home improvement chain Lowe's, which is headquartered there, to see about buying every mask the company had. The masks were already gone. After failing to heed warnings and stockpile masks and other gear, Kadlec and others within HHS were desperate and began personally entertaining solicitations from supposed middlemen who claimed to have access to masks, including people who'd never sold to any government and had no experience in medical supply. In one telling example, according to his emails, Kadlec entertained a solicitation from someone claiming to be a retired NBA hall-of-fame basketball player.

The solicitation was riddled with bizarre typos, factual errors, incoherent strings, and multiple fonts, presumably from cutting and pasting passages from various websites. The firm claimed it could deliver 14 million 3M N95 respirators, more than the 12 million the entire U.S. government had on hand. The email should have aroused skepticism, yet Kadlec set up a 7 p.m. conference call for March 11, according to HHS emails. It's unclear what occurred during that call, if it happened at all, but this is what the top leaders of the pandemic response were doing with their time.

On March 13, Trump declared a national emergency and, when asked about his administration's failure to roll out widespread testing, said, "I don't take responsibility at all."

The next day, the U.S. Department of Veterans Affairs, running the largest hospital network in the country, reached out to the stockpile, saying it had "immediate need" of 200 million N95s. VA officials estimated they'd be out of masks by the end of the week.

CHAPTER 5

"IT'S LIKE BEING ON EBAY WITH FIFTY OTHER STATES"

FROM HIS HOME IN THE U.S. NAVAL OBSERVATORY in Washington, D.C., Rear Admiral John Polowczyk was popping back and forth from his study to an adjacent kitchen, firing off work emails and tending to a pot of onion soup, when his cell phone buzzed and upended his life.

The screen said it was Lieutenant General Glen D. VanHerck, which was most unusual for a Sunday evening.

VanHerck reported to U.S. Army General Mark A. Milley, the president's top military adviser and the chairman of the Joint Chiefs of Staff.

"Heh-hey . . . Director," Polowczyk answered with some hesitation. "How are you today? What can I do for you?"

It was near 5 p.m. on March 15, 2020, the same day the CDC warned against gatherings of more than fifty people, just two days after President Donald Trump had declared a national state of emergency, four days after the World Health Organization declared COVID-19 a global pandemic, and many weeks after this call should have come.

"Health and Human Services has asked for some logistics planning help," VanHerck said. Polowczyk took that to mean that HHS secretary Azar or ASPR Kadlec had reached out for help from the Defense Department.

"Yeah, uh, okay," Polowczyk said.

As the Pentagon's top supply chain and logistics expert, he'd spent decades overseeing multibillion-dollar acquisitions of Tomahawk missiles and guided missile destroyers and the countless bits and pieces that comprise them and hail from different sources and manufacturers across the globe. He understood the intricate complexity of a globalized world and the delicate supply chains that live behind just about every product, commercial, military, or otherwise. But that week he had switched gears to piece together part of the Defense Department's pandemic response, which at this point was in its infancy.

As for the larger response taken on by the Trump administration, the thirty-three-year Navy officer wasn't yet plugged in, though he'd witnessed the same televised chaos as every other American.

"They just need some help planning," VanHerck explained. "And I got the green light from the secretary of defense and the chairman of the Joint Chiefs of Staff, to take a few people and go over to Health and Human Services and see what we can do to help."

"For how long?" Polowczyk asked.

"We don't know."

"John, just go," the general continued. "I just need you to go over there Monday—take some people—go see what they need and see if you can help them with logistics and supply chain planning for the pandemic."

Polowczyk alerted other relevant Pentagon officials to prepare for a trip to HHS the next day and returned to his simmering onion soup, which he shared with his wife, Karren. They would not see much of each other in the coming months.

Just hours later, on the morning of March 16, Trump held a conference call with a group of state governors. According to a recording that leaked to the media, the president told governors, "Respirators, ventilators, all of the equipment—try getting it yourselves."

As instructed, Polowczyk reached out to HHS that Monday, but no one seemed to be expecting him. He called Dr. Christian Hassel, Kadlec's deputy at ASPR, who said he hadn't been told to expect anyone and needed to hear it directly from leadership before he could invite a bunch of DOD folks over. It was the first sign, Polowczyk would learn, that officials at HHS were terrified to do anything without direct approval from a Trump political appointee, who were themselves terrified to do anything that might place them in a snarling presidential tweet. Finally, he told Hassel he was absolutely coming over. At about 2 p.m. on March 16, Polowczyk and a small entourage arrived at HHS headquarters, inside the Hubert H. Humphrey Building at the foot of Capitol Hill.

"That was Monday," Polowczyk would later tell me. "A very nonfulfilling day. But I will tell you, my first impression on that Monday? No one at Health and Human Services was walking around with a sense of urgency. I could not ascertain a sense of direction."

The next day the DOD entourage returned and set up shop in offices near officials working under ASPR. There was no one at HHS who had a background in supply chain logistics, let alone a team of people. The stockpile had for most of its history been housed under the CDC, based in Atlanta. So the agency largely responsible for disaster response, FEMA, was at best an arm's length away from the supply it would need for said response. For these reasons and others, Polowczyk would come to believe that, whatever the executive leadership, HHS was fundamentally and structurally ill-equipped for the occasion.

Perhaps most shocking to Polowczyk: The nation's stockpile, its first line of defense against a biological attack or a pandemic, was being managed by way of Microsoft Excel spreadsheets and a whiteboard, details confirmed to me by two other sources familiar with the stockpile in the Trump and Obama administrations. In fact, the method of tracking had not advanced since 2009, when Obama officials themselves were using simple spreadsheets on the fly to track inventory in response to the H1N1 swine flu.

You have got to be kidding me, Polowczyk thought.

Employees at about a dozen warehouses tucked in secrecy around the country kept tabs on their own inventories by manually updating disparate tables with varying formats, none of which gave officials in Washington a reliable or national view of what was on hand.

In other words, every drugstore, supermarket, and retail chain in America had a better grasp on its inventory than the most powerful country in the world did of its own emergency supplies.

Not that it mattered.

"I walked in, and the national stockpile had been given out," Polowczyk says. "I did not have a single—really—I didn't have a single N95 mask, surgical mask, isolation gown, nitrile glove. It had been issued."

This was news not just to Polowczyk but also to the many states that were still requesting materials.

That very day, emails show, the commissioner of Texas's Department of State Health Services wrote to ASPR and HHS officials that his state needed "a large cache" of respirators and other equipment. The agency had surveyed hospitals and found that hospital buyers were being told by manufacturers, including 3M and Cardinal Health, to expect back orders and delays as far out as fall 2020, maybe longer.

Polowczyk conveyed his concerns to Kadlec and other HHS officials. By Wednesday, Kadlec called him to his office and informed him of higher-level conversations about creating a special team to handle supplies. The effort would be "lifted and shifted" to FEMA, under the purview of the U.S. Department of Homeland Security, not HHS. And the administration wanted Polowczyk to run it.

Polowczyk had worked with FEMA during Hurricanes Sandy and Maria, deploying Navy resources where they were needed. In this role, he'd come to know chapter and verse what experts call the "Emergency Response Framework."

The framework is a detailed yet simple set of organizing guidelines that were developed over decades to help any administration work through any disaster. To be reductive, the response is tiered in this way: Execution falls to the lowest possible jurisdictions, meaning local fire and police departments are typically the front line; the state manages a broader strategy with emergency declarations, funding or routing state resources to hot spots, for instance; and the federal government wields its vast reach and resources to back everyone up, often based on what the lower jurisdictions say they need. The idea is that with this rubric, the response won't be made up on the fly, since that can lead to devastating failures, jurisdictional conflict, and oversights.

But unlike a localized crisis such as a hurricane, the COVID-19 pandemic presented challenges that had only been imagined in government drills or science fiction: a threat to all fifty states at the same time and a crisis in which all of them needed supplies that were either gone or running out.

Polowczyk was planning to retire in June but told Kadlec he would step in, and with DOD approval he was put on loan from the Pentagon to FEMA.

The next day, Thursday, Polowczyk met with HHS secretary Azar's chief of staff, Paul Mango, a fellow military man who'd graduated from West Point and obtained a master's degree from Harvard Business School. He'd also run unsuccessfully for governor of Pennsylvania before joining the Trump administration. Mango explained that the country was almost entirely dependent on products coming in from Asia, which was locking down.

"Man, we are in a lot of trouble," Polowczyk told Mango.

The two began to map out a "Supply Chain Taskforce" and discussed who should be plucked from where to lead a global hunt and buying spree. To do so, they needed to go to the White House and talk strategy with Pence, the chairman of the White House Coronavirus Task Force.

That Friday, March 20, Polowczyk reported to Pence's office at the White House.

Before Pence arrived, Polowczyk was greeted first by Jared Kushner, Trump's son-in-law. Kushner had inserted himself and begun dispensing free market principles into a complicated situation, for which many emergency experts thought the government should wield a very visible hand. Critics wanted to know why the administration hadn't executed on the Defense Production Act earlier to compel American companies to produce or ramp up production of ventilators and PPE and give the U.S. government first dibs on their purchase.

Instead, in conjunction with Pence's official task force, Kushner was cobbling together what would later be known as his own "shadow task force." It was composed of a small network of well-to-do friends, private industry consultants, contacts he had made in business, and other volunteers. Their task: to infuse the ingenuity and hustle of free market capitalism into the response by working the phones and email to quickly find supplies, buy them, and deliver them where needed, all outside of government red tape. Polowczyk would come to call this "dialing for dollars."

As the two waited for Pence, Kushner explained his plan.

"Oh, God, really?" Polowczyk said.

Kushner was taken aback.

"Uh, oh. Okay," the admiral said. "Well, you're not going to do that out of the White House."

Pence arrived, and so began the meeting with the admiral, Kushner, Mango, and a few straphangers to design a plan to protect the American people.

Kushner and the vice president described a fanciful list of wishes that had no obvious strategy or tactics behind them: They needed to get PPE to here, to there, from there, to here, with the help of this guy and maybe that company. They were not afraid to go around normal contracting channels. This was, after all, the Trump administration.

"I just sat there and listened," Polowczyk remembers. "I don't remember all of the, uh, words."

Finally, Polowczyk interjected, "Look, that's a lot of unfocused effort."

The two gazed at the admiral for a moment.

"How are you going to do transportation?" Polowczyk asked. "How are you going to get it here? How are you going to buy it? How are you going to keep track of the money, do the contracting?"

As the former governor and top executive of the state of Indiana, Pence knew well the mechanics of government purchasing. In normal times, there's a rigorous bidding process to ensure fairness and weed out fraud and firms that can't do the job. It can take many months. There are binding contracts, lawyers on either side, considerations for minority-owned businesses, background checks. In the federal government, contractors are typically pre-vetted before they are eligible to engage in the process at all. The money is accounted for by comptrollers and made public in government purchasing data. Audits are conducted.

In an emergency, some of this is thrown out the window to speed up acquisition, and purchasing officers might take a stance of awarding work first and asking questions later, but the process isn't completely demolished. Though the process might have seemed onerous in the context of a global pandemic, there remained numerous practical considerations—such as how might a volunteer consultant tap into government coffers to buy a lot of masks? How does a nongovernment employee approve a contract? How does the United States verify that the product is legitimate? Who is going to transport it?

"Yeah, how *are* we going to do all of this?" Polowczyk remembers Pence asking.

A core principle of the response framework had already been violated: A codified chain of command involving emergency response experts should be placed in charge of logistics, not politicians. The doctrine also guides that any response needs to be scalable, flexible, and adaptable so as to be executed nationally for any type of crisis to assist thousands of disparate local governments and agencies and to coordinate with nonprofits and the private sector.

It is not done from the personal cell phone of the president's son-in-law.

With reality sinking in, Polowczyk provided some inchoate goals that he would refine and call his "four lines of effort," which drew from the Emergency Response Framework. They were:

1. *Preservation:* We needed to ration masks and compel healthcare workers to reuse as much as possible.
2. *Acceleration:* We needed to hasten the acquisition and delivery of PPE to the U.S.
3. *Expansion:* We needed to increase manufacturing through private makers with either the threat of or invocation of the Defense Production Act.
4. *Allocation:* We needed to move PPE to where it was most needed.

The meeting lasted about a half hour. Polowczyk gave Pence a written brief on what he'd like to do under the FEMA flag. Over the weekend, Polowczyk says, Pence marked it up, added some edits, and asked staffers to rework it into the White House's brief format. The admiral was surprised to learn that he'd be standing up at the White House podium on Monday, March 23, to announce a new Supply Chain Stabilization Task Force to the American people.

That Monday, Trump spoke first, in his usual broken coherence. Then came Attorney General Bill Barr and Dr. Deborah Birx, the physician who was then directing the White House response. Finally, Pence spoke and introduced the admiral.

"Acceleration," Polowczyk explained, easing into his presentation after some initial hesitation. "We have a team of people that are searching the globe for personal protective equipment. Figuring out where it is, figuring out if we need to buy it or just transport it and get it here faster."

To his right, Trump looked on with pursed lips in that gravity-defying, forward-leaning stance of his.

"There are many vendors, many distributors, all on separate systems," Polowczyk continued. "Nobody has one-sight picture for that supply chain."

Polowczyk, who had grown up on submarines and spent his career in the dark recesses of the military-industrial complex, far from the news media's gaze, had just become the face of the nation's supply crisis.

The next week, inside FEMA, Polowczyk noticed a few fresh-faced strangers mulling around, out of their element. Polowczyk thought they were interns, but no, they were civilians inserted into the heart of the national response, armed with only can-do attitudes, personal wealth, and a laptop.

Despite Polowzcyk's initial skepticism, Kushner moved ahead with his shadow task force, recruiting a couple dozen volunteers. Most of them were in their twenties and had taken either vacation or leave from high-paying jobs at Google or consulting firms like McKinsey and Insight, while others hailed from Goldman Sachs and private equity firms. Their stint was short, a few weeks, but their fumbling and the chaos created by their presence would make for great media fodder. It would also result in a whistleblower complaint to Congress by a young member of the Kennedy family who had volunteered and become alarmed by what he had witnessed.

"They were very young," Polowczyk says. "It was finally FEMA that figured out that they were nongovernmental employees and then made them all sign, you know, nondisclosure agreements, and some said they couldn't and left."

When he realized the "Kushner kids," as he called them, were volunteer civilians, Polowczyk says he relegated them to perform his team's least enviable task: sifting through thousands of leads of potential PPE stock, the vast majority of them garbage, that were streaming into the task force from multiple directions, including the patronage-prone White House.

"Once we figured out—we being the adult leadership at FEMA— that these were nongovernment folks, we made them all go away," Polowczyk says, referring to mission-critical tasks.

For all its amateurish execution, Kushner's task force would in many ways overshadow the larger effort Polowczyk had undertaken to source supplies, which involved government officials working with manufacturers such as 3M, Cardinal Health, and Honeywell—under the threat of the Defense Production Act. As the kids dialed for dollars, Polowczyk says he and FEMA officials were scrambling to build what he'd call "the control tower," a computer dashboard that streamed in inventory, purchasing, and other data from legitimate PPE manufacturers and distributors. This information, paired with a view of where cases were spreading in U.S. cities, finally began to give the admiral and his team some visibility. It was imperfect and messy, but it was something.

To prop this up, the admiral and his team ran for weeks on just a few hours of sleep each night. They practically lived at FEMA, so much so that his wife, Karren, unofficially adopted Polowczyk's young assistant, helping with his laundry and groceries. She brought food for the team so they could stick to their desks as the world was falling apart.

If nothing else, Polowczyk says, the Kushner kids served a purpose in saving the adults from getting bogged down with bullshit leads.

"Between myself and the FEMA administrator, I probably had a thousand emails from people a day," the admiral recalls. But the truth was the federal government was desperate, so how could he ignore the tips?

"I had people run down every one of those leads," Polowczyk says. "So some of these volunteers helped with that. Somebody had to go do it. I did not want to pass a stone not overturned."

I empathize with this particular point. Over a year and a half of reporting for ProPublica and for this book, I too ventured down the rabbit holes, chasing dozens of leads that went nowhere, getting lost in emails between desperate government workers and would-be vendors and nimrod scammers. With the help of ProPublica researchers and a separate researcher I hired to help with this book, I reviewed thousands of purchasing and email records obtained via open records laws, from New York City, to New Orleans, Houston, Austin, California, and more.

It was an unmitigated bullshit bonanza, a nightmare for anyone receiving tips for PPE during the spring and summer of 2020. I wouldn't wish it on anyone—except maybe the Kushner kids.

But therein lies the true scandal. While it's true that the Kushner kids gave some cover for the admiral and freed up FEMA and military personnel to do other work, their mere existence speaks to the country's lack of preparation and the compounding tragedy of having this particular administration in control.

None of it had to happen.

Polowczyk's great fear in those harried weeks in March and April was that his team would miss an opportunity, and someone would tell the newspapers, "Hey, I had masks that the federal government didn't buy."

"We had thousands of leads. Now, ninety-five percent of those were just somebody that said, 'I have access to something.' But they didn't have it on hand. It wasn't in a warehouse."

In May, Polowczyk's fear was realized. The Kushner kids had sat on a promising lead from a South Carolina doctor who in turn had a lead on millions of masks from a Chinese factory. The lead went nowhere, and the doctor later told the media he sold the masks to hospitals.

As leads like that languished, the Kushner kids had placed high

priority on dead-end leads streaming in from Trump allies and prominent Republicans, going so far as to track those tips on a spreadsheet
called "V.I.P. Update."

On Friday, March 27, the *New York Times*' front page carried the
headline: "Job Losses Soar; U.S. Virus Cases Top World." With increased
testing came the data that proved the immensity of our failure—more
than 80,000 confirmed cases and 1,000 deaths, worse than China, Italy,
or any other country. As bad as that data was, the newspaper published
an alarming bar chart that was perhaps even more politically damaging
to Trump. It was a rolling bar chart of the number of unemployment
claims over time, which sat at the bottom of page 1 but for the singular
bar representing the most recent data. That bar burst past its predecessors and ascended the page, above the fold and just below the bold
headline, revealing a record 3.3 million unemployment claims in one
week. An unprecedented spike in jobless claims during an election year
is an incumbent's worst nightmare.

Later that day, Trump posted a shame tweet at Ford and General
Motors, urging them to "START MAKING VENTILATORS, NOW!!!!!!"

Among the thousands of replies, a Silicon Valley engineer named
Yaron Oren-Pines responded: "We can supply ICU Ventilators, invasive
and noninvasive. Have someone call me URGENT."

There was nothing to indicate that this guy could deliver—he had
seventy-five followers on Twitter and no experience in medical supplies
or government procurement. Nonetheless, his lead was given priority
status, and the Kushner kids forwarded it to emergency managers in
New York, who assumed the federal government had done due diligence. The state quickly awarded the man a $86 million contract for
1,450 ventilators—an extreme markup of three to four times the usual
cost of a ventilator.

Yet more astonishing: That deal paid out $69 million in advance.
No ventilators were ever delivered by Oren-Pines, and the state would
later fight in court to claw back its payment.

Although Kushner's involvement in the enterprise captured loads
of negative media attention and at the very least created unneeded dis-
tractions, Polowczyk was grateful for his presence.

"Mr. Kushner did nothing more than break down bureaucratic barriers and provide avenues for me to get shit done," the admiral insisted to me.

"And I never—ever—had to go ask permission from Mr. Kushner to do anything," the admiral said. "I went to him to say 'I need more resources.' 'Go find me more money.' 'Go bring me a lot more lawyers.' 'I need the White House counsel to do X.' And he got it done."

Still, it is undeniable that Kushner's involvement alienated would-be partners such as blue-state governors and cast a shadow over the larger effort. This was especially true with the execution of Project Airbridge.

The basic concept of Project Airbridge was this: Instead of waiting on traditional and time-consuming imports by sea, the United States could fly smaller international shipments of PPE directly to where they were needed.

Supplies like N95 masks typically arrive at U.S. ports by way of maritime shipping containers, which take about a month to arrive from factories and ports in Asia. Those avenues were shutting down as China nationalized its own supply sources. What supplies could make it out took far too long to reach U.S. soil by sea. And once they arrived at any number of coastal ports, the supplies would need to be handed over to FEMA, which would then have to handle further transport to areas in need. Lives were at stake. So FEMA envisioned a much faster, and much more expensive solution—paying companies like FedEx and UPS to pick up supplies and fly them to where the control tower said they were needed.

Contrary to what some envisioned, the federal government would not be constructing giant PPE factories, taking over 3M, or standing up behemoth warehouses as a nationalized effort. Polowczyk viewed his role as more of an air traffic controller whose job was to organize what existed, get more of it, and send it on its way.

Also contrary to what was reported or inferred during those whirlwind days, Polowczyk says Project Airbridge was his brainchild, not Kushner's, and that it was informed by conversations he had with supply chain experts at the Massachusetts Institute of Technology and elsewhere. Yet Kushner was made the face of the program when it was an-nounced on March 29, as the project's first commercial carrier landed at New York's John F. Kennedy International Airport with shipments of gloves, gowns, and masks destined for COVID hotspots in the Northeast.

In a statement released that day, Kushner billed it as a groundbreak-ing public-private partnership between the White House and American medical equipment distributors such as Cardinal, McKesson, Owens & Minor, Medline, and Henry Schein Inc.

"At President Trump's direction we formed an unprecedented public-private partnership to ensure that massive amounts of masks, gear, and other PPE will be brought to the United States immediately to better equip our health care workers on the front lines and to better serve the American people," Kushner said in a statement.

This gave the impression to the public that Trump and Kushner were directing the effort and diverting supplies where they saw fit. And it coalesced with complaints and some anecdotal evidence that states with governors loyal to Trump were being favored over blue states and that FEMA was commandeering and rerouting shipments ordered by other government agencies. Polowczyk maintains he was the one calling the shots, and that the rest was political theater.

"Mr. Kushner had nothing to do with Airbridge," Polowczyk says. "I did not run it past him. I voiced it. I told him—I said at a task force meeting: 'We are going to create an airbridge. I am reconfiguring the commercial marketplace, from maritime mode of transport to air.'"

"And everybody said, 'Holy crap, that makes sense,'" the admiral claims. "We're gonna fly it. We're gonna pay for it. And there were some other stipulations, but Kushner had nothing to do with Airbridge. I don't care what anybody said. It's not how it went down. He had nothing to do with Airbridge."

The program would be beset with allegations of secrecy and inves-tigative reports detailing gross exaggerations, but the bottom line was this: Polowczyk (and Kushner?) did manage to accelerate a not-meaningless amount of PPE to some U.S. hospitals, even if it was just a drop in the bucket.

Still, the lack of a real national strategy led to just the sort of confusion, unnecessary competition, and price gouging that had been pre-dicted. States facing an onslaught of patients, overrun hospitals, and supply shortages began to speak out and dispel the Trump administra-tion's lie that the nation was ready and well stocked.

Leading the frustrated chorus was New York Democratic governor Andrew Cuomo, who had stood up daily televised briefings on the state's coronavirus response. In just days, New York had become the epicenter of the outbreak, with more than 1,500 people dead. By the morning of March 31, Cuomo sat down at a dais, frustrated, two aides at either side, distanced.

Indignant and wringing his hands, Cuomo told reporters and a growing national viewership: "You now literally will have a company call you up and say 'Well, California just outbid you.' It's like being on eBay with fifty other states, bidding on a ventilator. And you see the bid go up, because California bid, Illinois bid, Florida bid, New York bids, Cal-ifornia rebids. That's literally what we're doing. I mean, how inefficient."

Other governors began to speak up, including Maryland's Republi-can governor, Larry Hogan, who said his state was "flying blind" be-cause despite what Trump officials said, there just weren't enough test kits to trace the virus's spread there.

Polowczyk was now in the crosshairs. He was the adult herding Kushner and his kids, a decorated military man who'd lost control of a political message, a logistician in a world throwing away logic. "I cannot overstate how stupid the politics were," Polowczyk told me. "On both sides, Democrat and Republican."

Accustomed to working in the context of confidential military op-erations, he was at first comfortable letting Kushner hog the limelight, though in time he'd come to wish he had been trained or had thought more about how smart public relations might have helped the story of his role in our national nightmare.

Despite his efforts, Polowczyk began to realize he might go down in the public's perception as something of a villain, a cog in the Kushner/Trump/Pence bungling of the pandemic. Finally, what tenuous hold he had on the message was eviscerated on April 2, when Kushner, riled by the comments of governors including Cuomo, addressed the media for a task force update.

"The notion of the federal stockpile was it's supposed to be our stockpile," Kushner said. "It's not supposed to be the states' stockpile that they then use."

It was a flagrant and verifiable lie. The entire mission of the national stockpile was to provide supplies to states or, as the HHS website put it, "to supplement state and local supplies during public health emergencies."

To conform to Kushner's televised reimagining of an entire federal government program, those words were deleted from the website shortly after the briefing and supplanted with new language that better matched Kushner's mental leap.

Kushner went on to say that the pandemic was revealing that some state leaders are "better managers than others."

"Some governors you speak to—or senators—and they don't know what's in their state," the man continued. "Don't ask us for things when you don't know what you have in your own state."

For no justifiable reason, medical supplies had become a political issue. And public faith in the Trump administration's effort to supply and protect America's healthcare workers was irretrievably diminished.

Connecticut governor Ned Lamont, a Democrat, said simply, "We are on our own."

And they were.

CHAPTER **6**

"YOU MIGHT BE BUYING A FERRARI"

IT WAS 5:58 P.M. ON MARCH 22. Trump had just ascended the dais in the White House briefing room to update the nation on the hunt for supplies, when a New Jersey used car salesman watching from home texted an accomplice.

"I think we are finally at a point of desperation where institutions and governments are willing to consider our pricing," Ronald Romano wrote to a friend, whom federal prosecutors would later refer to as Co-Conspirator 3.

He was referring to an alleged plan to sell masks at obscene mark-ups to New York City at its time of greatest need. With a potential payday still being worked out, Romano hung on to the words of the president.

In these whirlwind days, the White House coronavirus briefings offered a double whammy to the American psyche. The non-newspaper-reading public was often left to decipher truth from spin, hoax from reality, with help from televised experts of varying intellectual quality. Almost daily, the facts of the situation contrasted with the increasingly obvious lies of our president.

Yet, on this day, Trump managed to stick to the script.

"I want to assure the American people that we're doing everything we can each day to confront and ultimately defeat this horrible invisible enemy," Trump told the American people. "We're at war. In a true sense, we're at war. And we're fighting an invisible enemy."

"This will be a great victory," he continued. "This is going to be a victory. And it's going to be a victory that, in my opinion, will happen much sooner than originally expected."

As the president announced a wartime footing against COVID-19, most Americans registered bad news. The U.S. death toll was creeping into the hundreds and trending toward the thousands, with tens of thousands of confirmed cases, no vaccine, supplies running short, hospitals in New York City filling up. The country was at war with a virus, and also with itself, as cities and states and the federal government fought behind the curtain for the same supplies.

But Romano and others like him saw dollar signs. Increased national spending, acknowledgment from the White House of rising infections in California, Seattle, New York, and elsewhere—all could be a boon for business. And it would be a shame to let a good crisis go to waste.

Just days before the White House briefing, according to court records, Romano had elucidated his ambitions in a text message to a business partner that read: "I'm working on a few deals that if I get any of them (masks) you might be buying a Ferrari."

It was an absurd plan with a peculiar cast of characters. Romano, then fifty-eight, had no apparent experience sourcing medical supplies, nor experience contracting with New York City or any other government agency. Yet emails and text messages later obtained by federal prosecutors in the Southern District of New York showed he had decided early in the outbreak to endeavor to sell millions of 3M N95 masks at a cost of about $4 apiece, about four times the usual street price. To do so, he enlisted a friend who resurrected a defunct business through which the group could sell masks. To broker the deal, he leaned on another well-connected associate who happened to be the former foreign investment minister for Macedonia.

Yes, this really happened.

But about a half hour into the White House briefing, Romano began to worry that his plan might unravel. Navarro, Trump's trade adviser and one of the first in the administration who took the virus's threat seriously, took the podium to discuss the Defense Production Act and the administration's light foot on the pedal, which some criticized as insufficient. The Korean War–era law empowers the federal government to compel U.S. companies to produce goods needed to protect the nation, giving the government first dibs on those supplies, and activates criminal penalties for hoarders and price gougers. It is an extreme, if necessary, tool and one that promises to foment significant political hubbub. The Trump administration had thus opted to use these powers surgically, limiting any perception that it wasn't friendly to business while highlighting cooperation from the private sector.

"The Defense Production Act, sir, has given me quiet leverage," Navarro said, looking up to Trump at his right. "When you have a strong leader, you can take a light hand initially. So what we've seen with this outpouring of volunteers from private enterprise, we're getting what we need without putting the heavy hand of the government down."

(While companies like General Motors had already made moves to begin producing ventilators, later that week Trump would formally invoke the DPA to compel manufacturers to produce supplies.)

But it was what Navarro said next that caught Romano's attention, two hundred miles away in Manalapan Township, New Jersey.

"The last thing I will tell you is that I also get a lot of calls that are very disquieting," Navarro continued. "Brokers are offering millions of items—whether they're goggles, masks, or whatever—and you go through three different brokers, tracing to a warehouse in LA that's allegedly got ten million masks, and they want to charge you seven times what they cost. That's price gouging.

"A message to the hoarders," Navarro continued. "If you got any large quantities of material that this country needs right now, get them to market or get them to us. We'll pay you a fair price. But if you don't do that, we're going to come for you and make sure that doesn't happen in this country."

Just then, Romano picked up his phone and sent a typo-laden text to the broker helping him secure a potential mask deal with New York City, later identified by federal prosecutors as Co-Conspirator 2:

> *Romano:* Trump press conference not promising for us
> *Co-Conspirator 2:* What did they say
> *Romano:* Going after brokers. If your hoarding medical supplies come
>   forward with fair price and they will pay. If not we will get you

What's funny about this exchange is that Romano and his group were not hoarding or even conspiring to hoard in any real sense. That's because you can't hoard products that don't exist. Romano didn't have any 3M respirators, nor did he have a real chance of getting N95s out of 3M's headquarters in St. Paul, Minnesota. Rather, as a special agent with the U.S. Attorney's Office in Manhattan would later allege, Romano had fabricated a document claiming he had access to 7 million masks as a distributor. In an unusual sidestep of the standard procurement process, the city of New York had signaled that it would be willing to wire payment for medical supplies up front, before anything was delivered. This gave the city an edge over the competition, which was fierce, but also exposed the city to obvious risks.

The bulbous 3M N95 and its variants were the most coveted of the disposable respirators. It is the standard-bearer, the first "respirator," different from a traditional surgical mask in that it was designed to filter out harmful particles to protect its wearer as opposed to blocking spit to protect, for instance, patients undergoing surgery. Though the concept of using masks to stop the spread of contagion can be traced back to the bubonic plague, the 3M "respirator" is only a few decades old. Building on the basic concept of fabric masks developed during outbreaks in the early twentieth century, this new mask consisted of melted polymer blasted onto microscopic fibers, creating a haystack of sorts through which bacteria and dust particles became trapped. This more involved process provided filtration far exceeding fabric, while still allowing its wearer to breathe somewhat normally. Its earliest applications in the 1960s and '70s were for industry, protecting workers from harmful particles such as asbestos. The female inventor of 3M's N95 built on the design, inspired by, of all things, a bra cup. Soon after, the company added an electrical charge to the cupped fabric, which assisted this haystack with a static that grabbed bad stuff. This mask now filtered out 95 percent of particles. As it was applied more in hospital settings, during outbreaks of tuberculosis and for protecting immunocompromised HIV/AIDS patients, industry standards and government testing and regulation followed. Competitors emerged, but 3M's model remained top dog.

By spring 2020, the 3M N95 was so sought after and so prominently featured in news stories that it became perhaps the most enduring symbol of this most painful year—the thick white fabric bra cup, yellow bands, the ever-important stamp of approval by the National Institute of Occupational Safety and Health, or NIOSH.

As such, the 3M N95 was the subject of the most audacious and elaborate—if completely batshit—schemes that would arise in the coming weeks and months. Counterfeits entered the market. The volume of false claims from would-be profiteers that they had achieved the coveted status of being named an official 3M distributor, or that they had secret caches of millions of respirators, was such that the company devoted an entire team to help potential buyers determine who was phony and who was legitimate. Through emails and phone calls, the company fielded inquiries nonstop from buyers, brokers, government officials, and law enforcement.

The company would begin suing people and companies that were peddling counterfeits or striking deals outside the company's price limits.

Cities and states, left to their own devices, established amateur processes and teams for weeding out this type of fraud. It required the squandering of enormous resources at the worst possible time—at an incalculable and profound cost to taxpayers and the mental health of ordinary civil servants.

In New York City, the fishy inquiries were fed to an ad hoc group of purchasing staff that called themselves the GAG team. It stood for "I Got A Guy," a mocking reference to the multitude of solicitations filling city emails and voice-mail systems that often made reference to a friend or a friend of a friend who had a warehouse filled with masks.

From a command "bunker" in Brooklyn and from cramped apartments scattered across the boroughs, an overtired team of bureaucrats led a monumental effort to help supply masks and other equipment to the city's fifty-six public and private hospitals. Overnight, invisible procurement officers whose expertise was buying reams of paper, paper clips, and chairs, or managing city real estate, had become disaster aid workers and fraud investigators.

Romano's gambit was flagged by a purchasing officer and sent to the GAG team, which suspected his company planned to take the city for a ride. The GAG team confirmed with 3M that the solicitation materials were phony, and the company would sue to shut him down. The GAG team also forwarded his solicitation to the city's Department of Investigation, which built some of the case and passed it along to federal prosecutors. Romano's company offered the nonexistent masks at a 400 percent markup, for a total haul of $45 million. If New York had fallen for it and paid upfront, as it did with other vendors who'd run off with the money, Romano and his pals could have purchased fleets of Ferraris.

Instead, Romano would be arrested weeks later on three felony counts of fraud. He pleaded not guilty, setting off a long court battle.

The story of his arrest, a colorful and early example of the sort of opportunism that was transpiring in ways big and small across the country, provided a cautionary tale for mask buyers. But many other rip-off schemes and outright delusional transactions would slip through the ad hoc safeguards set up by hospitals and woefully ill-prepared municipal and state governments.

———

The month of March 2020 could be considered less a unit of time than a prolonged traumatic event. Dozens of people I talked with to retrace those crucial weeks, from different locales and vantages across the country and in varying degrees of frenzy, described the same sort of haze in which their faculties for processing cause and effect, recording the sequence of events, were so assaulted by stimuli they could not keep pace. Still, when pressed, almost everyone who had been called into action could paint in their mind's eye what they were doing as the immense gravity of the situation came into focus—the "Oh, shit" moment.

Jackie Bray's oh-shit moment came around the fifteenth of March. Her normal job, before COVID, involved advocating for New York City tenants and taking on unscrupulous landlords for the mayor's office. She was not an expert on infectious diseases, supply chains, medical supplies, or hospital administration.

But as COVID began to envelop the city, she was called alongside hundreds of others to fill shoes that had never been worn. Organized, hardworking, and respected among her colleagues, Bray was tapped by the mayor to be the city's version of what Admiral Polowczyk was to FEMA—the top air traffic controller. She became the connective tissue, gathering up data and new developments from several bureaucratic silos to turn it into information that could be used to make executive decisions and direct resources. The moment hit her as she reviewed models from Cornell, Columbia, and New York University on the predicted spread of infections and the corresponding strain on hospitals. In another life, Bray had been an administrator at the National Weather Service, so she knew to read models with a sort of careful skepticism. They can vary widely but can help prepare for a reality that may end up somewhere in between the rosiest projection and the worst-case scenario. Any way she looked at it, though, the picture was bleak.

Projections estimated the city needed something like 60,000 hospital beds and fast. Aghast, she looked into the city's data to see how many patients could be taken into inpatient care at that time—just 20,000.

"I remember thinking, *Well, how the fuck are you going to build forty thousand hospital beds in the next two months?*" Bray would later tell me.

The city was already shutting down. Broadway went dark. Shortly after her oh-shit moment, New York City schools closed. Then bars and restaurants. Then "nonessential" workers were ordered to stay home. A city of 8.8 million people, the city that never slept, lulling into a forced coma.

But city employees went to work, many of them reporting to the city's high-tech Emergency Operations Center in Brooklyn, aka "the bunker." Much of City Hall decamped to the bunker, which is reminiscent of a Hollywood action movie set. It was built with natural disasters such as Hurricane Sandy or a terrorist attack in mind, but it was now the central command for the city's hunt for masks, gloves, gowns, ventilators, and beds.

City bureaucrats broke the effort down into three front lines: space, stuff, and staff.

Bray knew the city couldn't do much of anything about staff—that was left to hospitals, and there is a finite number of doctors and nurses available.

Space—the city could get that. Officials began setting up makeshift temporary hospitals, looking into reopening shuttered hospitals and nursing homes that could house oxygen tanks and beds, and established a secret warehouse for supplies just outside the city. Another team worked to book hotels for an influx of medical staff.

Stuff was harder. Stuff they would have to buy, hoard, and make from raw materials. No one knew what they were doing at first. At random, Bray assigned a woman in the bunker to google for every manufacturer of ventilators she could find, then cold-call them and try to buy as many ventilators as possible. They did the same for masks, gowns, and gloves. Bray began the daily gathering of data from hospitals on their inventories and burn rates—information that took some cajoling with private hospital administrators unaccustomed to sharing business information. The delicate balance, the "just in time" method of restocking hospital shelves, was in shambles by late March.

By March 25, the city's hospitals were burning about 3 million N95s a week, an astronomical rate that would worsen with increased infections that were now a statistical certainty.

For the next four weeks, New York City hospitals would likely need 26 million N95s, Bray warned her colleagues in an email that day. Her spreadsheet indicated the city had in its stores just 1.9 million N95s, which were being distributed in push packs across the city. Out-of-work taxicab drivers were being dispatched across the city to deliver N95s and surgical masks to hospitals in small batches. Over the same time period, hospitals would also need something like 640,000 face shields, 1.2 million isolation gowns, and 71 million surgical masks to survive the month ahead. The city had just a tiny fraction of each. The notion of stocking even a week ahead felt like a dream—they'd be lucky to stay a day ahead of being totally naked to the virus. They were trying to outrun a wildfire.

Another team raced to award contracts to vendors who could deliver supplies. They coordinated with volunteers and philanthropists who had organized to donate supplies. Officials who oversaw real estate were working with industrial firms in the outer boroughs to produce clear plastic face shields instead of waiting on Chinese shipments that might not come. Officials got one company with a connection to a factory in Vietnam to commit to giving New York City first dibs on increasingly scarce medical-grade gowns.

The city's first COVID death had been reported March 14. And in just two weeks, by March 31, more than 1,000 city residents had perished. By April 1, there were at least 47,000 confirmed cases. In a press briefing that day, Mayor de Blasio said hospitals needed an additional 3.3 million N95 masks, 2.1 million surgical masks, 100,000 isolation gowns, and 400 ventilators to survive just the week ahead. A massive floating hospital with 1,000 beds, the USNS *Comfort,* had docked on Manhattan's West Side to take some of the strain off city hospitals. That week, Governor Cuomo extended stay-at-home orders.

Worried she'd bring the virus home, Bray stopped reporting to the bunker. She would coordinate the city's response instead from a six-hundred-square-foot apartment in the Williamsburg section of Brooklyn that she shared with Bryn, her girlfriend of twelve years, and Marlowe, the couple's fourteen-pound black and white Havanese. She'd wake to phone calls in the early morning, let some through to voice mail as she showered, post up at her kitchen countertop around 7:30 a.m., and then run through the day's fresh challenges: *What is the governor saying? What is the mayor saying? What are the numbers today?* By midday, the conversation shifted to tomorrow's crisis: *What's coming in? Who needs what? What's going out?* They'd brief the bosses and work into the late evening to prepare for the following morning. Rinse, repeat.

The days blurred together, none happy with the tight quarters but for the dog, whose scratches increased and whose morning walks were the only normal thing left for the humans.

Bray was among the first recipients of the anguish that would soon befall countless other invisible, small government bureaucrats. The failure to prepare at the national level, and the vacuum that welcomed aspiring profiteers, was cascading down through states and cities that would take turns addressing their own spikes in cases and death.

————

With New York City now the epicenter of the U.S. COVID-19 pandemic, those charged with buying ventilators, masks, and other supplies would unapologetically pursue them in ways that could at once be summarized as reckless, ruthless, prudent, and justifiable. The market for PPE was now accepted as the Wild West. The city was Wyatt Earp. It would protect its own.

The GAG team and the larger quest for stuff worked under the Mayor's Office of Contract Services, whose chief procurement officer was Dan Symon. He came from a family of frontline workers. Symon's wife was a nurse, as was his sister. Several family members were firefighters. Plainspoken, with a signature New Yorker patois and its accompanying rough edge, Symon had motivations that were visceral and personal.

As if that weren't enough, Mayor Bill de Blasio placed continuous pressure on Symon and his team to produce, while acknowledging they faced an agonizing catch-22. If the city signed big contracts that didn't work out, they'd take heat in audits and in the press. If they didn't, potential supplies might go to another city and New Yorkers could die. The mayor had issued an executive order that threw out the usual contracting vetting and gave his people unprecedented power to dip into the public purse. The mayor would keep those powers well into 2021, spending nearly $7 billion without the usual supervision, prompting a lawsuit from the comptroller to restore oversight.

"We were in a moral conundrum," Symon remembers, "of having to run down every lead, because what if it really does come through?"

By the first weeks of April, the GAG team and other purchasing of-

ficers had sorted through thousands of "resource offers" from middlemen brokers who claimed access to PPE. The city had learned to do
some due diligence, requesting FDA certification for any supposed
mask lot or proof of authenticity from SGS, a global firm that inspects
far-flung products for clients before they might be purchased sight un-
seen. They requested business filings and "proof of life," raw videos that
panned over the inventory and often included someone holding a newspaper or document verifying the date of the video. Vendors would send
different records, or sidestep questions, or change the product in the
middle of negotiations. In all that madness, few if any of the leads bore
fruit.

Symon and Bray realized the city was out of its depth, so the city
called in consultants who understood the medical supply chain. The
resources offers and the GAG team became less of a priority as the city
sought lines from more reputable sources. But the supplies just weren't
there. The city's public hospitals had some existing contracts with PPE
manufacturers such as Honeywell, but they had none to give. Manufacturing had ramped up, yes, but the federal government had corralled
roughly half of what was spitting out of industrial machines, while the
rest went to existing and more entrenched hospitals and buying groups.
The consultant recommended the city work outside of the entire morass, registering itself as an importer of record so it could work directly
with foreign factories, skipping the middlemen vying for a cut or wast-
ing precious time.

Miraculously, the city's effort to back up hospitals in their hunt for
supplies was mostly working. In dribs and drabs, from various sources,
the city gathered respirators, masks, and gowns and sent them on their
way, keeping hospitals a day or two ahead of an all-out depletion of supplies. But there would be no reprieve. If the city had masks and respirators one day, it didn't have enough gowns the next. Medical staff were
being asked to work impossibly long shifts while rationing and reusing
for many days gear that was designed to be used once per patient visit
and then thrown away.

To stay ahead of the wildfire racing up their spines, Symon and his
team had to beat out the competition—other cities and states. In those

first weeks, the fiercest competition hovered around ventilators. While few of the machines were lying around in the United States, it appeared thousands of units were available abroad for the taking. The city issued numerous large contracts for thousands of these machines at exorbitant markups to edge out the competition. Some of these deals blew up in their faces.

One was a $162 million deal the city struck with Reef Holdings 1 LLC, whose Atlanta-based owner, Bernie Tokarz, also happens to be a trustee for the Fulton-DeKalb Hospital Authority down in Georgia. Tokarz had learned of a supposed cache of ventilators collecting dust in Singapore, and through his large business network ended up in conversations first with the state of New York, and then the city, to import and parlay the machines. They were being sold at a significant markup, plus a commission of about 16 percent paid to him.

Tokarz told me that he remembers thinking at the time, "There was opportunity for a windfall here, but I don't want to do anything that would get me into trouble with the law."

The state dragged its feet, and Tokarz found himself instead talking to Symon and other members of de Blasio's contracts team. The two texted and talked late into the evenings because the sellers were providing updates from the other side of the world. Symon was determined to get the machines and willing to pay through the nose if it meant beating out the state. Tokarz was struck by the rabidity of the negotiations, particularly that Symon and other city staff voiced a desire to beat out Cuomo, who was already amassing notoriety and political capital for his perceived good handling of the outbreaks, which would turn out to be not so good. Mayor de Blasio and Governor Cuomo were famous foes, strong personalities with aspiring loyalists around them, and the dislike had manifested itself in contract negotiations in a way Tokarz, who dealt often with local governments, had never thought possible. Typically, civil servants, especially those buying stuff, stay out of the politics.

"The mayor and the governor don't like each other, and so they were negotiating against themselves," Tokarz remembers. "It is the most bizarre thing I'd ever seen, and it really left a sour taste in my mouth.

Really—the city basically said, 'Fuck the state. We want it. We'll pay more.' And I'm like hold on, hold on here."

The first week of April, the city consummated a deal for 3,000 ventilators, edging out the state. Tokarz didn't want money up front and instead took the purchase order to get financing from a bank that would release funds to the buyer, once the goods were shipped. But Tokarz ultimately backed out of the deal because he, like the GAG team and the federal government, had run into red flags. The deal didn't smell right; the sellers couldn't provide relevant certifications, the terms of the deal kept changing, the source would send over bizarre contracts that made reference to Indonesian law. There was just too much risk around the deal.

"Everything is crazy right now, but the rules of international business still applied," Tokarz says. "You can't just wire millions overseas without any guarantees or legal recourse."

He called to tell the bad news to Symon, who was distraught. Tokarz had spent thousands of dollars doing due diligence on a deal for which, luckily, taxpayers hadn't paid a dime.

But several other ill-fated deals signed in desperation paid vendors big-time. During the frantic buying spree, to beat competitors and to speed up the influx of supplies, the city paid millions up front to random companies. And I do mean random.

The city's deals included an $8.3 million contract for 130 ventilators—an absurd price—with Global Medical Supply Group LLC, based in Boca Raton, Florida. The company, founded by yet another car salesman just weeks before in March 2020, received half of the payment up front, according to court records. The company claimed to be able to deliver 130 ventilators. The company forwarded much of the city's advance to a man in China whose true business was exporting footwear. The money got stuck in China, the Florida company sued its connection, the city sued the company, and the company countersued, creating the legal equivalent of a venomous snake ball. And taxpayers got bit.

In these weeks, Symon ended each night wondering how long he and his staff could sustain. Twenty-hour workdays, no days off. No one knew how high the case and death counts would go, or when they might abate. Fielding scams and nonsense was a constant and outrageous irritation. The moral conundrum, signing deals that would never fly in normal times, created its own personal and professional burden. It was too much, too fast, and the consequences of every rushed decision could have profound impacts on the lives of his fellow New Yorkers, his own career, and the political fates of two men sparring for the political limelight. Symon packed on fifteen pounds that month.

Eventually the city got a handle on ventilators. With the help of the federal government and other sources, the city got more of them, and as knowledge of the virus and treatments progressed, demand for the breathing machines leveled. As the city's procurers tell it, it was the day the ventilator crisis ebbed, or maybe the day after, that they realized they faced a new wave of shortages of a product they never dreamed to surplus—body bags.

CHAPTER 7

RELEASE THE BILLIONS

TO UNDERSTAND HOW THE FEDERAL GOVERNMENT sent profiteers and swindlers to the races, rushing billions out the door while breaking all convention, it helps to first understand the man holding the starting gun.

Consider for a moment, if you will, if you dare, the mind of Peter Navarro.

Now, here's a man who gets things done. If he must, he'll do it around you, through you, in spite of you. Just ask Robert Kadlec. If he likes you, you might just like him back. Just ask Rick Bright. But the romance won't last. Just ask Rick Bright. Remember, he does not need to like you. Hell, he doesn't need to know you. If you call his cell phone, he'll tell you as much.

"If you called from a number I don't know, I ain't answering," he'll say in his recorded voice mail, instructing you to try a text message, which maybe you do repeatedly, only to be ignored, because screw you.

He's a blunt instrument, called prickly by some, worse by others. He just has that thing, you know, the *thing*: a persistence beyond reason, the confidence to outlast enemies and weather embarrassment, which only delusion or supernatural faith, or both, can provide. I suspect that's why Trump called him "my Peter"—that and his extreme protectionist views on global trade and perceived expertise on China. He's been described in the pages of the *New York Times* as having a Rasputin-like ability to whisper into Trump's ear thoughts that became policy.

While he was considered fringe even among colleagues in the Trump White House, from 1992 to 2001 Navarro ran as a liberal Democrat five times for elected office in California, failing each time. He stood next to Hillary Clinton and criticized then House Speaker Newt Gingrich, whose rhetoric ironically paved the way for Trump's ascent and thus Navarro's appointment. A veteran Democratic consultant who ran two of Navarro's campaigns told the online magazine *Politico* that his former candidate was "the biggest asshole I've ever known." And that guy presumably knows a lot of rich Californians.

He's written thirteen "academic" books, none cited by serious academics. Five of them quote Ron Vara, a nonexistent expert whom Navarro manufactured to support his arguments, with such musings as "only the Chinese can turn a leather sofa into an acid bath, a baby crib into a lethal weapon and a cellphone battery into heart-piercing shrapnel." Ron Vara: It's an anagram of his surname, get it? When academics and reporters called him out on it, Navarro acknowledged his fabrication and brushed it off, saying, "As Ron Vara might say, 'Lighten up and have fun reading the books.'"

He once got in an f-bomb-laden screaming match with Treasury secretary Steve Mnuchin in front of Chinese diplomats. He clearly believes he's highly intelligent, and maybe he is, an assuredness he exudes not with the erudite debate skills of someone who holds a doctorate in economics from Harvard, which he does, but with the bravado of a lumbering heavyweight, which he is not, talking trash before a street fight, which he would lose.

When Trump appointed Navarro to enforce the Defense Production Act and compel U.S. companies to prioritize manufacturing for the COVID-19 response, Yossi Sheffi, the director of the MIT Center for Transportation and Logistics, expressed disbelief.

"We have some of the largest companies in the world who are running global supply chains [and] have contractor relationships all over the world," Sheffi told *Mother Jones* magazine. "There are literally thousands of them. Any of them would be doing a better job than a crackpot economist."

I would not deign to resort to such hyperbole, as I've never met Navarro, nor do I claim to be an economist, crackpot or otherwise. Also, because I appreciate Peter Navarro for what he is: a uniquely American specimen. He's the Nicolas Cage of modern politics, unhinged but not always off his mark, beholden only to himself, amused by his own stunts. He might be fun to get a drink with, until maybe he isn't. I'd take my chances, anyway, but unfortunately Navarro did not respond to several attempts to reach him.

I suppose it is the tragedy of him that most fascinates me.

Congressional records, emails, and interviews with people who were in the room show that Navarro came close to becoming something of a hero in this particular story. Instead, he was Peter Navarro.

While the Trump administration was slow to establish a clear national effort to shore up supplies, Navarro was waging his brand of guerrilla warfare behind the scenes, starting with a March 1 email to Trump and other senior officials:

> Since the first news from China of a viral epidemic, I forecast a
> significant global pandemic. . . . Over the last month, I have
> presented the Task Force with action memos to combat the virus
> swiftly in "Trump Time," but movement has been slow. There is NO
> downside risk to taking swift actions as an insurance policy against
> what may be a very serious public health emergency. If the COVID-
> 19 crisis quickly recedes, the only thing we will have been guilty of
> is prudence.

Navarro's antics had lost him credibility in a White House whose credibility was tenuous at best, but he was right. He got a lot of things right.

In that memo, he recommended that a small White House team coordinate to gather up therapeutics that might run dry if supply chains congested. He urged the president to direct the "VA, HHS, CDC, and Commerce to identify current hospital system, wholesaler, manufacturer, pharmaceutical, and agricultural inventory levels and surge production capacity of essential generic medicines."

He raised fears that a vast array of imported drugs peripheral to treating patients, such as sedatives for those placed on a ventilator, could disappear if the United States didn't ramp up domestic drug manufacturing quickly. He called for more funding at HHS and BARDA, faster development of testing, faster testing itself. He noted that a vaccine was many months away and urged the administration to explore and invest in companies that had potential treatments on hand or in the works. He recommended the government get behind Regeneron's monoclonal antibodies, a cocktail of synthetic antibodies that could theoretically help COVID patients recover, based on its use in treating other ailments. He mentioned remdesivir, a promising antiviral developed by Gilead Sciences that some, including Dr. Anthony Fauci, believed could be useful in treating infected patients.

"In some cases, there is already SOME movement BUT the movement is NOT fast enough," Navarro implored.

In his exuberance, however, Navarro crossed lines that most scientists and serious public health officials would not: He advocated for remedies, drugs, and companies that hadn't been vetted. At the same time he listened to Bright at BARDA, he kept the counsel of Steven Hatfill, author of *Three Seconds Until Midnight*, which he revered as a sort of pandemic bible.

Navarro also did his own ad hoc research, which included talking with companies vying for government cash. The result was a muddled message that contained real and dire warnings as well as a sort of high-stakes gamble on unknowns and contingencies in the name of prudence. A key figure in preserving our national well-being was, in essence, throwing ideas at the wall to see what stuck.

Navarro was frustrated with the pace. So he did something cunning and historically remarkable: He took federal purchasing into his own hands.

Throughout the month of March and into late spring, Navarro

steered hundreds of millions of dollars to companies, working around career contracting professionals with blatant disregard for the formal channels meant to weed out fraud and corruption and ensure the government gets a decent deal. Tried-and-true processes developed after the spoils of the Civil War, fine-tuned through economic downturns and the advent of the military-industrial complex, refined after disasters like Hurricane Katrina—all of it was thrown out the window.

To stock up on medicines and the components needed to make them, referred to as active pharmaceutical ingredients, or API, Navarro used his position and his bluster to award a first-time government contractor a $354 million contract, with options that could have paid out as much as $812 million over a decade. The company, Phlow, had incorporated just months before, in January 2020. But its CEO, Eric Edwards, had met Navarro as early as the fall of 2019. It made sense that Navarro would know folks in the domestic pharmaceutical space, given his belief that China's dominance of pharma supply lines could one day kill us all.

Edwards was best known for helping launch the controversial drug company Kaleo, which marketed an anti-allergy injection pen to compete with the EpiPen. Kaleo's first epinephrine delivery device failed after it was pulled from shelves due to safety concerns, though it returned a couple of years later. Kaleo was also known for price gouging on a powerful opioid antidote at the height of the country's deadly rash of opioid deaths, raising the price of the drug from $575 a dose to more than $4,000 in three years.

Edwards moved on to a new venture, and as news of the coronavirus spread in February 2020, the company reached out to its valuable contact in the Trump White House, according to emails unearthed in a later congressional inquiry.

With Navarro's help, the company landed a meeting with BARDA officials in which it solicited a "a strategic API reserve," a stateside factory of compounds that can be made to cook up various drugs as needed.

After the meeting, on March 20, Navarro wrote to BARDA director Bright an extraordinary directive that, in sane times, aspiring government contractors could only dream of:

My head is going to explode if this contract does not get immediately
approved. This is a travesty. I need PHLOW noticed by Monday
morning. This is being screwed up. Let's move this now. We need to
flip the switch and they can't move until you do. FULL funding as we
discussed.

A week later, annoyed with the lack of movement, Navarro went
around Bright to several key officials, including DOD officials, Admiral
Polowczyk, and Kadlec at HHS.

"Phlow needs to get green-lit as soon as humanly possible. It is a
critical part of our Advanced Manufacturing strategy at [the White
House]. Please move this puppy in Trump time," Navarro wrote.

"I'm on it," Polowczyk replied. "Yes we need that contract."

If the influence peddling wasn't already obvious, a consultant helping Phlow land the deal told its CEO to keep Navarro fuming. "CC'ing
Navarro cranks up the pressure," the consultant advised.

Hatfill, at this point Navarro's brain trust, helped negotiate the contract awarded to Phlow. This is remarkable because Hatfill did not work
for or represent the federal government in any way. He was an adjunct
professor at George Washington University, a private school, who fre-
quently talked on the podcast by Steve Bannon, who just happened to
be an ardent advocate of an antimalarial drug called hydroxychloroquine as a treatment for COVID. Hatfill was given office space in the
White House, where he coordinated with high-ranking officials and
bragged to friends that he worked "an average of 10 hours a day, 7-days
a week, unpaid, as the senior medical advisor to one of the President's
senior advisors." He was a force in pushing the administration's obsession with hydroxychloroquine, records show.

At the same time Navarro and Hatfill worked out the Phlow deal,
Navarro's team was also trying to secure a $765 million loan to Eastman
Kodak, the photography company, to help produce hydroxychloroquine. The company showed interest but had no experience doing such
a thing, so after a few months of back-and-forth, nothing would come
of the Kodak moment. But the drug itself would be immortalized by
Trump, Navarro, and others who dangerously and falsely hailed hy-

droxychloroquine as a miracle drug. Navarro's advocacy for the drug, in fact, would soon place him at odds with his new pal, Bright.

I'll reserve judgment on Navarro's actions except to say they did break the rules and there were major consequences to throwing money around so willy-nilly. His personality and anti-China fanaticism blurred the lines between what might have been well-intentioned rule breaking and outright patronage and corruption. Still, I strain to argue that there is no higher morality than the arcane rules laid out in "the Federal Acquisition Regulation," or FAR as purchasing people know it. This was a crisis, and America will do what it does in any crisis—throw money at it. So, perhaps some rogue actions were warranted. We needed stuff, and we needed it fast. And, for better or worse, Navarro, with all his eccentricities, was the guy doing something about it.

The aforementioned contracts and the machinations behind them wouldn't be made public until about a year into the pandemic, but there was another deal that Navarro, with Hatfill and some other connected people, cooked up that slipped through the administration's smoke screen in early April. And I just happened to find it.

He had just given me more than a year's worth of stories.

———

I went into lockdown on March 10, 2020, a few weeks before much of the country, after learning that someone at a journalism conference I had attended in New Orleans was sick. The Crescent City was at the beginning of its first major outbreak following the close-quarter Mardi Gras festivities.

I am ashamed to admit I hadn't taken the coronavirus as seriously as I should have until that night, when I got the email from ProPublica's president that anyone who attended the conference could not return to the office. In that moment, what felt like an abstraction, a far-flung virus that some said was kind of like the flu, sharpened into a call to action. It was my oh-shit moment.

It was now clear this virus would be a major news event, and I needed to find my place in the coverage.

Sometime that week, much of the ProPublica staff joined a confer-

ence call in which we laid out some reporting lanes to cover the virus
and its impacts. I was assigned to a large team that would delve into the
deaths. In a moment of eerie prescience, one editor told the group,
"Poor and minority people are going to get totally screwed." I will never
forget it. So, through March, we gathered death records and data from
cities across the country to see what trends we could find. The best data
came out of Chicago, Milwaukee, and Miami. To our profound disappointment, the theory held true. The virus was ripping through Black
and Hispanic communities, disproportionately taking lives and destroy-
ing families. I crunched some of the earliest data in Chicago, mapping
out where those who died had lived and overlaying it with census data
that broke down neighborhoods by income and race. The contrast was
as stark as it was heartbreaking.

This line of reporting would not stop, at ProPublica and elsewhere, as
the virus exploited the deep institutional racism and inequality of our
healthcare and social systems and laid bare the contemporary consequences of our historic and enduring sins. It was the most important story,
but I had begun to feel like deadweight, as reporters more qualified and,
frankly, better at covering race and science eclipsed my contributions.

So, as a member of a very new reporting team in Washington, and
seeing the frenetic pace of developments at the federal level through
March, I switched gears for what amounted to a less emotionally taxing
but foundational journalistic pursuit—following the money.

On March 27, Trump signed into law the Coronavirus Aid, Relief,
and Economic Security Act. The CARES Act unleashed $2.2 trillion in
stimulus relief and spending. Among many initiatives, it authorized rare
direct welfare in the form of $1,200 to most single Americans, subsidies
to keep small businesses afloat, and more than $100 billion in spending
for hospitals and supplies. To citizens and business owners, it represented a lifeline. To aspiring profiteers, the new money and the president's authorization of emergency no-bid spending meant opportunity.

By the first week of April, transactions from the first wave of COVID
spending were added to a massive public-facing federal purchasing database. My colleague Derek Willis, a data journalist who had spent un-

godly amounts of time with this data over a long career, jumped on it. Together with a group of reporters, we spliced up hundreds of thousands of lines of data and queried for trends, outliers, and totals. Reviewing contracts might sound on the surface like the most boring endeavor imaginable. But starting all the way back to my amateur muckraking days at Colorado State University, I had developed a nose for finding explosive stories hidden between the legalese and in the footnotes. There is always a story in government contracts—always.

We noticed potential stories right away. First, the delivery timelines for many of the contracts involving PPE, hospital beds, and testing equipment extended well into the summer and the fall. This meant that, despite what the Trump White House would have Americans believe, the executive branch was preparing itself for a long slog well into 2020, or worse. Money talks. This was existentially depressing, but we needed more to craft a story.

Next, we did some standard categorizations, placing chunks of data into what we call "buckets." When we grouped by total agency spending, the Department of Veterans Affairs stood out, as did Kadlec's office at HHS, ASPR. It stood to reason that these agencies would be the big spenders—ASPR was central to the pandemic response and the VA oversaw the nation's largest hospital system. But when we narrowed the totals to just contracts awarded without any bidding, the VA jumped out especially. In just the initial gusher of contract awards, the VA awarded something like $365 million in emergency awards, much of it for PPE. They were freaking out. We doubted the agency could have done much, if any, due diligence on that many awards in so little time.

From there we dug deeper into the granular data to examine the vendors being paid. Following the same process—grouping, totals, sorting, drilling down—we could see the vendors who landed the largest paydays, and those who did so without any bidding. In general, data can point you in the direction of the story, which one must next unearth through sourcing, paper records, and going out into the field. Federal purchasing data is limited on qualitative detail, such as, crucially, describing what the damn contract is actually for and why it was awarded.

Gathering what clues we could required reading line by line by line. Luckily, we'd filtered down to our buckets and made some top-level targets. We split up what was now a few hundred rows apiece and started picking through spreadsheets.

That's when I stumbled on the Easter egg Navarro had unwittingly left me.

The single largest no-bid contract, at the time, was a $96.4 million deal that FEMA awarded to the American subsidiary of a Canadian defense contractor called AirBoss of America, which made various things out of rubber. It was for the production of powered air-purifying respirators, or PAPRs, those full-faced hoods that actively filter to make breathable air, as seen worn by hazmat teams and Dustin Hoffman in *Outbreak*. In the cell describing why the contract was awarded without bidding, someone had written "ordered by the White House."

That was odd; these descriptions are by design almost always too short or lacking enough detail to be interesting on their own. I wondered if some smart, lower-level contract official added it to CYA, "cover your ass," to ensure auditors would later know who was responsible. I ran a few queries in the larger purchasing data and found no other instance of that wording. It was an outlier. The White House, a political office, is not supposed to single-handedly order payments to private businesses, for obvious reasons, so we had a story. A couple of days later, a colleague and I published the story confirming that the White House had taken the extraordinary step of ordering agencies what to buy and from whom. Trump and his men were writing enormous checks without any real vetting or oversight.

What could go wrong?

But why did the White House order this specific deal? We had two theories: Either the government was so desperate and clueless that it was doling out checks like Oprah gives out cars, or there was some type of old-school corruption afoot. Or both. We looked under what rocks we could and noticed some loose connections between the company's leadership and people adjacent to Kushner, but it was all innuendo that amounted to nothing. We had to let it go, and I'm glad we did.

We wouldn't learn for about a year that the contract was directed by

Navarro, with help from Hatfill. All it took for the company to land the deal was a second-degree connection to Navarro and an email with a price quote.

When the company emailed its price for 100,000 of its high-end respirators, Navarro, who had no authority to approve contracts, simply ordered it done.

"This will be sent forthwith for swift approval up the chain and consider it done," he said.

In normal times, a deal of that magnitude would take many months to complete, but Navarro did it in two days. When the company announced its deal with FEMA in a press release, it included a quote from Navarro that read "[T]his is war, and President Trump is using the full force of the federal government and the full power of private enterprises," like AirBoss.

The next week, the parent company's stock price doubled.

The company would almost triple its sales volume, thanks in large part to Navarro, and see a $12 million increase in profit from April to June 2020.

As Ron Vara might say, "God bless America."

CHAPTER **8**

BUCCANEERS AND PIRATES

ARMED NOW WITH THE REASONABLE SUSPICION that our government had no clue what it was doing, we dove back into the data. It was a treasure trove.

Looking at large contracts for important things, we focused in on companies that sounded funny, that we didn't recognize, or that promised stuff we now understood was hard or impossible to find. Then we looked to see when the business entities were created, if they had done previous work with the government, if their proprietors had previous legal troubles or political connections.

Our subjective honing process was hit-or-miss, but always entertaining. My colleague Lydia DePillis, a brilliant economics reporter, noticed a $14.7 million contract the VA awarded to an Ohio company named "Aunt Flow," which sold tampons and other menstrual products that are dispensed in women's restrooms. It sounded absurd, but DePillis called the company's CEO and learned the company had done something clever and maybe useful. As its orders slowed due to the pandemic lockdowns, the company converted its own manufacturing facilities in China to produce surgical masks and began selling them to the government and its clients. The company also tried to delve into making N95s—much more complicated. The CEO told us she had to cancel her deal with the VA because the Chinese government seized her shipments that were bound for the United States.

In the data we found another peculiar deal awarded to Zach Fuentes, Trump's former deputy chief of staff at the White House. Just eleven days after he formed an LLC, he was awarded a $3 million contract for masks by the Indian Health Service, an agency within HHS that provides medical care to Native American tribes, which were hit hard by the virus. Fuentes delivered a tranche of the Chinese version of the N95, called KN95s, destined for the Navajo Nation, but the agency would determine that most of what he delivered couldn't be worn by medical staff because it didn't meet FDA standards. The agency would later request a refund, which Fuentes would refuse.

In the data we'd find former telemarketers whose records included allegations of fraud, but who were now entrusted with delivering millions of masks and coronavirus test tubes. Dozens of the companies we plucked out had been created just days before landing multimillion-dollar contracts. It appeared that anyone who paid a nominal fee to create a limited liability company could land a multimillion-dollar contract in the very same week.

One of the largest orders for masks, at the time, went to Panthera Worldwide LLC, which despite its grandiose name was a tiny company in Virginia. A quick court record search showed the company was in bankruptcy and its owners were being sued by former business partners for fraud. And the IRS had placed tax liens on both owners in 2018 for failure to pay taxes. Yet FEMA awarded the company a no-bid $55.5 million deal for 10 million N95s.

For surgical masks, FEMA also hired a boutique liquor company in California, which was in the middle of fighting a high-profile fraud suit, which, to be fair, doesn't bar someone from becoming a major federal contractor.

A nuanced picture was emerging. The United States was desperate, China was holding back, manufacturers and entrepreneurs were filling the space, and money was being sent to whoever dared to play the game. The stockpile was empty, and every level of government was struggling to restock.

Our national well-being now rested with mercenaries.

The money was going out so fast that what math we did was irrelevant the next day, but by late April the government had handed out more than a billion dollars and counting to hundreds of first-time contractors. A cottage industry was cropping up around federal government purchase orders, fueling an emerging black market and frustrating the search for the same supplies by states, cities, and hospitals.

We pitched a story and, from our apartments and homes, we set out to call each company to gather responses and relevant context and break what we in the business call a "quick hit" investigation.

I was most intrigued by the VA. The department had denied news reports of widespread shortages of protective gear for medical staff, but the data seemed to agree with doctors and nurses. The department's contracts people were panic-buying on an unprecedented scale.

In late April the department granted a $14.5 million contract for N95 respirators to Bayhill Defense in Pittsburgh. We found the company was listed to the home address of Andrew Taglianetti, a former University of Pittsburgh football player and an aspiring arms dealer. Bayhill Defense had never won a federal contract, according to federal data, but Taglianetti's website claimed it sold ammunition, assault rifles, grenade launchers, and more to the United States and other "friendly nations."

Seeing what the VA was doing, I wanted to look a little closer at the contractor who had landed its largest order for masks, about $34.5 million for 6 million of them. At nearly $6 a mask, that was a whopping 350 percent markup for a mask that usually costs about $1. It was Federal Government Experts' first-ever government contract. Of all the no-bid contracts at the time, this company ranked number 10 in total value. Its owner, Robert Stewart Jr., didn't stand out in court records and the usual places we look.

But there were other reasons to wonder.

First, the company's name, "Federal Government Experts," aside from being a little on the nose, suggested the company was devoted to federal contracts, yet on its website it advertised a robust private sector client base. The website was also filled with stock art and ambiguous descriptions of the firm's expertise. For instance: "With continued growth and increasing competition in the Federal sector, we have developed a dynamic business management consulting process. . . . Our process has yielded unmatched results for our clients."

I could not discern what that meant. This company was expert at everything, from temporary staffing to IT consulting to a "block chain" AI solution to government procurement, whatever the hell that meant. Yet there was no evidence that anyone besides Stewart worked there, and there was no record of the federal government ever hiring the firm.

The company was based in Virginia, but had little footprint there besides a tiny office in Falls Church. Stewart did know his way around contracts, though, because he'd worked for years as a procurement officer at the Pentagon. His posts on social media gave the look of a one-man operation being run from an old desktop computer.

The workday was nearing its end, and I was still doing the due diligence, planning to call Stewart in the morning, when a colleague sent me a link to a news article. My heart sank as I read the headline from the *Wall Street Journal*: "U.S. Pays High Prices for Masks From Unproven Vendors in Coronavirus Fight."

The article mentioned Federal Government Experts and Stewart, Panthera, Aunt Flow, and more. It was the exact story we were working. I flipped my laptop to sleep and cursed the news gods.

I coped in the usual way. I poured a tall scotch. Then another.

———

The morning after realizing the *Journal* had already executed the story we had in mind, I woke to a headache and the self-loathing any reporter who's been beaten knows all too well. It was the last Friday in April. I knew I'd need to dust myself off and come back with something stronger the next week, as this whole pandemic thing showed no signs of abating.

I cooked eggs and bacon to the din of bad news spilling out from the morning CNN announcer and thought about what that article did and did not say. The truth was—it didn't tell us all that much.

It was too early to tell who was legitimate and who wasn't.

In the end, it was what data reporters refer to as "fancy arithmetic."

It added up contracts, gave some totals, pointed out the outliers, and filled the numbers in with a couple of interviews and cross-references to public records, such as the articles of incorporation that every company must file with their state's secretary of state. I don't begrudge this whatsoever. It was, after all, the exact story I had pitched.

There was also one bit, near the end of the article, that just didn't sit right with me. The *Journal* had quoted Stewart, the CEO of Federal Government Experts LLC, as saying, "I'm getting ready to step on a Boeing 737 to bring the masks to the VA." This felt oddly specific, and at this point, airports were still ghost towns.

The thirty-three-year-old entrepreneur told the newspaper he was at the Port of Los Angeles, about to go through customs. "I'm looking at a few million masks right now."

But how? How did this guy, who had never won a federal contract, who had no apparent experience buying, importing, freighting, or reselling medical equipment even in the bustling days before the world shut down—how did this guy with a tiny office in suburban Washington, D.C., manage to do what no one else seemed able to do?

I decided to click a little deeper into the company's website and noticed something I had overlooked. My spidey senses were tingling again.

A detailed outline of his firm's process included a "hierarchy of consulting purposes," a pyramid that one could climb toward greatness. As someone who's watched countless consultant firms do their best to destroy American newspapers while using inane buzzwords, I'm skeptical of consultants. Setting that bias aside, though, there was something off here. It described eight tiered purposes of any consultant, starting with the two building blocks of "providing information to a client" and "solving a client's problems." A successful consultant could ascend all the way up to tiers seven and eight: "facilitating client learning" and the final pinnacle, the apex, the nirvana of consultant achievement, "permanently improving organizational effectiveness."

This was deep nonsense. But more than that, it struck a different tone from the vagaries and puffery that littered the rest of the website. This section read almost academic. Here's where I turned to one of investigative journalism's most powerful tools—Google—and plugged in a particularly grating and likely unique passage in quotes: "The lower-numbered purposes are better understood and practiced and are also more requested by clients. Many consultants, however, aspire to a higher stage on the pyramid than most of their engagements achieve."

And bing. The search engine zipped me straight to a 1982 article in the *Harvard Business Review* titled "Consulting Is More Than Giving Advice." Large passages were lifted verbatim. It was funny, but big deal, I thought. It wasn't even worth a tweet, let alone a story. But it did tell me something about the guy. It told me he was willing to deceive.

That's when I decided to call him, even though we'd been beat, just to see what he would say.

A couple of hours later, Stewart returned my call, sounding agitated. He said he had only a few minutes to talk as he sealed up his $34.5 million deal with the VA. He'd be boarding a "noncommercial" flight the next morning for Hines, Illinois, outside of Chicago, to supervise delivery of 6 million N95 respirators. His deadline was two days away, Sunday, at midnight.

When I asked how he managed to get such a big contract even though he had very little relevant experience, he told me the contract staff at the VA "liked my technical approach." He did not specify what that technical approach was. That didn't mean too much to me just yet. Because he is a Black owner of a small business and a veteran of the U.S. Air Force, the government is required to give companies like his preference in certain circumstances.

"We don't like China," Stewart offered, unprovoked. "But when our ass gets jammed up, who do we go back to?

"They know they have us by the balls because we're a consumer nation. We don't produce anything anymore."

The irony of us being so reliant on China, our sources of PPE being yet more reliant on labor in, of all places, Wuhan, the epicenter of the outbreak, was worth reflecting upon. But my reporter brain was still stuck on the "noncommercial" plane.

My research didn't indicate he had the kind of scratch that can cover a private jet, so I asked who was footing the bill. A veterans organization, he said, though he wouldn't specify. He claimed he'd signed a nondisclosure agreement with this organization, which seemed odd. If this mystery organization had, in fact, paid for the delivery of masks to the VA, that would be fabulous public relations fodder. Famously, Robert Kraft, owner of the New England Patriots football team, had lent out his plane to deliver some supplies, to some applause.

Stewart also offered that he was exhausted beyond belief because he'd been working the phones day and night while quarantining in his Virginia home with a newborn baby.

"Quarantining?" I asked. "Didn't you tell the *Wall Street Journal* that you were in LA, looking at a shipment of masks?"

The *Journal* misunderstood him, he claimed. He meant he was "figuratively" looking at a shipment of masks. This was not how the article read. But while we were on it, Stewart needed to vent about the *Journal* article, which he said was unfair and made him look like a crook. I told him I thought the article was fair and that he was barely mentioned at the end of it.

"That's the thing that was kind of fucked up," Stewart said. "At the end was 'Well, he was a contract!' That infuriates me to no degree. I don't do stuff like that."

"Like what?" I asked.

"My mom wrote the editor of the *Wall Street Journal*," Stewart said, dodging the question. "My mom and dad raised me to be a man of integrity."

I had not questioned his integrity. But he seemed to need to defend it, so I obliged and asked him if there was reason to question it.

"No!" he responded.

The real story, he said, was the intermediaries, the middlemen with whom he'd found himself dealing late into the night. He described, and I'd find it to be true, that the overnight craze to buy and sell masks had produced multiple inefficient layers of private profit and government waste without any of the transactions seeing the light of day.

I got a guy . . .

This deal was much more complicated than anyone knew, Stewart said.

"If I had these things in my basement ninety days ago, shit yeah, I'd be rich!" Stewart told me. He would indeed. He could have delivered the cache to the VA and collected the agreed-upon 350 percent markup—fast, easy, simple.

But Stewart didn't have any product on hand, so he had to take the not-unusual but seldom-advertised route of essentially becoming the master contractor who builds the deal, working with various subcontractors who take their negotiated shares, the ultimate buyer none the wiser. It's sort of like when a homeowner commissions a repair job with a general contractor and that contractor hires an electrician, a tile guy, and framers and in turn maybe each of those tradesmen contracts out some of the work.

So, armed with his government purchase order, or PO, for $34.5 million worth of masks, a figure that was broadcast to the world, Stewart sought to find a guy who knew a guy who had masks or knew of someone who might know of someone who did.

He called it a broker chain. In these chains, secret intermediaries collected handsome fees for setting up deals and greasing the skids from the comfort of home. Everyone involved signs a nondisclosure agreement to avoid any potential scrutiny.

I needed to learn the mechanics of these broker chains. As Stewart explained it, after all this wheeling and dealing and doling out everyone's cut, he didn't expect to pocket as much as he had hoped, maybe creeping up on $1 million, he said.

"It's a bunch of buccaneers and pirates!" he said. "But so were the men who made America. You're gonna have a lot of millionaires that come out of this. They're just scoundrels."

"You have this black market," he continued. "When the cat's away the mice will play. It's like robbing Peter to pay Paul."

We were on the record, and the guy was on a roll, so I spoke as little as I could while he talked. He was not one of these pirates, he explained, but he stood to gain from the lack of government oversight just as they did.

"Because of the fact that there is a lack of oversight, there is an opportunity that wouldn't have existed to prove I can do these things," he said.

One thing I've learned about liars over the years is that many will overshare on details peripheral to the truth they hope to conceal. The blunter and more truthful they are about certain things, they might believe, the less likely someone is to think they're lying about the subject at hand. It makes sense on a human level—liars only succeed if they are trusted, and bonding begets trust.

For a second, I admit, it was almost working. I genuinely liked the guy. I laughed and told him he reminded me of a wonderful quote from Lord "Littlefinger" Baelish, the evil schemer in HBO's *Game of Thrones,* who once said, "Chaos is a ladder."

I wish I had remembered the complete quote at the time because it would have been prophetic: "Many who try to climb it fail and never get to try again. The fall breaks them."

My head was spinning. I told Stewart I agreed that this underworld of broker chains and investors was the bigger story, and I'd love his help in telling it. No problem, he said. As a veteran, he found the whole affair disgusting.

"You and I could go and start a cartel and it would be less conspicuous than this. It's a multilayer hidden society of people. It's sketchy shit, man. You gotta see it for yourself."

That was my opening. I said that was a great idea and asked, Well, how about I get on the private plane with you?

Sure, he said. He had nothing to hide.

I got off the phone and immediately called my editor, Marilyn Thompson.

———

After the lockdowns came in March and April, ProPublica's top brass made the ethical decision to make no effort to purchase N95 masks for reporters to go into the field, so as not to further deplete supplies for healthcare workers, whose need was greater. Reporters were ordered not to go out into the field whatsoever.

Our charge was to cover the largest and only story on earth, most likely the biggest in our lifetimes, and it had to have investigative impact, but we couldn't go anywhere. I did not disagree with this policy, but I needed to ask that we break it. And being that I was one of the newest and youngest reporters on a fledgling team in D.C., and knowing I had zero political influence, I was almost certain I'd be told no and

I would have to resort to being a pain in the ass, an area where various bosses have told me I excel.

I dreaded this. I was in just about the worst position a reporter can be: I hadn't yet published anything big, I had nothing big coming down the pike, and now I was about to make trouble for overtaxed editors who were very aware of both of those facts.

"We have to get on that plane," I told Marilyn, who agreed but said we needed approval from New York.

As expected, I got on a conference call with senior editors and was met with skepticism. I understood. They were worried about my safety, of me sharing air with random people as we soared over the earth in a tin can.

I reiterated my case. *It's a PRIVATE PLANE! There's something off about this guy. Red flags! Government money! People are dying!*

They weren't buying it. We ended the call with a tentative no, but we agreed to take the matter to the top editor.

A few hours later, my editor and I got on a call with Stephen Engelberg. Aside from being a thoughtful and nice guy, Engelberg was once a foreign correspondent for the *New York Times*, whose enduring appetite for a big story is as ravenous as any journalist I've known. One gets the sense that the guy really, really misses being a reporter. He was all over this story when it seemed to me that it was just some bug in China, and, having cowritten a book years before about germs and biological weapons, he knew his stuff.

It was the day's end at the end of a trying week in our new reality. The other editors who were trepidatious had gotten tied down with childcare and other duties and couldn't make the call to offer counterpoints to my pitch. Engelberg gave it his usual insightful, out-loud breakdown of the variables and potential consequences and came to the conclusion that, if I was aware of and willing to take the risks, and as long as I understood that in no way was management asking me to take such a risk, he saw no reason to keep me grounded.

Chaos is a ladder.

Engelberg offered sincere and detailed caveats and asked for my reassurances that I would mask up and quarantine for fourteen days when I returned. I was also told that the company life insurance policy might not pay out if I went down in a private plane. We were in agreement, and I was given permission to be the first ProPublica reporter to go out into a contagious world.

———

Stewart almost came to his senses.

We had switched to texting, and after several attempts to get him to divulge who was paying for the plane, something we needed to know to ensure we weren't wading into any ethics issues—like, say, what if the Trump campaign was funding it?—Stewart finally said his company was paying the bill. He sent a photo of the charter receipt, which showed a $22,080 charge to his company's account. We agreed that we'd reimburse him for my seat at the prevailing rate for a similar commercial flight, which is standard journalistic practice for reporters who travel on Air Force One, for instance. It came out to about $200.

I packed a bag filled with surgical masks, notepads, a camera, and a change of clothes and booked a one-night stay at the Hilton near the VA warehouse outside Chicago, where he said he and a few employees would stay. Everything looked good—until he sent an ominous text message at 11:11 p.m.: "Sir trip has been cancelled. Do not want to speak on it at this time. Beyond my control."

"Oh wow," I replied. "Cancelled for everyone or just me? Will you reschedule?"

I was disappointed. But something about the way I responded, I suspect, made Stewart want to prove he was the real deal. Just seconds later, he pinged: "We will still make the trip."

Followed by: "Keep the course."

We agreed to meet at 7:45 the next morning at the executive wing of Dulles International Airport, just outside D.C.

CHAPTER **9**

AIRBORNE

WE WERE ALREADY LIFTING OFF in his private jet when Stewart admitted that he didn't have any masks.

There were none in Los Angeles or Chicago, and he didn't have a line on masks at all, anywhere. He'd been up all night making calls, and he believed he had a new lead. He was acting on faith now, and armed with it, he intended to find another source and deliver 6 million masks to the VA by midnight.

He enlisted the help of someone he erroneously said was the attorney general of Alabama, his home state. I'd soon learn he was working through a cagey broker who, in fact, was once the AG of Alabama but was no longer. To get the deal done, he needed to get a bank to give him a loan against the VA's order. If he found masks, he'd still have to figure out how to get them to Hines, Illinois, ASAP.

That was a lot to put on faith, I thought. I didn't yet know the half of it.

The flight plan had also changed. En route to Chicago, we were stopping first in Columbus, Georgia, on the opposite end of the country, to pick up his parents, so they could come along on a chartered jet to Chicago. I asked why he felt the need to fly more than six hundred air miles to pick up his parents for a business meeting.

He gave a long pause, took a breath, and said, "That *Wall Street Journal* article really affected my parents."

He'd made me a liar. I told my editors that it would be just me, him, and a couple of employees. Now a couple of senior citizens were involved. I didn't have an N95, so in that moment, I was mortified that I could get someone sick, or worse.

He broke down the perverse mechanics of a COVID-19 mask deal in this way:

The VA awards a contract for goods at a set price per unit to Federal Government Experts, aka Robert Stewart Jr.

The federal government typically doesn't pay this up front. Instead, the hired gun gets a purchase order from the VA, a piece of paper, which proves the deal is backed by Uncle Sam. The contractor can then seek purchase order financing, where a bank or deep-pocketed private investor gives a high-interest loan to buy stuff. If the stuff is delivered, the feds pay up and the company reaps a profit minus whatever it owes the bank or investor. Thus, for the company to make this work, the markup on the actual item must be substantial.

The repayment terms on these high-risk deals are short, a few days or weeks. In return, the banks or private investors collect steep interest, as high as 20 percent, according to some brokers I'd soon meet.

That's just the money.

Because he wasn't a direct mask maker, he needed to find a legitimate supplier. To do so, he would need to go through a distributor or a broker. The big companies like 3M had already clamped down on distributors and were going after anyone trading on their brand. So he turned to the world of brokers. They'd collect a broker fee, usually a few cents or as much as a dime, per mask. Multiple brokers might be involved in any one deal, whether they help negotiate for the seller or the buyer or even between brokers.

So in the end, a deal that would appear to the public to go like this . . .

The VA pays $34.5 million to Robert Stewart, aka Federal Government Experts, and the company delivers 6 million masks to VA.

. . . actually looks like this:

The VA issues a purchase order to Federal Government Experts

LLC, and the company takes that purchase order to a lender and gets a high-interest, short-term loan roughly equal to the cost to acquire masks. It's wired to the company's bank account. Stewart then coordinates with Broker A, Broker B, and Broker C to locate a seller. Each broker has an agreement with Stewart to collect a "finder's fee" or commission. Once Stewart and the various brokers locate a seller, Stewart releases payment into an escrow account. Upon closing the deal, the funds are released, the seller is paid, and various brokers collect their fees. Then, masks in hand, Stewart delivers to the VA, which in turn wires a payment equal to the contracted rate. Stewart would then repay the loan to the lender plus the agreed-upon interest due.

This is not accounting for the cost of storage, cargo planes, freight forwarding, shipping insurance, and other ancillary costs that can add up quickly. The remainder after all the overhead, the payouts, the interest, and the purchase itself equals Stewart's profit.

If this sounds stupid, that's because it is.

As we approached our pit stop in Georgia, I had chicken-scratched through an entire notepad while Stewart explained his business, his predicament, and the logic behind whatever it was we were doing.

This was the second time that a shipment of masks was within his sight but evaporated. He claimed that, earlier in April, he had a line on N95 masks, sold by a distributor and allegedly made by a Chinese factory, Shanghai Dasheng. Everything looked good, he said, until the CDC put out a warning that loads of ineffective counterfeits bearing the name of this manufacturer, and falsely labeled as NIOSH approved, were flooding the market. Naturally, the VA didn't want those masks, so he was starting from scratch with only days left to deliver on his deal.

Also concerning Stewart was news that the FBI and the Justice Department were beginning to round up mask brokers and counterfeiters and charge them for various nefarious schemes, including price gouging. Stewart's contracted rate of nearly $6 per mask was well beyond what some government consultants recommended. But that rate was what this crazy, unregulated free market was demanding, he said.

"I'm just trying to fulfill my obligation and not go to jail," he said.

This was at least the fourth time Stewart had mentioned jail or prison without provocation.

"We don't want to do anything nefarious," he said. "The goal here is not to get rich. The goal is to get crucial equipment to the government."

With his deadline looming at 11:59 p.m. that night, Stewart said he still had faith that he could find 6 million masks and get them to the doorstep of the VA. The latest plan had come together just twelve hours before, when one of his contacts connected him with the former attorney general of Alabama, a guy named Troy King, a Republican lawyer who held a variety of LLCs and side hustles and whose name has often appeared adjacent to scandals in the newspaper.

Further aiding his efforts was a mysterious woman to whom King had connected him, a Juanita Ramos, who allegedly had a relationship with someone on Vice President Mike Pence's White House Coronavirus Task Force. This was the officially official one, not the Kushner Kids assembled by the president's son-in-law.

Now he had legitimate channels, Stewart said, and all the ingredients to pull off "a miracle."

Stewart held a tattered daily devotional Bible, plucked from his briefcase, as he explained how he would triumph in the face of adversity. As someone who had completed a proper Christian education, and won several Bible memory award ribbons, long lost to movements of a rambling journalism career and doubt, I had an idea of where this was going.

He flopped the book open and referenced Joshua 24:15, which in the New International Version ends with a familiar passage etched into many a Hobby Lobby tchotchke: "But as for me and my household, we will serve the LORD."

He said this was a perfect analogy, but it was a bit lost on me. I might have picked Proverbs 13:16: "All who are prudent act with knowledge, but fools expose their folly."

After all, he said, it was a miracle that he'd gotten this important job in the first place.

"Awarding a $34.5 million contract to a small company without any supply chain experience," he mused. "Why would you do that?"

He added: "I've been reminded in this engagement that the road to hell is paved with good intentions."

Our tangent into the heavenly was cut short by our rapid descent to earth. At 11 a.m. on Saturday, April 25, tail number N407FX skidded onto warm asphalt in Columbus, Georgia, with two men in the narrow and empty fuselage and two bemused pilots in the cockpit.

As Stewart dropped through the plane door, I stopped in the tiny bathroom and stared in the mirror for a long second. Wild as this assignment felt, I noted that I myself looked a tad unhinged. I hadn't been able to get a haircut before the lockdowns, and my hair was already on the longer side. Now my shag and beard tufted out at the seams of my mask as if Teen Wolf had grown up and become a surgeon. I took a couple of selfies for posterity. They're not great.

I gave myself a silent pep talk. Part of me was worried that my more cautious editors were right—this might all be for naught. A dud. The scene before me had its elements of comedy, but I was heartsick with the knowledge of all the death and despair playing out in the hospitals whose staff and patients were praying for capers such as this to be a success.

Surely Stewart must have given some assurances to the government that he could get the job done, right? The government was desperate, and there was no meaningful oversight of how $17 billion in new emergency cash was going out the door, despite what the administration claimed, but I had to believe there was at least an inquiry as to his plan, his sources. My reporting is often guided by a solemn faith that people invariably do stupid and selfish things and systems inevitably fail—call it job security—but I never could have imagined recklessness of this magnitude.

I was last to step out of the cabin and into the balmy Georgia air, where Stewart made calls from the asphalt and entered and exited the empty regional airport where his parents would soon arrive. Earlier that morning, Stewart had exuded the confidence of a world-class magician about to perform a career-defining trick, but now he showed obvious signs of stage fright.

In between calls, Stewart chatted up the pilot.

"Let me ask you," he said, admiring the contours and angles of a status symbol shimmering in the sun, "at what point does it make sense to buy a plane?"

When his folks arrived, we greeted and boarded the jet as members of Stewart's extended family watched and said goodbye from behind a chain-link fence.

"I paid for it!" Stewart announced to the cabin. "Eat all the snacks."

(Narrator voice: He didn't pay for it.)

Also with us was Dawn Lockhart, Stewart's childhood friend and remote-working human resources director.

"This is the first time I've worn heels and a skirt in probably three years," Lockhart said. "Most days I work at home in my sweatpants."

She, like me, had been told by Stewart that everyone on board would have access to an N95 mask, but there were none. So I sat about as far away from the other guests as I could, nearing the cockpit.

Stewart's parents sat in the rear, his mother enjoying M&Ms, his father settling in for a nap.

Despite his company's moniker, it appeared there was nothing expert about this operation. As we zipped skyward, Lockhart began to flip through a large college textbook labeled *Strategic Staffing.* Meanwhile, Stewart was poring over the weighty federal government tome *Federal Acquisition Regulation,* or *FAR,* as those who've endured its contents call it.

Stewart was building his company, like this deal, in midflight.

That very day, if I hadn't been aboard that flight, I would have been watching the televised NFL Draft. I thought of those amazing moments when you see an entire family lifted up by the unlikely payoff of a young man's hard work and ambition, screams and shouting and crying, and often, that unmistakable sigh of deliverance.

In a similar way, Stewart had been drafted by the federal government to the tune of $34.5 million, and he too wanted to share the glory with his family and literally lift them into his new world. Whatever his crimes, his belief that he could move up in a system stacked against him was precisely what we Americans preach. In this moment, for the sake of his family and the country, I wanted him to succeed.

As Stewart said, "When you're a poor kid from Alabama, you do what you need to do to get the job done."

————

Once again, it would not go down as Stewart had promised.

He had said that once we landed at Chicago Midway International Airport, he would drop his folks off at the Hilton Oak Brook Hills Resort and he and I would take a taxi over to the VA distribution center in Hines and wait for a mask delivery "even if we have to wait until three a.m."

Instead his entourage rented a few SUVs and I took a separate Lyft ride to the hotel, where everything and nothing went down.

After two very bored employees sitting behind Plexiglas checked us in, we met in the vast lobby facing out into a rolling, empty golf course. The capaciousness of this convention center hotel was made larger still by its emptiness, the unlit and shuttered cafe, the pool with no people. It was only us in what could have been the Overlook Hotel denuded of its history, charm, and spirits. Disturbing the eerie quiet was Stewart and his crew, who had formed an unofficial mission control from the lobby, where he worked two smartphones with increasing anxiety. He needed the VA to sign off on his new arrangement, but to win approval, he needed invoices and other documentation that he said Troy King, the former attorney general of Alabama, hadn't yet provided.

"Troy is not the first vendor," Stewart said. "Every time we go to a vendor and get ready to say 'Give us six million masks,' they'd be gone by the time we got to the due diligence part of it, right?

"I finally got to a point after, like, the third time, when we got with Troy, I said, 'Hey, man, before we go through this deal, I need to see some proof of life.'"

It sounded like something out of a hostage negotiation, but it was the standard parlance. Brokers would share a video showing that inventory, including some sort of time stamp to prove it existed, wasn't old footage, and was ready to be shipped.

Just before 2 p.m., King had sent the proof of life. The grainy cell phone video pans over what appear to be hundreds of boxes labeled 3M, but it was unclear what was in the boxes or where they were housed.

Was that really how these mask deals were going down? I thought.

The video breathed new life into Stewart. He wanted to believe they were real, that he could get them, that the VA could get them, and all would be well.

"Those are in Atlanta," King wrote beneath the grainy video.

"They have 6.5 million," King continued. "Our cost is $4.90."

King didn't explain who "they" were, but Stewart responded with gullible immediacy: "Okay, I'm good with that. . . ."

Stewart had just agreed to pay $4.90 apiece for masks that should have cost about a dollar, which he would flip the very same day to the VA for about $5.90 apiece. A dollar was his cut, less the costs he would bear to get them to their final destination, and payouts to the various brokers in the chain and lawyers managing escrow. In other words, if he could get $29.4 million to the seller, he'd stand to make several million dollars.

By 3 p.m. we were joined by an outside attorney, two consultants, and a friend of Stewart's from Houston who made his living clearing debris after natural disasters such as Hurricane Harvey, the category 4 storm that inflicted $125 billion in damage and killed more than one hundred people. It was Roosevelt "Trey" Daniels III of Frontline Recovery who had connected Stewart to King and, I'd later learn, at least two other politicians representing Texas and Louisiana.

Emboldened by the video, Stewart and Daniels made dozens of calls, in frantic succession, to trucking companies, to supposed cargo jet owners. Daniels didn't want me around and tried to block his sound, but some slipped by.

"Hey, Frank," Daniels said at one point into his cell phone. "Who is a good freight company?" And that would lead to the next call and the next.

"Well, I talked to Tess," Stewart said in another conversation. "Prefers twenty-four-hour notice to get people in to unload the truck.

"Well, when I talked to Daniel it was eighteen trucks," he continued, referring to what it would take to transport thousands of boxes carrying millions of masks that, although individually light, amount to tons and tons of weight and volume.

The next call . . . "Got a 727 that can get to Atlanta in three hours?"

Stewart got on the phone with King and walked out of earshot. When Stewart returned from his call with King, he said to me: "Troy still says he's putting his foot on the gas, man."

As the clock ticked near 6 p.m., Daniels had suggested they send a portion of the shipment by truck to Illinois, while they figured out how to get the rest on planes. But Stewart insisted that he wanted to get the whole shipment there at once.

"There's just a lot that's going to go wrong with multiple logistics companies involved," Stewart said. "I'd rather be late with all of it than on time with half of it and then the other half coming in damaged because it was in a hurry."

I began to suspect that with each new call, each aside, and each curious huddle with Daniels and the other consultants, maybe Stewart was putting on a show. If the performance wasn't for my benefit, then perhaps it was for his compatriots, or his parents.

Also concerning Stewart was that his lender, whom he wouldn't disclose, was showing signs of backing out of the deal. They wanted clearer proof that the merchandise was real and that the VA backed the sale.

Then a new idea emerged. Maybe they could buy some time by getting the VA to agree to an extension. Daniels had worked as a district director for U.S. representative Sheila Jackson Lee, a Houston-area Democrat, and got her office to draft a letter in support of FGE on a deadline of just a couple of hours.

I had covered politics off and on for more than a decade, including in Texas, and was astounded that these guys could sway a legislator to intercede in a contractual affair on such short notice. Even on the state level, that sort of help would require substantial lobbying influence and money.

The letter read: ". . . Mr. Stewart, a remarkable and heroic disabled veteran, used every resource available and took every step to ensure the United States Department of Veteran Affairs would receive their supply on-time.

"Unfortunately, it has come to my attention that unforeseen circumstances may possibly cause an interruption in the scheduled delivery for the Department of Veteran Affairs. In the event that this delivery is off schedule, I am respectfully requesting your office to grant Mr. Stewart a 72-hour window pursuant to FAR 52.249-14. . . ."

This explained why Stewart, who had spent years as a contract officer at the Pentagon, was reviewing the *FAR* on the plane. All day he had been looking for a way out. He had passed this provision to the congresswoman's staff. Stewart also drafted his formal extension request, citing the same procurement code, and emails I'd later obtain would show King had coached him on what to say to the VA to keep the deal alive.

As Stewart and I talked in the lobby of an empty hotel, VA contract officers were growing concerned that Stewart was full of it. One manager instructed a subordinate to go ahead and give Stewart an extension anyway because it was easier to appease a member of Congress than deal with explaining why the VA terminated the deal, according to emails I'd later obtain.

"We won't lose anything except a little time," the VA official said. "But at this point, that's all we really have."

Stewart's parents popped in and out of the scene, looking worried for their son but not altogether invested, like dutiful but bored parents fulfilling their obligations at a Little League game. He sent the group to fetch some TGI Fridays takeout and got on the phone with the VA contracting officers overseeing his deal. His promises had turned to excuses.

"Look, man, I don't drive trucks!" he said into the phone. "Well, look, man, we're going to get the memorandum from Pence's team. We have the proof of life video. We have the attorney general calling over there. I don't know what else we can do."

By Pence's team, Stewart meant the mysterious Juanita Ramos, who he hoped could draft a letter and pull strings in Washington with the vice president and VA secretary Robert Wilkie. While Stewart had heard this woman's voice on a previous phone call with King, he told me that he had no clue who she was. And by attorney general, Stewart meant King, who was no longer the attorney general of Alabama. In fact, King was now a private citizen, having just lost an election for one of that state's seats in the U.S. House of Representatives.

The whole mess would take months to unravel to my near satisfaction, and much of what Stewart told me would prove false or impossible to confirm. What was clear is that the man who had so decried the nature of unscrupulous mask marauders had sailed into the storm and become captain of his very own sinking ship.

As daylight slipped away, so too did any reasonable hope of this miracle working out. Stewart and Daniels's frenetic string of calls had succumbed to venting and finger-pointing.

Between calls, I asked Stewart to share his communications with King, and he agreed. He also agreed to show everything he had submitted to the VA to get the deal in the first place. But when I asked if he would just go ahead and forward the records, using email and the hotel's free Wi-Fi, so I could review them from my hotel room, he pointed at his MacBook and said he couldn't figure out how to access his files. This was from the CEO of an IT consulting company.

Stewart's parents returned with dinner, and the group huddled around takeout appetizers in what Stewart joked was "the last supper." His father patted him on the back. As they sat and ate in disappointment, I took up a section of floor.

"I don't love defeat," he said to the crew, "but I do feel as though we've exhausted all resources."

As I texted an update to my editor back in D.C. on what I'd just seen, Stewart transitioned into small talk about Netflix and TV shows, telling his colleagues, "That's actually one of my favorite shows— *American Greed*."

I looked up that CNBC program on my phone. Its subtitle read: "Some people will do anything for money." It's about con artists.

———

The next morning, the dejected party boarded the return flight, back to Dulles International by way of Columbus, Georgia. Just before liftoff, the pilot asked, "Anything I can get you before we take off?"

"Yeah, six million N95 masks," Stewart quipped.

An awkward hour and a half later, we landed in Georgia, where Stewart's parents and HR director deplaned. Stewart got out and snapped photos with his family in front of the jet and reboarded the plane to endure an even more awkward hour alone with me.

The CEO was in the same gray suit as the previous day, though it was now wrinkled, and his bold red tie had slacked, the trappings of a successful federal contractor tattering in real time. He said he'd been up all night. I had no reason to doubt him.

With his friends and family now gone, his joviality had given way to exhaustion and the realization that the article I was about to write wasn't going to be fun for him. The optics of the private jet, he realized, would not be good.

"The only reason I took the plane was because of my parents," he said. "They're old and I didn't want them to get sick, and I wanted them to see this. I wanted to say thank you."

Stewart said he had severed ties with King the previous night. The nail in the coffin on this deal, Stewart said, came late at night when Daniels knocked on his room and urged Stewart to just walk away. His friend convinced him something was off.

Further fueling their suspicion, Stewart said he and his team couldn't track down any Juanita Ramos, the connection King purported to have to Pence's task force. I, too, had spent much of my evening trying to find this person—searching LinkedIn, all the social media, LexisNexis, and other expensive databases to which ProPublica subscribes to track down people, most of the time with success. Nothing turned up on the mystery woman who had serious White House connections.

"I absolutely do believe he made her up," Stewart suddenly disclosed. "He's the one that made up this figment Ramos lady. I didn't make that up."

(Narrator voice: She exists.)

"So, Troy King was saying he had an in with one of these distributors, yeah, and a stockpile of N95 masks. Because he is a legal representative for one of these distributors and that's acceptable," Stewart explained.

"Which distributor?" I asked, sitting closer than was wise so I could hear his words through the clamor of wind ripping at our sides.

"I don't know who he represents," Stewart said. "He wouldn't give me a name. And that's generally how these things work."

Over the course of our conversations that day, Stewart had rambled about his dreams, his integrity, his mistakes. He revealed that he held ambitions to one day become the governor of Alabama. That was long term. In the short term, he aspired to go into business with a friend who had a large tract of land in Macon, Georgia, to build a factory for nitrile gloves, which were also in scarce supply and reliant on tangled supply chains stringing back to Asia. He planned to acquire a classic Oldsmobile 442, then paint it white with a royal blue racing stripe and white interior. He mused on and on, but it was my job now to bring him back to reality and make him aware of what this article would have to say.

"You know, I don't know if you're going to like the article as it is now," I told him. "I really don't."

"I don't know exactly who did what," I said, according to one recorded conversation. "I can only write about the facts in front of me, right?

"I didn't want to ask you in front of your mom," I continued. "But I wanted to ask you about these conversations—Why is Troy King involved? He's taking a cut, you know, but what's the actual price of acquisition versus what's going to be charged to the VA? And it sounded like Trey [Daniels] had many of the same questions."

I encouraged him to send me the communications and records. He would forward most of the materials, with the notable exception of the actual bid documents he'd provided to the VA, which would tell us how he'd represented himself and gotten this monster deal. (Emails I'd later obtain would show he got the deal just by sending an email full of promises to a contract officer who said, "Let's see if he can actually come through with the product. Guy seems to be legit.")

As he and I drilled down, we got closer to the heart of my inquiry. Was all of this just a show? Did he take me, his friends, the VA, the American people for a ride? Were there ever any masks?

"Right now, you just think I'm full of shit," Stewart said to me. "Because I haven't delivered. . . ."

"I didn't say that," I responded.

He said his new plan was to come back to the VA with a much lower cost estimate. He had found a more reputable distributor, he claimed, and he could deliver just as many masks for half the cost. I told him that if that worked out, I would of course make it a prominent piece of the story.

The story I should write, he offered, was one of a dedicated businessman paving his way to hell with good intentions, a caveat for hospitals and government bureaucrats seeking masks. It was he who had been taken for a ride.

"It took me a while, but I broke through the bullshit," he professed. "I would rather be late, and you go, and you bash me in your article about me being late and being right, doing the right thing, than deliver something on time that has blood money on it, and it's going to get people hurt, and I'm going to end up going to jail for it, right?"

Again, jail.

———

After we landed in Washington, D.C., Stewart went on his way and I waited for a ride. I called my editor and attempted to explain what I'd just seen. I made a pitch I'd not made since I worked for an alternative news-weekly where my angsty post-college drivel streamed down pages filled with advertisements for medical marijuana. It was a pitch I assumed would be met with eye rolls: We should write the story in first person.

I thought just conveying what this world of mask brokering looks like and how odd it was to witness would be the best way forward. There were too many moving parts, ins and outs, and what-have-yous, and too many unanswered questions to write it like a straight news article with demonstrative findings. And people needed this information faster than a full-fledged investigation would allow.

She told me to give it a shot, and we agreed I'd take a couple of days to get what answers I could.

When I reached out to Troy King, he ignored my calls but had a spokesperson from his failed campaign shoot me an email.

"After several conversations over the weekend, Mr. Stewart informed us that he had secured these masks through another source and that he would not need our services to secure the masks," King's spokesperson said. "There have been no further conversations between Mr. Stewart and me. No agreement was ever made, no contract was ever executed, and no money was ever exchanged."

King didn't respond to my inquiry about the mythical Juanita Ramos.

I reached out to the Pence task force and the White House, but no one had ever heard of Juanita Ramos. I had no idea who she was, I couldn't find her, and I'd have to include that in the story.

I reached out to the VA and recounted what I had witnessed, and the agency's spokesperson informed me the next day that Stewart's contract had been canceled and the case was being referred to the agency's inspector general. As we entered May, the agency was waiting, along with much of the federal government, on FEMA, the spokesperson said. While manufacturers like 3M were ramping up to produce hundreds of millions of masks under the Defense Production Act, some of which were destined for VA hospitals, the VA decided not to wait. So it hired contractors like Stewart to scour and scrounge for any domestic loot.

The agency maintained that it did rigorous vetting of its contractors, which was bullshit, but we would publish their response nonetheless.

In the end, VA hospitals, where at the time more than 2,200 employees had tested positive for the virus, ended up with zero additional N95 masks from its deal with Stewart, and as a result the agency had paid nothing to Stewart. However, I would later learn that Stewart had been bankrolled by the government through a separate hustle.

Just before publication, I did the routine follow-up with Stewart. He had not been informed that his contract was dead, which was unfortunate, so I delivered the news and asked if there was anything he'd like to add to the article. He said he just wanted people to know he gave it his best.

"Stuff just never materializes," he said. "It's a bunch of smoke and mirrors and ghosts."

After the article was published, Stewart ghosted on me, which wasn't unexpected. It would be nearly a year before we'd meet again in person—in federal court.

CHAPTER **10**

HISTORY RHYMES

The man who is admired for the ingenuity of his larceny is almost always rediscovering some earlier form of fraud. The basic forms are all known, have all been practiced. The manners of capitalism improve. The morals may not.

—John Kenneth Galbraith, economist and author

MORE THAN A HUNDRED YEARS before COVID-19, the Great Influenza brought death and the spoils that follow in its wake.

Racistly dubbed the "Spanish flu" and contemporaneously referred to as "the grippe," the H1N1 influenza A-strain caught the United States on its heels as it waged an expensive and exhausting war in Europe. Supplies and food were already being rationed to support the Great War effort. Restaurants and food halls, essential to many city dwellers, faced federal scrutiny over price hikes created by both diminished food supply and advantageous greed. Government orders to vacate public spaces and to wear homemade gauze masks were the subject of localized controversies and resistance. Spiking infections and deaths wrought fear and desperation for protection, remedies, and information.

Crooks saw their opening.

A Brooklyn pharmacist named Joseph M. G. Tukay sold flu patients thousands of boxes of aspirin tablets, marketed as a remedy. Even if aspirin could treat more than flu symptoms, the pills he sold weren't aspirin at all but rather a cheap and dangerous compound of mostly talcum power, cornstarch, and an unstable acid.

Tukay was caught and sentenced to a $500 fine and three years in prison. When the *Rochester Democrat and Chronicle* reported his sentence, the headline curiously referred to Tukay as an "Influenza Pirate."

An advertisement printed in the *Kansas City Times* just before the 1918 Christmas holiday warned readers of the dangers and high transmissibility of the virus, saying, "It is the duty of every man, woman and child to do everything in their power to keep well and prevent further spreading of such a dangerous disease." The advertisement resembled a news story, explaining for several frightful paragraphs the symptoms and characteristics of the illness, before offering to customers an exciting remedy:

Snake oil.

"Hundreds of letters and testimonials from all over the country tend to prove that Miller's Antiseptic Oil (known as Snake Oil) has already prevented the spread of Influenza, and this had no doubt saved many lives."

By then snake oil had been marketed for more than a century as a panacea, on street corners and in stores, in countless iterations, and with some vendors using the moniker to mask elixirs containing addictive drugs like cocaine, amphetamines, and opiates. Those potions, and their sale, had already become synonymous with hucksters and quackery in the early twentieth century with the passage of the Pure Food and Drug Act in 1906 and new federal regulation. Yet snake oil was flying off drugstore shelves a decade later.

To the left of the snake oil ad in the *Kansas City Times*, another company marketed in bold letters a drug called Laxative Bromo Quinine, claiming it keeps one's "system in condition to throw off attacks of Colds, Grip, and Influenza." The tablets, marketed by entrepreneur

Edwin Wiley Grove, had been around for a couple of decades as a treatment for colds and would become widely marketed as an actual cure for the flu, though people who believed the latter were shitting themselves.

Grove was a self-made pharmaceutical mogul and puffery genius whose products bore his signature as a gesture of authenticity to consumers. His two most popular products, including his Tasteless Chill Tonic, combined the bitter and hard-to-swallow antimalarial drug quinine with other elements to produce a more palatable drug to combat fever and chills. It was a legitimate innovation, even if its benefits were overblown.

On a smaller scale, unscrupulous doctors sought their own fortunes. The Ohio state medical board received thousands of complaints about doctors and nurses charging exorbitant fees for treating patients suffering from the flu. In Nebraska, the *Omaha Daily Bee* ran an above-the-fold dispatch titled "Omaha Doctors Coining Money Off People's Misery."

In castigating doctors for charging as much as ten dollars to treat patients, the city's health commissioner offered a local reporter fabulous quotes that would be unthinkable in today's staid bureaucratic culture: "Some of the doctors who are getting plenty of practice for the first time in their lives in the present Spanish influenza crisis are proving themselves nothing but human vultures. . . . I'm going after those fellows if they don't stop it."

In Tampa, Florida, journalists noted that the citrus industry, poised to charge inflationary prices for fruits, was a good stock buy.

"We are advised that fruit retailers are taking advantage of the epidemic of influenza to profiteer to a very great degree, especially on oranges and lemons, both of which are badly needed," the *Tampa Daily Times* wrote in October 1918.

Reports of pandemic profiteering coalesced with broader frustration surrounding shortages of basic household items limited by rations and exports for the war effort. Many of the nation's grocers, restaurants, and mills, which newspapers from Chicago to Selma and San Francisco dubbed "food pirates," were hoarding goods such as sugar and wheat and selling them at obscene markups, sometimes double the price. The concerns were widespread enough that the Justice Department stepped in to regulate prices and prosecute price gougers. By December 1919, federal law enforcement had identified more than 200 food pirates and pursued criminal charges in about half of those cases.

Perhaps the vilest example of profiteering seen over several waves of the Great Influenza from 1918 to 1920 was that of the coffin trusts. Influenza would take some 675,000 Americans, and as the bodies stacked up, many U.S. cities experienced devastating shortages of containers in which to bury their dead. In West Haven, Connecticut, for example, the body of a dead woman was left to deteriorate in a house for seven days while the family's undertaker searched for a casket.

The shortage was most troubling in larger cities such as Philadelphia and Washington, D.C., where some undertakers banded together to fix and raise funeral costs. As Dorothy Ann Pettit wrote in *A Cruel Wind,* her 1976 dissertation on the Great Influenza, "The problem seemed two-fold: the short supply, and the high rates being charged by some unscrupulous believers in 'free enterprise.' Evidently more than a few undertakers thought that raising their funeral charges during the pandemic was only part of the natural law."

The cost of living in Washington was already high, as an influx of wartime workers had overcrowded the city and its housing supply. But now the cost of living paled by comparison to the cost of dying. Families could not afford to bury their dead. As with most scams, it was the poor and vulnerable who suffered most.

At one point, the city had so many dead it couldn't keep count. Washington's newspapers couldn't keep up with traditional obituaries, opting instead to list only prominent Washingtonians taken by the flu. Many D.C. residents embraced public health measures like wearing masks, but it had already overtaken the city. On one "Black Saturday," more than 1,300 people were found to be infected, and 92 died. Cops and federal government workers were out sick. It became a crime to cough and sneeze in public, punishable by steep fines. Schools closed. The city opened two emergency hospitals.

But for all the bureaucratic and medical measures officials could take to address the crushing wave of deaths, there was simply nowhere to put the corpses. To secure coffins, the city's top health official publicly attacked those who had raised the price of funerals.

"Such preying on unfortunate families in this direful time is nothing short of ghoulish in spirit and unpatriotic to the point of treason," Dr. William Fowler told the *Washington Post* in October 1918.

City leaders protected their people at the expense of other cities, at one point hijacking a train shipment of caskets en route to Pittsburgh, which experienced arguably the worst sustained beating of the 1918 pandemic.

Much was the same as the virus spread to other states and cities, where local leaders each experienced their own versions of hell, made different only by their proximate political and cultural forces.

It is tempting to judge the rampant stupidity and blatant profiteering of the past, but the thrill fades upon further inspection of our present. Parallels abound between COVID-19 and the flu that killed between 20 and 50 million people worldwide a century before. In both times, people were shot and killed during conflicts over mask mandates. In both times, local officials fought with state governors over business closures and mask requirements. Governors fought the federal government, invoking states' rights. Theaters and restaurants became flashpoints for public angst. In both times, hospitals were overrun, medical staff died, bodies piled up with nowhere to put them. In both eras, we had presidents who embraced white supremacists. In both times, people looked to an antimalarial drug for salvation, despite a lack of scientific evidence. It is remarkable that hydroxychloroquine, falsely touted by the Trump administration as a cure-all, was discovered by scientists trying to synthesize a drug that was similar to the naturally occurring quinine contained in Grove's Laxative Bromo Quinine. Our blind adoption of these pharmaceutical relatives a hundred years apart says something about our gullibility when a plague we don't understand starts killing our kin.

Robert Stewart's invocation of "pirates" as we journeyed across an infected country in search of masks seemed odd and anachronistic at first, but it somehow ties neatly back to the shenanigans exhibited a century before, when both literal sea pirates and the profiteering kind shared headline space in American newspapers.

As I attempted to reconcile the schemes I was chasing in real time against those stored in the torn and yellowed pages of our past, I began to feel that perhaps we are doomed to repeat history. It was all there, in textbooks and the Library of Congress and various online archives. We knew everything, yet it seemed we had learned nothing.

CHAPTER 11

"JUANITA RAMOS IS EITHER A STRIPPER IN ATLANTA OR A NATIVE AMERICAN MEDICINE WOMAN"

AFTER PROPUBLICA PUBLISHED THE STORY of Rob Stewart's private plane and doomed contract, I was inundated with hundreds of tips and inquiries from across the globe. In emails, on Twitter, and through encrypted apps, broker after broker reached out, claiming they could deliver masks. Or they knew a guy who knew a guy who could.

A few got through on my cell phone, including a man near Seattle who asked if I could connect him with the top brass at FEMA or the VA, so he could try to sell masks to them. I told him journalists don't do that sort of thing. But I'd love to know more about his business, I said, and after a few basic questions such as "what's the name of your company?" and "how did you get these masks?" the man ended the call.

My favorite tips were those that included "proof of life" videos, cell phone footage claiming to show millions of masks on the ground, waiting for a lucky buyer. Almost always, the video showed boxes labeled 3M but didn't reveal much else. I connected with as many of these brokers as I could and was shocked to learn that, during this particular time in lockdown, people were wiring fortunes to strangers based on little else than a grainy video.

I was beyond bored in my apartment at this point and thus followed each lead down its own rabbit hole. The jackpot, I hoped, was in there—finding a warehouse where masks were being sold at extreme markups. I engaged with a South African who reached out via Twitter and claimed to have a surplus of KN95s. I obviously wasn't going to buy any, but I couldn't help myself.

"Do you have proof of life?" I responded.

"Yes my contact has proof of life. . . . I will connect you with my guy," he wrote back.

He forwarded a video that appeared to be from China, featuring a woman holding a sheet of paper with his name on it, boxes allegedly containing thousands of masks behind her. Another video sent to me included a date stamp and showed a man loading the boxes into a truck. Each time, I'd ask the broker a couple of follow-up questions, and they'd disappear.

I managed to turn a few domestic mask brokers into sources and asked them to walk me through their business. A few claimed they had just seen a multimillion-dollar windfall because of COVID.

"It's like stumbling into the drug business," said one broker, Rick B., who talked to me on the condition that I not publish his last name. Using public records, I independently confirmed his full name and business associations.

"You start out as a guy on the corner holding a little bit of product, and the next thing you know, you're making calls and connecting people."

Rick B. was about to open a marijuana dispensary in Nevada when COVID scuttled his plans. On the suggestion of a friend in the mari-juana business, which is tangential to medical supplies in some ways, he pivoted his business and made six figures in a couple of weeks. But the guys who got into the mask racket early, he said, "made just stupid amounts of money."

"There are scandalous brokers out there," Rick B. said. "There are people that just make me want to take a *Silkwood* shower at the end of the day," referring to the classic film about radiation exposure. "There are brokers out there who are buying at $3 and marking it up to $6 or $7."

I learned resellers pursued three avenues to attain masks:

The first was the all-cash spot buy, done fast to keep the feds from confiscating inventory. In this scenario, a seller broadcasted, typically via email or messages on WhatsApp, that they had a mask lot on the ground. A potential buyer bid for the product and provided either a purchase order or bank records to show they had funds backing the deal. In return, the seller would usually provide proof of life. The money was funneled through an escrow account, similar to a real estate deal— and released to the seller upon mask inspection.

The second type of deal was a direct buy of existing stock from a manufacturer such as 3M or Honeywell. To pull this off, and avoid scrutiny from the feds, a purchase order needed to come directly from a hospital or government agency. This approach was less attractive to brokers because it required more paperwork, oversight, and the masks sold for near the list price, so as to avoid allegations of price gouging. I could not find a single broker who had a productive conversation with 3M, other than to confirm that masks they were looking at were counterfeits.

The third type of deal was to purchase a production line—a commitment to buy X amount of masks at X price over X period of time from a reputable factory. It's sort of like a futures buy. I came across multiple documented deals attempting this, but I am unaware of one that worked out in the buyer's favor.

The mechanics of the deals were clear, yet determining with 100 percent certainty how a specific box of masks bought with taxpayer money traveled through this gouging daisy chain proved beyond difficult. I'd connect a node here, and a node there, and then hit a roadblock or come to learn the deal was altogether a fantasy that never materialized at all.

I was swimming in mysteries.

But there was one question driving me especially crazy: "Who the fuck is Juanita Ramos?"

I couldn't get the question out of my mind.

I had hit a roadblock on my search for the alleged fixer that Robert Stewart said was pulling strings with the White House Coronavirus Task Force. Stewart had claimed she had the political clout and connections to save his $34.5 million deal with the VA. It teased a potentially big story about yet more cronyism and profiteering within the Trump machine, this time in the context of his administration's most consequential failure, that of abdicating responsibility to protect the American people. I considered that the story could be complete bullshit, of course, but it did seem too specific for Stewart to have manufactured the whole thing. He'd also taken the extraordinary step of name-dropping Ramos in his letter of appeal to the U.S. Department of Veterans Affairs.

"I am providing a 'proof of life' video that demonstrates these masks are on hand and will be released upon review of the final details of the additional vetting. We've been instructed by Vice President Pence's task force that this will be concluded within the allotted extension requested. Ms. Juanita Ramos, leader of this vetting effort, will be contacting the VA Secretary directly on our behalf to explain this situation further," Stewart wrote to contract officers in late April.

His words were specific and confident, suggesting at the very least that he believed it. But the White House, the VA, the Pence task force—none had any idea who the hell Juanita Ramos was. And dammit, neither did I. Despite my best efforts, and bringing to bear the know-how and resources of ProPublica's formidable research team, I had struck out.

For a day or two, on Twitter and among friends, it became something of a meme: "Where in the world is Juanita Ramos?" After that story was published in May, a Colorado friend of mine named Crizno texted: "Juanita Ramos is either a stripper in Atlanta or a Native American medicine woman."

This comment fit with the sardonic and random nature of our friendship, so I dismissed it as a joke and did not respond. I moved on to other leads, but the question would nag me for months to come—unnecessarily.

Pro tip: Listen to your friends.

CHAPTER 12

HOW TO MAKE MILLIONS SELLING MASKS, IN THREE EASY STEPS!

IT WAS 10 P.M. ON A TUESDAY in early May 2020 when Tim, a juicer salesman, called from California.

"My name is Tim, and I heard you're looking into VPL," the man said nervously.

I heard the faint but recognizable crackle and exhalation of vapor from his lungs. He was pacing. I got the sense he'd never spoken to a reporter before.

A few hours earlier, I had called the owner of Viral Protection Labs Medical Inc., or VPL Medical, a freshly minted company outside Los Angeles that had gotten about $21 million in contracts to supply three-ply surgical masks to veterans' hospitals and the national stockpile. It was a standard inquiry, but my call had freaked them out, Tim said, and someone at the company had passed my number along to him.

What was his interest in the story, I asked.

"I distanced myself from the company because they weren't delivering what they said," he continued. A couple of weeks earlier, after the industrial juicer business came to a halt because California juice bars had shuttered, he had taken his shot at joining the craze and becoming a mask broker.

"I went and got myself eight thousand dollars in cash. I was on my way with the money in a briefcase. . . ."

I dashed over to my kitchen table, shuffled through the detritus of mail and scribbles and stale takeout, and grabbed my notepad.

———

Boredom was the reason for this encounter.

By now, the novelty of working from home and trying out Instagram food recipes was swiftly eroding. I had grown wistful of even the obligatory weekday D.C. happy hours. Bereft of such mental stimulation, I returned to the data we'd already crunched and sorted, and I ran a few additional queries in search of clues. I went back over all of them.

Among what we dubbed "curious contractors" listed on a shared drive were a few other companies that popped out just as Federal Government Experts had. One of them was VPL Medical, whose footprint was suspiciously new. In our blitz of calls for a broader story aimed at accounting for something like $17 billion in new federal spending, we had reached out and been given the company's explanation that it had a good product, had been vetted by the federal contract officers, and was ahead of schedule. The delivery date hadn't passed yet, so there was little to push back on at that time, and we moved on to other targets.

My recent caper with Robert Stewart had renewed my suspicions, however. Just four days after the company had formed, on April 12, 2020, VPL managed to land a $6.4 million deal for 8 million surgical masks from the VA, which by now I had reason to believe was giving anyone with an email address a contract. That same week, the data showed VPL also landed another $14.5 million deal with the HHS team overseeing the national stockpile. This was a big and important deal.

It was an amazing turnaround that raised questions yet again about whether the federal government was doing any due diligence. Imagine starting a company with only the $100 fee to incorporate with the California secretary of state and landing more than $20 million in orders backed by U.S. taxpayers in the very same week. That's an extraordinary return on investment, especially for an obscure company with no obvious connections to the greasy beltway mechanics of federal procurement.

Odds were that this company hadn't formed because its proprietors had a secret warehouse stocked full of masks that, most of the time, would be a money-pit investment. My guess was that they, like Stewart, probably ventured they could get a purchase order and wrangle the masks later—hopefully.

The listed owner also had a track record that piqued my interest. We learned this from a basic "scrub," which we do for any company we're examining. I start with the secretary of state filings that will provide key dates and the names of owners and various officers of the company, which can often be cross-referenced to find other interesting companies they may have owned, sold, and/or ruined. Unscrupulous businesspeople tend to open and shut down many businesses in their wake, so we're always looking for that trend.

VPL was incorporated by Bobby Bedi just as the Trump administration released the billions and was based inside a commercial strip mall in Rancho Cucamonga, about an hour and a half outside Los Angeles, in the Inland Empire. That was the same address listed for another of Bedi's companies, "Rock On IT," which aside from having a delightful name, advertised expertise in website optimization for Google searches and the like. The office was small, clearly not for the manufacturing of anything.

I saw nothing that indicated he and his associates had any background in sourcing medical supplies, either. The N95 mask they advertised was the exact type, with the ear loop instead of the headband, that the CDC warned were Chinese counterfeits not to be used in medical settings without additional testing. The company had recently issued two press releases, announcing plans to open two U.S. mask-making outfits, which called into question their claim that they already had stateside infrastructure to make American-made masks. They were getting big, fast. I wondered if they'd put the cart before the horse.

The secretary of state filings are also a handy guide for our next step, which is running names of people and businesses in state and federal courts databases to see if they link to any interesting lawsuits, divorce records that might detail personal financials, or any actions from government regulators against the companies or their operators. This is standard due diligence.

Long story short: Bedi had operated numerous California businesses and been subject to multiple tax liens and about a dozen civil lawsuits, including allegations of fraud, lease manipulation, and breach of contract. It did not take the vast resources of the federal government to dig this up.

Just hours before Tim the juicer salesman called, I had followed up to ask Bedi about this ordeal and other tidbits I'd noticed while poking around that day.

I got Bedi on his cell and identified myself as a reporter. He explained that his $6.4 million deal with the VA was going off without a hitch. The masks were all being shipped in from China, though he hoped to start manufacturing masks in the United States by the summer. The deal with the stockpile would be fulfilled next, he claimed.

"David, look, no one has been in this situation before," Bedi said. "We've never been in this situation before."

He was doing his part, he said, leveraging connections in Asia to help Americans through this crisis, another capitalist savior. Having a string of tax liens, lawsuits, and fraud allegations was nothing more than the inevitable cost of doing business in a litigious world, he said. But when we moved to my basic question of how the company got this contract to begin with, Bedi became cagey and opaque in his responses.

"I don't know," he said. "I can't speak to how the government fulfills the order. There was a bidding process. There's a huge vetting process."

This time, however, there was no bidding process because the deal had been awarded under emergency contract rules following the president's order. And no government contractor I had ever met couldn't recite, chapter and verse, how they got their contract and why someone else didn't. I asked what he submitted.

"I don't really recall because we're doing so many projects right now. The important thing is right now there is a global pandemic, there is a shortage of masks, and we are fulfilling it on time.

"It all happened quickly," he continued. "There was no time for anybody to think."

That piece I believed.

That's when Bedi said he had to go to a meeting and that he'd call me back. I asked for his assurance that we'd reconnect, something I often do because for some reason people often don't want to talk to me more than once. The guilt of breaking a promise sometimes works. Bedi assured me we'd reconnect. But he didn't call back that evening, and he didn't return my voice messages. That's because, according to Tim the juicer salesman, he was on the phone with other people, totally losing his shit.

I landed in Los Angeles just a couple of days after Tim Zelonka had told me of his encounter with VPL. The story rose to the level of being worth some cautious travel because Zelonka said that, as curious as I found Bedi, he wasn't even the true owner of the enterprise. The true owner, he said, was a former Mercedes-Benz car salesman named Jason Cardiff, who was yet more interesting.

On that day in April when he zipped east on Interstate 10, breaking the thin shadows of palm trees overhead, a briefcase stuffed with cash in the passenger seat, Zelonka said it was Cardiff whom he was meeting. Cardiff had identified himself as the owner of VPL, though his name was nowhere to be found on the aforementioned business filings. Zelonka came to know of the company through a friend who'd been hired to help with marketing, which I'd later find out meant she was paid a handsome vig for selling the VA on the deal. Intrigued, Zelonka thought he could buy a sample lot of masks and maybe sell them around town and then come back for more if the product was legit, and buyers would place larger orders.

But halfway to the office park from his West Hollywood home, the deal fell through as Zelonka made basic inquiries during a cell phone call with Cardiff. Zelonka thought perhaps he had asked too many questions of Cardiff—about where the masks had come from, if they were kept in sanitary conditions, and about the company's credentials.

"He said: 'They're not in boxes. They're in Ziploc bags,'" Zelonka told me, recounting his conversation with Cardiff. "And I said, 'That's not what you're advertising. You're advertising made in the USA and in sealed packaging.'"

So, a few days after our late-night call, we met outside a closed coffee shop in the Venice Beach district, which I chose because, if I was going to fly over the country in a pandemic, on the cusp of a panic attack the whole time as some passengers still weren't wearing masks, I would probably need an afternoon on the beach. Also some tacos.

We couldn't order coffee, so instead we sat outside as he rifled through files, which were just printouts of webpages I had already seen. I was struck by how this guy could be a walking advertisement for California. His sun-scorched dyed blond hair, his yellow-gradient aviator shades, the teenager's wardrobe, his svelte physique, it all belied his age of nearly fifty. He made a point of it.

"Do you mind if I ask how old you are?" he said to me.

"No—sure, I'm thirty-two."

I assumed he was asking because people are often surprised that I'm not as ancient as I sound on the phone. No, he meant I looked like shit.

"Oh, wow, I would have guessed older, you know."

"Thanks?"

"I just mean out here we worry about these things and have cosmetics and everything. So, I don't look fifty." He paused in solemn repose. "I'm an LA fifty," which he estimated looked about fifteen years younger than fifty elsewhere.

Despite this microaggression, I liked Zelonka. I admired his pluck. He was an odd guy, maybe an unlikely and bemused hero à la Ace Ventura or any Keanu Reeves character. Or he could have been a midlevel Bond villain. I wasn't sure yet which he was, and something told me neither was he.

Like many others in the burgeoning underground mask business, Zelonka didn't have expertise in the medical supply chain. He handled

U.S. distribution for a Spanish commercial juicer company whose equipment can hold dozens of whole oranges, allowing customers the tactile satisfaction of selecting their own blend of juice and watching the machine, pluck, press, and pummel the juice out into eco-friendly cups.

His was a familiar American pandemic story. He had been furloughed from his juicer gig, so he was looking around for a way to bring in income. He started making calls and meeting with people who had tangential knowledge of imports from China and how to manufacture masks. In his research, he said, he'd begun to differentiate the bad guys from the good guys.

"VPL is a coyote company that should be in jail," Zelonka said. "You can quote me on that!"

Zelonka's plan was more novel than what other brokers had told me in recent weeks. His plan was to sell masks, gowns, and gloves to the food service industry and workers at places like Jamba Juice. He was looking ahead to when the lockdowns lifted, eyeing a cottage industry within a cottage industry.

We left the deserted coffee shop and dropped into his white Infiniti sedan to meet up with the proprietor of a T-shirt factory who had pivoted his business to make cloth masks for, among other buyers, Comcast and the sprawling Kaiser Permanente hospital system. These were the good guys, he said, and I should meet them before we headed to Rancho Cucamonga to surprise VPL the next day.

Zelonka fidgeted with a dirty yellow cloth mask as he cruised his Infiniti through unusually sparse traffic on I-10. I kept silent as Zelonka filled the uncomfortable void, reciting his many run-ins with oddballs and ganjapreneurs whose claims to have legitimate 3M masks or KN95 masks fell apart each time.

He retold his various strange conversations with mask suppliers, detailing how they didn't make sense, or there was no product, or the supplier couldn't answer basic questions.

"It would be like if you went to buy a gallon of milk and you asked, 'Is it whole milk or skim milk?' and they didn't know the difference."

That's when I realized I forgot to ask a pretty damn important question—had he actually purchased any masks?

"I have purchased none because everyone's full of shit," he said.

I asked if he'd made any money yet, to which he replied, "Nope."

We arrived at the garment district, and I began to turn over in my head how I'd just wasted about a thousand dollars of my company's money to meet up with a guy who didn't have any masks—again.

Was this my job now? My role in the middle of such an important story—to be the idiot chasing idiots chasing masks?

I set that discouraging thought aside and hoped this journey would take us somewhere worth writing about.

The tour of the T-shirt factory was interesting—a few dozen workers feverishly stitching together masks and gowns and dropping them in large bins—but it was, from a reporting perspective, a waste of time. I wasn't sure why Zelonka wanted to take us there. Perhaps he wanted in on the business and thought I was a fluff writer who might help place him into the good graces of these businessmen, whom he'd known for all of two weeks.

But it wasn't entirely pointless to go along for the ride. On the way back to Venice Beach, Zelonka piqued my interest with a comment about a venture capitalist in Florida who claimed to have connections with 3M and was interested in sinking a billion—with a "B"—or so into the mask trade.

Zelonka would play back for me some of a recorded videoconference call:

"We've got several billion dollars sitting in escrow to procure product right now, and we need it yesterday," said the man on the phone. "We had no idea what we were doing, to be honest with you."

Zelonka provided a misspelled version of the guy's name and said he was a venture capitalist working for a company called something like "Oasis."

This was quite an escalation from $8,000 in a briefcase, and I questioned whether this investor was legitimate. He said that he wasn't sure, but that he was working to secure a pipeline for masks from a source in Mexico.

"I think he's looking for a credible source that isn't 3M that he could use to supply the federal government with masks," he said.

Anxious yet quizzical, Zelonka appeared to be suffering from an internal moral dilemma: Can one make a profit off a global crisis without becoming a vulture? And where is the line?

"Then I would be what you're investigating," Zelonka joked. "A profiteer."

———

The next day, Friday, we met outside a Walmart in Rancho Cucamonga, around the corner from VPL's modest headquarters, where he told me his plan was to just walk in with a reporter in tow. I told him that we don't misrepresent ourselves or go undercover in any way, and that if I was asked, I would identify myself as a reporter.

I'd gone inside to get a Starbucks double espresso, and he got his own Monster Energy drink, which in between spirited guzzles he joked would be "my last nonalcoholic drink of the weekend." After this he'd be heading to Mexico, he said, to see a guy about some masks on behalf of his mystery investor in Florida.

As Zelonka and I talked that whole week, he had told me he was still in contact with VPL and had arranged with Cardiff, VPL's alleged shadow owner, to view some new product, this time KN95s, the Chinese equivalent of the N95 whose origin and efficacy were the subject of much speculation and fear.

I had done my due diligence on Cardiff that week and discovered an array of scams that he employed to live the life of a rich Californian. In 2018, for instance, the Federal Trade Commission filed suit against a company that Cardiff and his wife operated, which regulators described as a pyramid scheme. Regulators said the scheme involved robocalling people and making "false and unsubstantiated claims for dissolvable film strips advertised for smoking cessation, weight loss, and male sexual performance."

I did not expect this mask broker trail to lead me to dick pills, I admit, but there we were.

In response, a federal court shut down the Cardiffs' operation, froze the couple's assets, and required a third-party receiver to control and monitor their money. But in March 2020, about a month before

VPL was born, Cardiff had been found in contempt of court for flouting that receiver and the judge's order by, among other infractions, hiding assets in Canadian currency worth about $1.5 million. This filing was the one Zelonka had found through a basic Google search. I dug into the filings a little deeper.

The trade commission accused Cardiff of opening a secret account in his ninety-year-old father's name and using those funds to continue his lifestyle.

"The Cardiffs are spending nearly $17,000 per month," court records stated. "On Bentley, Porsche, and Range Rover lease payments, private elementary school tuition, restaurants, phone and cable bills, salons and spas, pet grooming, a 5-star hotel in New York City, music lessons, taekwondo lessons, ride shares, movie theaters, and other lavish expenditures."

The couple also stopped paying the $12,000 a month mortgage on their home. Oh, and that secret account in his father's name? "Strikingly," federal regulators said, it was not paying for his father's retirement home bills.

These records made we wonder if Zelonka was right—that Cardiff was the actual shadow owner of the company hired to get masks to the federal government and healthcare workers who were dying without them. Subsequent court filings would later reveal Cardiff's history to be even more colorful, but I had enough intel to tag along with Zelonka and see what gives.

Together in Zelonka's Infiniti sedan, we drove around the corner and meandered through an asphalt maze of nondescript, eighties-style buildings in search of a door that would lead to the suite number registered to Rock On IT and Viral Protection Labs Medical Inc. It was then that Zelonka revealed we did not have the element of surprise that he had envisioned. That's because he'd called his friend Stacey, who worked marketing for the company, and told her he was coming with me that day. Also, Zelonka revealed in the parking lot, Cardiff wasn't even answering his calls. There was no briefcase. No meeting time. No element of surprise.

I didn't understand Zelonka's decision to give the company a heads-up, but it wasn't my place to manipulate the situation. I was along for Zelonka's ride, to see what he saw, and he was in the driver's seat.

The point of this adventure now unclear, I followed Zelonka inside the building. As someone who's knocked on countless doors with nothing but a hunch and a prayer, I believe all doomed reporting missions should be seen through to their end.

Besides, Zelonka was a funny dude, and I'd come all this way. So as the world outside was falling apart, we roamed the empty halls, two guys in masks, one with fogged-up glasses, the other aviators, one zapped on Monster Energy, the other on Starbucks. We knocked on the door for Rock On IT. Predictably, there was no answer. After many tries, we returned to his car, where he called and texted Cardiff to no avail.

Without any masks or much of a story, we drove back toward the Walmart parking lot, and Zelonka expressed remorse that his promise to show me the seedy underbelly of mask brokers had petered out.

"Well," he said, "at least you can go home with a suntan."

———

When I returned, I attempted to answer the obvious questions. Who was Zelonka's mystery investor? Did he blow up the VPL surprise visit because he had a deal in the works? What was Cardiff's actual role?

I took these inquiries as far as I could before publication. When I called Cardiff, he pretended not to be Jason Cardiff. Said he'd never heard of him. But I knew it was him, and we'd later have several conversations via the same phone number. In an email, Bedi, the owner listed on VPL's official paperwork, did acknowledge that Cardiff was involved, but claimed he was "a consultant."

I wasn't sure how to tell what just happened, if anything had happened, but my editor invoked the adage "Just tell people a story." This madness, she said, was outrageous in itself when you consider the tens of thousands of Americans who are dying, whose best defense against the virus, it was becoming clearer each day, was access to a decent mask.

A couple of days before publication, as Zelonka and I plodded through the routine follow-ups and clarifications, he texted me and said his investor "is looking to spend $1.8 billion on 3M model" at a cost of $6.25 each (they list for about $1.27).

"Anyway," he continued, "I'm meeting him in Texas on Wednesday, and if the Mexican supplier works out, I'm going to visit them the following day."

I called the firm and investor that Zelonka named, and while I could see the investment firm did exist and was interested in PPE, I didn't get enough evidence to meet publication standards for printing the firm's name. Zelonka said he had proof, but he'd signed a nondisclosure agreement and didn't want to be sued. In the end, I'm not sure it mattered. Also, I doubt Zelonka was able to become the profiteer he'd pondered becoming. Could they all just have been bored, ambitious people blowing smoke up each other's asses?

I reached the VA and HHS to tell them what I knew about Bedi and Cardiff and to see if they had any response or complaints about their dealings with the men. The VA confirmed it had received masks from VPL and they were satisfactory. But HHS was still waiting.

"HHS has taken appropriate steps available under Federal Acquisition Regulations to request the company provide assurance that it will uphold its contractual obligations as we consider our options moving forward," a spokesperson for the Strategic National Stockpile told me.

(Narrator voice: they didn't.)

The day before publication, I connected with Zelonka, who said he was in Dallas to show clients how to sanitize high-end juicers. The prospect of being the star in a story about the absurd world of mask trading had soured on him. He was on defense. He'd pulled out of his promise to have a profile photo taken. I told him the story wouldn't say all that much about his business, as it wasn't even clear what business he'd done. It's just a tale, I said, and his experience gave us an unusual entrée into this world.

He's not in the PPE racket, he insisted. He never really was, he now claimed. His sole focus was juicers now.

"I'm not going to comment on anything because I'm not sure how that will go," he said.

I reminded him of what he'd said about billion-dollar investors, the alleged Mexican supplier, and his aspirations to break into the business.

"You're breaking up," he said. "I can't hear you."

The call ended. I never heard from Zelonka again.

———

The headline read: "The Secret, Absurd World of Coronavirus Mask Traders and Middlemen Trying to Get Rich Off Government Money."

The story recounted my time with Zelonka but was filled in with a great deal of context from federal purchasing records and a few dozen other interviews I'd done. I wasn't exactly proud of the story, which began with a suitcase full of cash and ended with all the satisfaction and resolution of a Richard Linklater film.

But if we hadn't published the story, pulled on the thread to see where it led, we never would have gotten back to the dick pills.

Someone involved in the Federal Trade Commission case must have seen the story and followed up, using their power and that of the court to find evidence that Cardiff was, in fact, the shadow co-owner pulling the strings behind VPL and its gambit to get rich selling masks—all while hiding the true profiteer behind the enterprise.

The court receiver had obtained emails that showed Cardiff had delineated how he wanted the company formed, who its board would be, and how he would control it.

"I am not going to lose another company," Cardiff told his lawyer in an April 5 email.

He was referring to the alleged pyramid scheme that had the FTC crawling all over his finances. One of the ventures that had been shut down, Prolongz, claimed to offer men "increased ejaculation control."

He went on to detail a list of people he'd hope to lure to the board of this new company, including a right-wing pundit with ties to the Trump White House. The emails showed Cardiff wanted to cement controlling stock of VPL and the ability to buy out his partner, who would later be the listed agent on corporate business filings.

"As I [have] raised all the capital and done all the work once again," Cardiff wrote. "I am not going to lose out on perhaps my biggest company to date. Further I have a group that wants to put in 10 mil this week."

VPL was incorporated seven days later, sans Cardiff's name. And twelve days after Cardiff's email, VPL began landing multimillion-dollar federal contracts to supply cheap surgical masks for healthcare workers. Any money gained from that enterprise, then, would have escaped the gaze of the FTC and the court receiver.

The chain of emails, the business ledgers, and other exhibits that the court receiver included in the filing confirmed a few of my nagging suspicions, such as Cardiff being a co-owner and that there never were any American-made masks. They showed that Bedi and Cardiff would pocket about $2 million in profit each on the VA cash alone.

Zelonka's friend who was handling the marketing, Stacey Barker, got paid about $257,000 to set up the deal with the VA, which records suggest was easy money.

The emails showed that when Barker set up the deal with the VA, which appears to have taken only a few emails, she told the agency that Cardiff was, in fact, the CEO. A simple Google search would have revealed with whom the VA was truly doing business: the dick pill guy.

In consideration of the masks that the VA did ultimately purchase and receive, records show VPL paid a Chinese manufacturer just $2.26 million. That's less than half the total taxpayers would eventually pay.

Another $1.2 million went to shipping and logistics. After overhead and the personal payouts to Cardiff, Bedi, and Barker, the company invested another $285,000 from the VA deal to buy machines from China that could make masks, ostensibly to fulfill the company's purchase order with the national stockpile.

But, perhaps more important, the documents committed to the official record illustrated the trend I had been reporting in bits and pieces—the federal government and states were throwing out billions in seed money to all kinds of unsavory characters.

This time, after I contacted his attorney, Cardiff agreed to talk with me. He put in plain words how he managed to get rich off the pandemic, as one federal agency paid him millions at the same time another agency was suing him for millions.

"The tough part is not getting the government purchase order or the financing," Cardiff told me. "The tough part is executing."

While he maintained he wasn't the true owner of VPL, just a consultant, which is very clearly refuted in court records, he explained in detail how the company worked. His ticket to riches, and that of many others, followed a simple three-step process.

Step One: Get a purchase order from a desperate government
   agency.
Step Two: Use the purchase order to get financing from private
   investors.
Step Three: Buy masks from China.

"As you can see, the government is desperate for its citizens, so it reaches out with a broad reach and says, 'If you can get masks, I'll pay you,'" he said.

At the time the follow-up story was published, my unscientific perusal of Amazon found the less effective surgical masks pricing anywhere from $7 to $25 for a box of 50—often less than a quarter per mask, depending on quality. The VA paid about 68 cents per mask.

The VA paid Cardiff's company at least $5.4 million, federal purchasing data shows.

After the stories ran, officials overseeing the stockpile canceled the $14 million deal with VPL. According to court records, the company's contract with HHS included the stipulation that any masks received must be made in the United States.

CHAPTER **13**

"I'M NOT GOING TO TAKE ANY OF THIS"

DR. RICK BRIGHT HID FOR WEEKS in a friend's house in rural Virginia, alone but for the company of his partner of fifteen years, his punishment for telling the truth in an age of lies.

His Washington, D.C., address and phone number had been accidentally released by a major newspaper rushing to break news of a whistleblower complaint he filed upon being fired from BARDA in late April 2020. Careful and private, Bright's life as a gay man had suddenly been spread and weaponized against him—by top Trump officials, he believed. His phone had been overrun with death threats, graphic pornographic images, and general harassment since he'd risked his career to fight back against the Trump administration. People were walking by his house and launching eggs but nothing lethal, yet; he got armed guards to watch over. His adherence to science and reason had been manipulated to make the case that he was somehow a secret Democratic operative.

To escape, he and a few confidants made plans to ditch his car somewhere between D.C. and his secret refuge, where he hopped into a friend's car and then transferred to another, to ensure no one could trace him to a vibrant compound with a gravel road, barking dogs, and roosters that woke with the sun. The scenery was peaceful, though it could not ease the anxiety he felt in the days before his life's defining moment—a nationally broadcast congressional hearing where he would outline the compounding and catastrophic failures of the Trump administration to prepare for and combat COVID-19.

Bright's complaint described egregious and destructive efforts by HHS to downplay the pandemic, ignore warnings of mask shortages, and rush dangerous and unproven remedies to appease Americans' fear, including a plan to "flood the streets" with hydroxychloroquine sourced from suspect factories in Pakistan and India. It was known that the drug posed serious health risks to certain patients, including heart complications. Bright was reluctantly on board with authorizing the drug in certain controlled situations, with doctor supervision in hospitals for critically ill patients. But the White House and HHS leadership, desperate for a public relations win, wanted to rush the drug to pharmacies, where anyone could get the drug and take it without medical supervision. It was irresponsible and dangerous, so Bright leaked information and emails to the media to warn Americans. Navarro, his once-uneasy ally, stopped talking to him. In return, ASPR Kadlec transferred him to a toothless role at the National Institutes of Health, which welcomed him with insults and suspicion. Kadlec had framed it as a promotion of sorts, but Bright knew that he had just been sidelined and silenced.

When news broke of Bright's eighty-nine-page whistleblower complaint, fastidious and damning in its details, Mike Bowen, the mask guy, texted him.

"Give 'em hell, Rick!" Bowen wrote.

There was no response. Bright had changed his number and gone into hiding.

Bright took his ouster hard. The eldest son of seven children, raised by a single mother in the flat and dusty small town of Hutchinson, Kansas, Bright had long been fascinated by disease and the human capacity to mitigate it. The 1918 influenza, some researchers believe, began in Kansas and spread to the world as soldiers flew to the front lines of the

Great War. The first COVID-19 death a hundred years later also appears to have occurred in Kansas. Then, as now, the disease was allowed to spread freely due to politics and local leaders' desire to keep businesses open. For decades, Bright had dreamed of applying everything he knew from history and science to become "the boy from Kansas who stopped a pandemic." As a reminder, he kept as his computer screen saver, in bold, the words "SAVE THE WORLD." But access to his computer and emails had been revoked by the lead architects of the American failure to address the pandemic.

D.C. has a way of crushing such idealism. He was now the man from Kansas who tried, but failed, to save the world.

The night before the hearing, he and his soon-to-be husband returned to the city. They'd gone over and over what he intended to say—just the facts, no emotion, no partisanship. As a coping mechanism, Bright told himself, "It's just five minutes. I just need to survive five minutes at a time," referring to the time allotted to each member of Congress, some of whom would be hostile toward him. He practiced living his life in five-minute increments. Each five-minute block represented his capacity to handle what awaited. He could do it. Just five minutes at a time.

The morning of May 14, ahead of a hearing that promised to be devastating to his administration, Trump tweeted, "I don't know the so-called Whistleblower Rick Bright, never met him or even heard of him, but to me he is a disgruntled employee, not liked or respected by people I spoke to and who, with his attitude, should no longer be working for our government!"

Bright's partner, Travis Elliott, a lawyer, told him to ignore the noise. "You got this," he said.

The couple met up with Bright's high-profile whistleblower attorney, Debra Katz, and the entourage entered together into the hearing called by Representative Anna Eshoo, a California Democrat. Bright, wearing a gray suit, red patterned tie, and an American flag pin, took the hot seat. Elliot sat behind him, taking notes. Katz sat at a safe distance to his right, out of frame, giving the sense to millions of viewers that Bright was alone. Before Eshoo called the hearing to order, Bright noticed that a couple of Republican congressmen on the right side of the room bumped fists, one of them saying audibly, "Don't worry. I got this."

Bright had been through the wringer before and understood the theatrical nature of such hearings, where everyone had already made up their minds and came with some preplanned grandstanding. After Eshoo called the hearing to order, the Republicans pulled the legislative equivalent of calling a time-out to ice the kicker just before a field goal attempt, lobbing several parliamentary inquiries to raise objections to the hearing, without eating into their five minutes. The Energy and Commerce Health Subcommittee, which is not an investigative committee, was not the venue, they argued to no avail. They hadn't been given all the materials, they claimed. Bright knew it was all an attempt to fluster him. To pass the time, he compulsively sipped at his water, which worried his attorney.

Testimony is no fun when one must run to the toilet.

Finally, after thirty minutes of preamble, Bright removed his mask to speak to a few socially distanced House members and a panicked nation. Just five minutes.

"I am Dr. Rick Bright, a career public servant and a scientist who has spent twenty-five years of my career focused on addressing pandemic outbreaks. I have a bachelor's degree in biology and physical sciences and a PhD in immunology and molecular pathogenesis . . ." he began.

"Americans yearn to get back to work, to open their businesses, and to provide for their families. I get that," Bright continued. "However, what we do must be done carefully and with guidance from the best scientific minds. Our window of opportunity is closing. If we fail to improve our response now, based on science, I fear the pandemic will get worse and be prolonged. There will likely be a resurgence of COVID-19 this fall. It will be greatly compounded by the challenges of seasonal influenza. Without better planning, 2020 could be the darkest winter in modern history."

And it would be.

"First and foremost, we need to be truthful with the American people. Americans deserve the truth. . . ."

To a sparsely filled room, with most who were present wearing masks, he reiterated his warnings that the United States needed to increase domestic supply of masks and to develop a coherent national strategy for testing. We had lost several precious months to inaction, laziness, and stupidity. But it wasn't too late to get back on track.

"We will either be remembered for what we did, or for what we failed to do, to address this crisis," he said as he closed his first five minutes.

During her five minutes, Chairwoman Eshoo asked, "When you look at the first four months of this year, would you describe the government's and the administration's response as a success or a failure?"

"We've known for quite some time that our stockpile was insufficient in having those critical personal protective equipment," Bright answered. "So once this virus began spreading and became known to be a threat, I did feel quite concerned that we didn't have those supplies. And I began pushing urgently in January, along with some industry colleagues, as well. And those urges, those alarms, were not responded to with action."

As the chairwoman passed to the ranking member of the opposing party, our pernicious tribalism was thinly veiled. Bright had questioned the sitting president and his men. Now *he* would be questioned.

Texas Republican representative Michael Burgess, a medical doctor, pointed out that BARDA had funded research into hydroxychloroquine, among other potential remedies. Just before his time expired, he suggested that BARDA had not done enough to investigate anecdotes from some doctors who said they had treated patients with the drug—which is not, in fact, scientific evidence.

"I'm hearing from a lot of doctors in my state, around the country, who have experience using hydroxychloroquine and chloroquine coupled with azithromycin and zinc, and they're reporting significant benefit if it is used early enough. . . ."

His five minutes were up. But Bright answered, "I've heard those anecdotal stories as well, and they were not conducted in the context of a randomized, controlled clinical study. . . ."

The hearing would continue in this way for nearly four hours, going back and forth, from Democrat to Republican, friendlies to adversaries, giving either side of a divided nation what they wanted to hear, five minutes at a time. Something as simple as a documented chronology of events could not escape the politics of blame and accountability.

Finally, Bright was dismissed. He stood and walked to the back of the room, looked back and nodded to Eshoo, who gave him a salute. He turned toward the door, brushing past a balding, silver-haired friend whom he had never formally met, Mike Bowen, who was up next.

Bowen is not of D.C.

He had been summoned to provide context for dozens of emails Bright included in the whistleblower complaint—of his partnership with Bright and Navarro and years of warnings to the federal government. Though he was honored to appear before Congress, his respect for the decorum of such pageantry was thin. He was tired and frustrated, and he'd brought a little bit of Texas with him.

"I can confirm that the emails in Dr. Bright's complaint are mine," Bowen said in his opening remarks. "They are merely the latest of thirteen years of emails I sent to BARDA in an effort to get HHS to understand that the U.S. mask supply was destined for failure. . . . In my opinion, they didn't have enough authority. Their hearts were in the right places."

The enormous mask machines Bowen had offered to the federal government in January were never fired up. While Bowen had talked directly to Peter Navarro—who told him the administration "would move heaven and earth" to get masks—the White House grew distant and eventually stopped responding. Instead, the federal government leaned into Project Airbridge and deals with companies like 3M, whose offshoring had put the nation in a bind in the first place. Bowen had concluded that Navarro was nutty. Navarro in turn would tell the press that Bowen was difficult to work with. The truth, I would later find, was somewhere in the middle.

It was a failure to communicate between two strong personalities. Navarro, pressing for immediate solutions in "Trump time," wanted the brass tacks—a set amount of masks at a set price, even an obscene price.

Bowen, on the other hand, wanted a long-term commitment from the government to buy masks off of new manufacturing lines. Frankly, both could have happened, and it probably would have saved lives.

In emails, they talked past each other. Bowen's proposal was convoluted and lacked the bluster of other pitches that had won multimillion-dollar contracts, such as Robert Stewart's or VPL Medical's, neither of which had a factory or expertise in *manufacturing* masks. Bowen could have delivered. He didn't have any lobbying experience or know-how to navigate the mechanics of government purchasing. Navarro, firmly in control of government contracts in early 2020, could have directed tens of millions of dollars to Prestige Ameritech and procured millions of masks for less than a dollar apiece—a major victory for both the company and the nation. As the Federal Government Experts saga told us, had Bowen simply said he could deliver 6 million masks at $6 apiece, he almost certainly would have been given a no-bid contract and many millions to do so. He could have made a fortune.

Bowen would also harbor suspicions that Navarro didn't want to give Prestige Ameritech a major contract because he was not a fan of Trump and had been quoted saying as much in the press.

Instead, the company was thrown a bone—a $10 million deal with FEMA to deliver batches of masks over more than a year. At less than a dollar a mask, it was a far better deal for taxpayers than the dozens of mask contracts I'd chased down. That small contract was enough to blunt the bad press of having passed on an offer for masks in the first weeks of the pandemic, but not enough to make a dent in the stockpile. It was also a small piece of the company's business, most of which was with hospitals that made long-term commitments to avoid the Wild West mask market.

As members of Congress inquired further into his business and his relationship with Bright, Bowen's penchant for plain-spoken defiance began to slip through. He was irritated that his friend Bright was being maligned.

"It seemed that everybody who was beating up on Dr. Bright was a Republican, and everyone who was defending him was a Democrat. I'm a Republican. I voted for President Trump and I . . . I . . . I."

He took a moment to consider what he would say next.

"I admire Dr. Bright. I don't know what he did in all of his other activities, but I think everything I've heard, and every time I've talked to him, and everything he said here, made a lot of sense, and I believe him."

Despite his many years of prodding the country to prepare for this exact scenario, Bowen's insistence that the government invest in manufacturing lines and labor—instead of orders that might disappear—was used against him.

In his line of questioning, Representative Brett Guthrie, a Republican from Kentucky, implied that Bowen had not done enough.

"I know that the president has asked General Motors and Ford to make ventilators," Guthrie said. "And everybody's business is their business, and they make decisions based on what's right for their business, but during a pandemic there is an upload, and if every businessperson says we're not going to adjust our lines during a pandemic . . ."

Bowen stared daggers at the congressman. The nuance had been ignored. Prestige Ameritech had ramped up its production of masks, with his business partner parking an RV outside the warehouse to keep the N95 lines running 24/7. They had built new machines to get more out to market. The workers were dog-tired. But it was those four machines they had sitting idle, and which needed significant investment, that was getting the attention.

Guthrie offered some equivocation.

"And I understand," Guthrie continued, "that Ford and GM have different access to capital than some others. . . ." He trailed off. "It's just something that everybody needs to be concerned about because, in a pandemic, you do have increased orders, but I understand you want some long-term guarantees as well, but there are a lot of people making decisions. . . ."

Nowhere in that ramble was there a question. Bowen had just been accused on national television of being unpatriotic. He was furious.

Guthrie brought his comments back to a technical question about the company's masks. Bowen answered. Next he questioned why Bowen was dealing with Bright and not trying to sell masks to the Strategic National Stockpile, whose officials had for years ignored Bowen.

"You got it all wrong," Bowen said, now agitated. "I wasn't looking for business. I don't need your business. My phones are ringing off the wall. I just—I thought of BARDA. . . . I thought of them as brothers in arms. I knew they couldn't buy my products. I knew that. But they were the only people who believed it."

On defense, Bowen listed off everyone he'd warned over more than a decade—Trump, Obama, BARDA, the NIH, CDC, the stockpile, hospitals, the media, Congress.

"My conscience is clean, Mr. Guthrie," Bowen said, staring down a member of Congress. "I've been working on this damn issue for thirteen years, trying to save lives. Nobody listened. And now . . ."

He took a breath.

"I'm not going to take any of this, what you're trying to do."

Guthrie talked a bit more, apologized to Bowen, and yielded to chairwoman Eshoo.

"I think my colleagues will agree that my description of Mr. Bowen is that he is a force of nature," the chairwoman quipped.

As members of Congress quibbled with the men who tried to warn us, the real force of nature was ripping through communities, killing without regard for political preference. As of that day, the United States had confirmed more than 1.4 million infections. More than 85,000 Americans were dead.

CHAPTER **14**

"IT WORKS AS HAND SANITIZER, TOO!"

IN THE SUMMER OF 2019, Lucas Rensko and his wife sold their twelve-year-old Mitsubishi Outlander, along with most of their belongings, packed up, and left the breezy, tropical hills of Honolulu, Hawaii, for the oppressive heat and wide river plains of San Antonio, Texas. His wife, a doctor, took a job at a nearby hospital while he hunted for odd jobs on TaskRabbit, the handyman-for-hire app. He delivered groceries and assembled furniture to help pay the bills until something more permanent came along. Then the pandemic hit, and after weeks of pressure, Texas governor Greg Abbott begrudgingly locked down the state—well, sort of.

As the lockdowns eased and the public established new levels of comfort and acceptable boundaries, the TaskRabbit gigs began to pop back up, and thirty-six-year-old Rensko made his own risk calculations and decided to pick up a task from a stranger that he thought entailed a simple delivery. The task took him to a tattered row of appliance and car repair shops in northwest San Antonio, to a leaky-roofed warehouse that was being rented month-to-month. It abuts a Mediterranean food distributor's chaotically organized stockroom, where wafting scents of exotic produce coalesce with that of nearby hot garbage and the vermin that feast upon it.

Rensko, a not-small man, approached, and a very large man met him and introduced himself as Jaime Rivera. The man politely informed Rensko that this was a modest bait-and-switch of sorts, but that he had good work lined up for him.

"He was like, 'Okay, well, listen, this isn't really a delivery,'" Rensko would later tell me. "What we're doing is basically repackaging masks and we're going to sell them to hospitals."

"He's asking, 'Well, how much time can you commit?'" Rensko said. "'We've got a whole lot of work for you.' He's basically in this large warehouse with large tables set up—he's got five or six people in there doing this. And he kind of takes us on this tour of his facility, which is essentially a shelled-out warehouse."

"They're from China," Rensko said, referring to thousands of masks that "Taskers" were repackaging. "And he was saying they were designated for personal or residential use, not for medical, and so what he was doing was basically putting them into other packaging where the city of Antonio and the state of Texas are able to look at them and [buy] them for medical purposes," he continued.

"He's giving me this background of why it's legitimate," Rensko remembers. Rivera, he said, told him that state and local governments "won't even look at them if they're not in this packaging."

"I said, 'Listen, man. I'm going to dip. I don't feel good about what you're doing. It doesn't seem moral to me.'"

Rensko told his wife, who told a friend, who later told me. When we connected by phone the first week of June, Rensko agreed to take me to the warehouse, and I told my editor I needed to head down to the Lone Star State, where, under the leadership of a waffling governor and his cryptic directives, cases of COVID-19 were surging out of control.

————

It was fascinating to see both California and Texas, economic and cultural foes through and through, at this point in the pandemic, when COVID cases had already surged and scared the hell out of the coasts, and cases were beginning to rise in the inner kingdom, where leaders had much more time to prepare, and to equivocate. In California, a blue state, residents were militant about masks, even in open-air situations. In Texas, a red state, people were galvanized against the oppression of a basic, if inconvenient, public health measure. Part of me wished I could gather up a few representatives from each state and place them in the octagon for a winner-take-all battle royal to settle our differences once and for all. In one corner, self-righteous indignation at the enemy's rejection of reason and the communal good, and in the other, formidable courage built upon a sort of cultural entitlement to individual freedom, whatever the cost. The Texans would destroy the Californians, bless their hearts. But we'd all lose.

It was 96 degrees, though it felt hotter on that day in mid-June. I met Rensko at a Starbucks around the corner from this shelled-out warehouse where people hired on a smartphone app conspired to deceive Texas hospitals. We made introductions in the empty patio area, where chairs were stacked and locked, and with sweat on our brows discussed his encounter with the man who appeared to be leading this repackaging operation.

"He called me the next day and apologized," Rensko said behind black Oakley shades. "So, he knew something was up."

In California, a dearth of customers afforded me a free rental upgrade to a black convertible Ford Mustang, which was wonderful. In Texas, the folks at the counter at the San Antonio airport said all I could get was an older-model Dodge Caravan, which was the opposite of wonderful. We masked up, piled into the suburban monstrosity, and whipped around the corner to a 5,000-square-foot warehouse in disrepair.

The large metal garage door was closed as I passed by, hoping to get a sense of what to expect before parking in front. There were two men chatting just outside the warehouse—one peering out of a blue taxi and the other gesturing wildly at him, giving the impression they were locked in a spirited but friendly debate.

The latter held a small bottle of amber liquid sloshing about, which I mistook for rum or whiskey. We introduced ourselves, and before I could balk, I was locked in the first handshake I'd participated in since early March. It was a reflex, I suppose, from the before time. I made a mental note to not touch my face and to sanitize once I returned to the van.

I told them I was following up on a potential story about a mask repackaging operation. Instantly the two men indicated they knew what I was talking about. The man with the sloshing bottle said, "The FBI is looking for them!"

"He was going to sell these masks to a guy I know," the man, who introduced himself first as Ricardo, only to amend it later, said. "They just disappeared. They've been gone two weeks now."

Before the mysterious neighbors disappeared, the man said he watched U-Haul trucks pop in and out with loads of masks. Between sorting, shuffling, and transporting boxes of imported Mediterranean goods, he tried to peek in a couple of times but was shooed away by "the big guy" and another man, a well-to-do white guy from California.

"The guy's name is Brennan," the man said of the white guy, sweat soaking through a worn blue Burberry shirt. "He's an American, but he was in China."

"He had about a million masks," he added.

The man said he'd set Brennan up with a private buyer he knew, a guy named Sam, who was his cousin. He wouldn't provide a last name. I handed him a business card and asked that he pass it along to this mystery Sam.

But the deal fell through, the man said, when Sam realized the masks weren't on the FDA's ever-changing list of masks that were roughly as good as the American-made N95. The guy recited recent amendments to the list, for masks allowed under emergency use authorization in hospital settings, which told me he knew more about the business than he divulged.

Soon after, he said, Brennan disappeared. "He felt that someone was looking for him," he said.

It was the first truly hot day in Texas, the day the weather breaks, signaling an approaching inferno. In the dead of summer, the Texas sun doesn't just beat on you. It demoralizes you. It insults your mother and makes you consider your life choices.

Lamenting as much, the man pressed on the cap of the bottle I'd mistaken for liquor and spritzed the neckline of his Burberry shirt. The cologne he'd been holding: Obsession for Men.

"It's because I'm sweaty," he said, nudging at me, next pointing to his hands. "Look, it works as hand sanitizer, too!"

———

Having failed to catch the action in real life, I did what any good millennial would do—I turned to social media.

A quick perusal of Jaime Rivera's Facebook page told me he spoiled and doted on his six children, often dancing in the yard and driveway with them. He shared memes critical of Donald Trump and privileged white people. He had a good sense of humor. He posted a photo of himself from inside a supermarket, wearing an unsoiled diaper as a mask, his eyes wide open, as if he were a Pampers-themed luchador. His favorite shirt appeared to be a classic blue Superman tee, which I also own and wear too often. He was just a guy trying to get through this morass without going bust or getting killed.

It was clear that he worked hard, routinely updating his virtual friends with his exploits and the fruits of his labor—a few hundred bucks for assembling furniture here, a few more for some landscaping there. He was a generalist handyman, and judging by the comments, his friends adored him for it.

This habit of sharing his latest odd jobs would reveal his culpability, however. As I scrolled through his happy feed, a few posts stood out. They began in late April 2020, when he posted a series of photos that showed dozens of beaten-up boxes stacked in his San Antonio garage, in between his wife's craft tables. Bursting through the seams were more than 150,000 KN95s, the Chinese masks that often didn't pass muster with the FDA or NIOSH, and without further testing shouldn't be used in healthcare settings, where tiny particles with the virus can seep through. While the ear loop masks might offer some protection, the FDA warned healthcare workers against using them.

The six-foot stack of boxes came from a Chinese manufacturer that had been called out by the FDA as producing ineffective KN95s. The Centers for Disease Control and Prevention found in test results it posted online that those which Rivera was peddling filtered as few as 39 percent of particles—a far cry from the 95 percent of a bona fide N95 mask. These particular masks were so ineffective that Canada had issued a recall. But before the CDC warned of their ineffectiveness, the FDA had hastily approved them and other masks—often relying on paperwork provided by the manufacturers themselves—for healthcare use at the beginning of the pandemic, as the Trump administration tried to atone for its original sin of ignoring the coming onslaught. I wondered if those masks had been imported before the FDA's about-face; the time stamps on Rivera's posts suggested as much. And once they were in—who would buy them? And what was someone who had invested in them, hoping to make quick-turn profit, to do with their potentially worthless bounty?

Also intriguing: Rivera had posted a $2,000 payment he had received from a sender noted as BM through Venmo, the person-to-person payment app I knew from the days when I could hang out with friends and split a bar or restaurant tab.

The payment memo read "4/17 kn95 37.5 drop off and 50k hand-off . . ."

"A day's work!" Rivera announced to his friends. He had used a U-Haul rental truck to deliver nearly 100,000 masks to two buyers that day, according to a separate post.

"Looks like code for a drug deal," one of his friends commented beneath the post.

"From China?" another friend asked.

To which Rivera responded: "Yup. [On] its way to medical facilities all over Texas. Soon I MIGHT have a trip to Los Angeles as well."

Rivera left a series of these posts.

"Off to Dallas to pick up 200,000 masks."

"3 hours to go pick up a load of 47000 masks," another post read. "Tomorrow 4 am start for delivery to Houston Texas for 3 facilities. Upon return looking at picking up another shipment from the airport for another load. Looking at HOPEFULLY a 15-17-hour day at 50 per hour! GOD BLESS U FEMA!! Lol."

My god, I thought. *He's been delivering these masks all over Texas. But for whom?* It was clear someone else was paying him to do it. One of his public posts included a text message exchange with BM, and the iPhone text app showed his first name was Brennan, the same name the mystery man with the cologne had mentioned.

When I used Venmo, I typically added a cheeky comment, a mildly inappropriate but not untrue inside joke, such as the time I paid a friend who helped me retile a bathroom and appended the note: "That thing you did with your hands!" Each time, I marked my exchanges as private so only those involved could see the exchange. I pulled out my iPhone, tapped the app, and searched for Rivera, using the moniker he'd published online for the world to see. God bless 'em—Rivera and BM left their comments public.

Venmo showed that Rivera's payments from Brennan Mulligan, aka BM, included one for "131 boxes to TDEM," an acronym for the Texas Division of Emergency Management, the state's version of FEMA. I knew, from watching my former state's muddling response to the pandemic, that this agency had been charged with receiving and routing supplies and lifesaving gear directly to hospitals coping with COVID-19 cases.

I hopped to Mulligan's public Venmo profile and could see he had been paying Rivera and a dozen other people for weeks. He also detailed what he had paid them for.

"5/18 packaging," he noted in payments to twelve different people in late May.

He was paying them about $20 an hour.

"6pm to 11pm repackaging on 5th."

"12 to 6pm 5/5 repackaging."

I had knocked on numerous doors across sprawling San Antonio and hadn't been able to find Rivera. So I called him, and to my surprise, over a series of calls he outlined the business in which he found himself.

It didn't take much persuasion for Rivera to walk me through it. In mid-April, he responded to a delivery gig sent to him through TaskRabbit. "Need to pick up a truckload of boxes at Southwest Cargo near San Antonio Airport (SAT) and drop off at Texas Dept. of Emergency Mgmt. [TDEM] warehouse," according to a screen shot Rivera later

shared with me. It would take an estimated two to three hours and required a truck, which Rivera rented from U-Haul.

This was easy money, Rivera explained, and it came just in time. He
made most of his income through jobs on the TaskRabbit app, and after
the lockdowns most opportunities for cash dried up because people
were no longer inviting strangers into their homes to build Ikea furniture. He was desperate, and his obligations to his family were immense.

Once he got to the TDEM warehouse in San Antonio, he dropped off
the boxes, and the state's emergency workers would process the masks
and distribute them to hospitals across the state. After his first delivery,
Rivera and Mulligan cut out the digital middleman and began working
together through text messages and exchanging payment using Venmo.

"So, I went from picking up packages in San Antonio to Houston to
Dallas to Austin, bringing them back over for processing, and that's
pretty much it," he told me.

Receipts that Rivera kept show Mulligan was importing Chinese
masks to Los Angeles and then placing them on a Southwest Airlines
cargo jet destined for various Texas airports so they could be delivered
to his far-flung buyers, primarily the state of Texas. To my knowledge,
this was the first close-up view of how subpar and ineffective masks were
seeping into the pipeline and ending up on healthcare workers' faces.

Rivera was just a courier at first. He delivered 94 boxes and 2,444
pounds of masks on April 29, according to shipping records, and another 52 boxes and 1,300 pounds on May 4. The masks were different
brands, but none were approved for medical use by the FDA, according
to the receipts Rivera shared.

But in May the job changed. The FDA was cracking down on bad
masks as they made their way into hospital settings, vexing and endan-
gering frontline workers who trusted their lives to devices that came
through such dubious back channels. Further complicating the new
business partners' efforts was the refusal by TDEM and other buyers,
growing wise to the sea of subpar masks, to accept anything that had
been labeled as not for medical use. Dozens of mask brands that the
FDA had hastily approved under emergency use authorization were suddenly unacceptable.

Mulligan had sent a massive shipment of masks that fell into this limbo, and that's when the two came up with a plan to pull the masks, ten at a time, out of their packaging and place them into new packaging so they could be cleared for sale by TDEM and forwarded to hospitals.

Rivera was put in charge of finding local help to speed up this repackaging scheme, and he turned to the app that was functionally his employer. He'd gone from courier to a manager of sorts, supervising workers' hours and recruiting people like Rensko, who'd later tip me off.

"All we're doing is we're just omitting," Rivera explained, unaware of why this was bad. "We're taking off anything that says 'nonmedical.'"

This wasn't a big deal, he said, because those labels were a perfunctory disclaimer that Chinese officials had onerously required for masks that were being exported. If the masks arrived in their original packaging with the disclaimer, state inspectors would notice the warning and reject the masks without further inquiry. He was just clearing up red tape in pursuit of getting masks to people who needed them, for a little bit of money. He was one of the good guys.

"It's stupid," Rivera said. "These KN95s—they're much easier to use for just day-to-day activities." While that is true—the ear loop masks are far less cumbersome than the tightly fitted 3M N95s with elastic headbands—he wasn't selling them for day-to-day use. These weren't going to grocery stores. They were going to hospitals. I explained my concern.

"Before it gets to the hospital level," he attempted to explain, "it has to get past the red tape."

FEMA was trying to capture ineffective and counterfeit masks before they reached domestic supply chains and, ultimately, hospitals. This scheme circumvented that effort by sending smaller, less noticeable shipments zigzagging across the country, to be picked up by a guy in a U-Haul in Texas.

"These masks are being taken and are being denied for arbitrary reasons," he said. "Those are lives that are being impacted."

Rivera claimed the repackaging enterprise had slowed down in mid-May anyway because the warehouse was too small and "there were leaks everywhere." I didn't even bother to mention the safety concerns—

having a few dozen people in tight and unsanitary quarters, a leaking roof, and open air as they removed and replaced packaging of products that hospitals expect to be hermetically sealed, sterile, and otherwise unadulterated.

We talked at length, as long as I could keep him on the phone, but in that time Rivera could not provide an explanation as to why he needed to repackage the masks if it weren't for the sole purpose of removing an important medical disclaimer. There was nothing stopping the men from selling these as nonmedical masks to the general public; at this point I had collected a few dozen nonmedical KN95s at various retailers, for instance. The key difference, I suspected, was that medical facility buyers paid a great deal more for legitimate KN95s.

Rivera at first said he'd have no qualms about meeting me in person to go over all this, but each time I tried to pin down a time to meet, he would back out.

Growing more worried as I asked questions, Rivera finally offered that the real reason the repackaging operation had halted was that he and Mulligan had been approached by an investigator with the U.S. Department of Homeland Security's Homeland Security Investigations, or HSI, which investigates counterfeits, among other potential crimes.

That visit, he conceded, had given him pause. That's when I asked, "Are you worried you were complicit in a crime?"

"The more we talk about it, yes," he said.

Before he hung up, and later rebuffed my text messages, he added, "I'm not the brains of the operation, and I'm definitely not the wallet for it."

———

The wallet was Brennan Mulligan, a San Francisco businessman with connections in China. He had founded a company whose proprietary software allowed brands like Reebok and Nike to customize products using computer simulations, and he later sold that enterprise. So, he knew a little about tech and a little about Chinese imports and the textile industry, which had largely shifted to mask production in those dark and austere months.

Mulligan was at this point CEO of SKYOU Inc., a newer venture. This firm's "manufacture on demand" business provides 3-D design software for companies to create unique shirts and hoodies, which are manufactured in and then shipped from China. Using the internet archive, I could see that the company had been advertising various PPE, including the KN95s, on a since-deleted webpage. As others were, the company was charging well beyond the usual list price.

It might have seemed odd that a tech/clothing entrepreneur would wade into the get-rich-quick absurdity of mask trading, but it did fit with what I'd seen in California and what I'd heard from the dozens of mask traders I'd encountered. Behind every mask deal, there is a mysterious investor. By now I knew Rivera had likely told Mulligan what I was up to, so I saw no harm in emailing Mulligan to ask him why he was using technology and low-wage workers to deceive Texas emergency workers.

"I would be willing to share my opinion re: your questions, off the record, but I don't feel comfortable being quoted publicly," Mulligan wrote back.

I informed him that if he chose to talk with me it would be on the record because his business was the subject of the story. He didn't respond, so I kept reporting out the story.

I had routinely analyzed Texas purchasing data—a vast database of payments, receipts, and so forth—so I was surprised when I found no trace of any payments to SKYOU or Rivera or Mulligan. I called the Texas emergency agency, and a spokesman said the agency had no record of dealing with the company, either. I followed up and emailed a photo of the masks that were being repackaged, which Rivera shared with me, and asked if they looked familiar to TDEM staff who were vetting and receiving loads of masks from various brokers.

The agency recognized them, and through a public records request the agency provided a photo they had taken of shipments they had received but rejected. Comparing Rivera's photo and TDEM's, the packages were identical but for the important words that were missing from the final packaging:

"MEDICAL USE PROHIBITED."

The brand of masks had never been cleared by the FDA.

The reason the Texas emergency agency didn't initially know anything about SKYOU, Mulligan, or Rivera is that the two were routing their product through yet another third-party vendor, which had landed a deal in mid-April to hunt down KN95s for $6 apiece—a flagrant ripoff. SKYOU, it turns out, was a subcontractor selling to a master contractor. This kept SKYOU and its emissaries out of public view—save for some unforced errors on Venmo and Facebook. It was another broker chain, which by design hiked up prices and spread profit among people who, for the most part, would never face any public scrutiny.

Texas canceled its deal with that master contractor and its subcontractor, SKYOU, in late May "because the products we were receiving were fraudulent," a spokesman said. The master contractor would blame Rivera and Mulligan for getting the deal killed, alleging they "went above and beyond" to work around roadblocks and get subpar masks to hospitals. In total, Texas paid more than $14.8 million for masks through that master contract and its invisible broker chain, records show. My reporting would find that Texas had one of the more rigorous processes for weeding out bad masks, but it also found that whatever Texas rejected would just be sold to another state or hospital that lacked such a process.

Nearing the end of my trip, I decided to extend my stay and head about 180 miles east to Houston to see a guy about why he was screwing over his country. FEMA had agreed to pay him $10.5 million to supply COVID-19 testing tubes, but a public health official had slipped to me that the test tubes were actually unusual mini soda bottles that were worthless to labs.

I didn't want to leave San Antonio, however, before following up with the outlandish guy outside the shuttered warehouse, the guy with the cologne. I popped into his storeroom, where he offered a refreshing fermented, nonalcoholic fruit beverage but no more information. His businessman cousin, Sam, the man who almost bought masks from Mulligan, was a busy guy and wasn't going to speak with me. But, more than once, he'd gestured behind him as if Sam's place of business was nearby.

I went out to my stupid Dodge Caravan, popped open Google Maps, typed in "Sam," and soon came upon Samy's Embroidery Club, just eight miles away. It was worth checking out, I thought; he was in textiles, so that's not a completely unreasonable leap.

When I entered Samy's Embroidery, it was alive with the tinny thrum of industrial sewing machines that mended together ornate biker gang apparel, local sports team jerseys, and what you might call designer COVID-19 masks. I waited for about an hour as Sam helped customers, and then we sat on a couch in the middle of the noise to talk about Brennan Mulligan, whom he did indeed know.

"The guy, you could tell from the first minute he was hiding something," said Bassam "Sam" Hasan.

Hasan had met with Mulligan shortly after TDEM declined to purchase SKYOU's masks. Thanks to his connections and experience importing from Chinese textile factories, Hasan said, he had become a modest supplier of PPE to the city of San Antonio and the local jail. He also had a cousin in Illinois who had a potential contract with a hospital system there, so he was interested in getting good KN95s. He was connected with Mulligan, he said, by his cousin Yasar, the guy with the cologne, who worked next door to the pop-up mask warehouse.

"If they are one hundred percent approved, I said, why not," he said.

According to text messages Hasan showed me, Mulligan was offering a couple of different brands of mask. "[T]hey were on the CDC [Emergency Use Authorization] list before," one text from Mulligan's number reads. "They've since been removed so we can't say whether they will meet the KN95 standard."

"He wanted to do the deal immediately," Hasan said. "This was like a million dollars, and I said you can't do that."

Instead, on Memorial Day, Hasan met Mulligan and Rivera, his right-hand man from TaskRabbit, at an IHOP off Loop 410, a couple of blocks from the warehouse.

"When he told me he was repackaging them, I was out," Hasan told me. "I'm not a little kid. I've been in business for twenty-seven years. C'mon, man. This guy—I can tell you he's not doing it right."

Near the end of our forty-minute chat, Hasan took out his phone and said he could prove he had nothing to do with Mulligan. He called and put Mulligan on speakerphone, which I did not ask him to do. I took notes as the two talked.

"Did you solve the masks you had, or what's the deal?" Hasan asked Mulligan. "What happened?"

"No, I've just been contacting people," Mulligan responded. "But you know, there's just a lot of masks out there now."

"Well, I sent the merchandise to the hospital," Hasan said. "But they said they didn't pass, you know?"

Hasan continued: "So legally, like, you can't really sell them to them. If they're not—if they're not matching the criteria they need, you know?"

This was an act of CYA—cover your ass.

Hasan told Mulligan he'd be interested in trying again to sell to an unnamed Illinois hospital, but he'd need masks that were NIOSH approved.

Mulligan said he was aware of a couple of warehouses in Los Angeles that did have masks that would pass U.S. standards, but he probably couldn't scrape a million together on short notice. Hasan asked what the deal was with the repackaged masks. Mulligan told him it was just a formality.

"So, you know, the China customs, they passed this dumb law," Mulligan said.

He was referring to rules the Chinese government imposed on exporters after masks sent to other countries like the Netherlands resulted in complaints that dangerous, subpar masks were being sold as effective in medical situations. The rules slowed down exports, bugged exporters, and exacerbated a global shortage of PPE, but they also may have saved lives by slowing the flow of untrustworthy masks.

"They said, 'Oh, you have to have 'nonmedical' on the packaging," Mulligan said. "And so the factory—this is like a law in China. So, the factory provided us with the nonmedical use packaging and their original packaging. . . ."

Mulligan said he was just undoing China's vetting process and replacing the packaging so it could be sold to hospitals. He did not address the fact that his masks had not been tested or cleared by the FDA. As a rule, if China, whose consumer and worker protections are notoriously lax, tells you something shouldn't be used in a hospital setting, it's wise to steer clear.

"It's a Chinese law," Mulligan said. "So, in a very technical sense, we're breaking a Chinese law in America."

After this awkward call, I followed up with Mulligan myself. He didn't return my phone calls but sent an email.

In the end, Mulligan said, all the effort and expense of repackaging the masks was a waste. He shared photos of scores of boxes outside a self-storage locker, millions of masks he said he couldn't unload. He made his Venmo transactions private.

"We did not sell ANY repackaged KN95s to TDEM or any other customers in the US," he wrote.

If that's true, the only people who made money on the repackaging shenanigans? The Taskers.

A spokesperson with Homeland Security Investigations responded to my inquiry about its look into SKYOU and Rivera's operation. The agency responded in an almost bemused tone, something of a federal law enforcement version of "¯_(ツ)_/¯."

"At this time, HSI, along with its law enforcement partners, is assessing these allegations in an effort to determine if any violations exist and/or if mishandling occurred," the statement said.

We like to say that when we sink our teeth into a story, we don't let go until it's dead. I felt like I was gnawing on the tendons at this point, and barring illegal travel to China to chase down likely untraceable threads, I decided to move on. I had a four-hour drive of wide, flat Texas scenery ahead of me and a Texas mix that included ZZ Top, Stevie Ray Vaughan, and Leon Bridges—plenty of time and headspace to reflect on the conditions that made this state such a fascinating and outrageous case study.

CHAPTER **15**

"GREG ABBOTT CARES ABOUT GREG ABBOTT"

OUTSIDE OBSERVERS COULD BE FORGIVEN for thinking Greg Abbott leads Texas.

Many governors made mistakes when it came to balancing human lives versus keeping capitalist enterprises humming. These were— forgive the cliché—unprecedented times, and some deference should be afforded. But none were so blatantly self-serving as Abbott, who abandoned any pretense that he was working to protect anything but his own political career.

By design, Texas has a weak-governor system. The long-standing joke goes that the most powerful person in Texas is actually the lieutenant governor, who controls the Senate and therefore the legislative agenda and wields the power to quash or pass legislation that the governor may want.

That's the system, but as both Abbott and his predecessor, Rick Perry, have shown, even a weak governor can consolidate immense power through personal relationships, moxie, and good old-fashioned nepotism, placing those indebted or loyal to him throughout the tentacles of

the bureaucracy where they owe him, and he may call upon them. Abbott oversees the vast executive bureaucracy of a state that was once its
own country, and sometimes still acts like one, with 29 million residents, the tenth-largest economy in the world, a place where one can
drive fourteen hours straight and still be within its bounds, with state
revenues of more than $250 billion a year.

With his seat, Abbott has the influence to pick, prod, pressure, and
push out agency heads who palm the levers of government and command
some half a million government workers. Those agencies include the
enormous Health and Human Services Commission, the state's equally
troubled iteration of the federal HHS. Add to that education, the state
police and Texas Rangers, insurance, public utilities, emergency management, the child welfare system, and more.

While Abbott is charged with directing this unwieldy bureaucracy,
insiders often describe his disinterest in it, or how it works. His interest,
I'd hear over and again, had to be spurred by an inconvenient headline.
And when things go awry, he would blame whichever bureaucracy oversaw said cockup and push somebody out of a job.

In this way, he wears his crown without the weight.

As a former reporter for the *Austin American-Statesman* and the *Dallas Morning News,* I covered Abbott's entire first term and some of his
second, and while reporters in Austin shy away from this phrase, I came
to refer to the apparatus as the "Abbott administration," for he works
his executive branch in much the same way as a president. Thus Abbott
should be held accountable for how he wields this power, just as legions
of D.C. press corps reporters hover around the machinations of the
executive branch of the federal government.

But despite a robust and talented group of reporters in the state
capital, Abbott expertly evades consequential scrutiny of his administration's mistakes and failures, which are numerous. I marveled as many
definitive and damning exposés from the state's powerhouse newspapers bounced right off him—everything from government waste, political patronage and nepotism, systemic neglect of disabled and abused
children, to purging Hispanic names from voter rolls, and more. In that
time, I came to believe Abbott's Teflon is created from a shrewd under-

standing that it ain't really Texans to whom he is accountable. Hell, it's not even the finely curated electorate that voter suppression measures and gerrymandering have afforded his controlling party, despite demographics that are hueing blue.

No, Abbott has consistently shown, with such predictability that it's almost boring, that he holds himself accountable to the right-wing media and, by extension, those who use it to force his hand.

I first observed this trend in 2015, during "Operation Jade Helm 15," a routine exercise led by the Pentagon to place soldiers in unfamiliar terrain and train them to better navigate social and economic conditions in conflict zones.

For eight weeks that summer, the operation took place in Texas and six other states. But what was a routine military exercise also happened to be a routine exercise under President Barack Obama's leadership, to which Texas and many Texans were openly hostile. Abbott had gained notoriety in his previous elected seat, Texas attorney general, by suing the Obama administration more than thirty times, focusing on issues that could be a Mad Libs, Fox News Edition, party game: immigration, the Affordable Care Act, climate change, drilling, and more.

The influx of soldiers to communities of folks prone to conspiracy ideology created a statewide hubbub, including in a community outside of Austin that had been beaten down by natural disasters and disillusioned by inadequate government response. I was sent to Bastrop County to report the story after residents whooped and booed and lobbed angry questions during a county commissioner's meeting that was called to address rumors that the exercise was a martial law takeover. One attendee held up a sign that read "No Gestapo in Bastropo." It was stupid.

Much of the hysteria was stoked by Alex Jones, the Austin-based talk radio host and millionaire whose website, InfoWars.com, regales its audience with tales of the merely absurd, such as that lizard people exist and chemicals in the water are turning frogs gay, to far more damaging and outrageous lies, like the claim that the Sandy Hook Elementary School shooting, which left twenty-six dead, including twenty children, was a hoax. In his unbearable way, Jones and others spread fear that

Jade Helm was a precursor to the martial law takeover of the United States at the direction of Obama, a sort of Trojan horse. Military training in Texas, a bastion of military jingoism, was suddenly and inexplicably controversial.

Such folderol could be expected to dissipate, but in one of his first acts as governor, Abbott validated the fringe of his party and the rampant conspiracy theories spreading online. He ordered the Texas State Guard to monitor the situation—that is, somehow watch over the Pentagon—"to address concerns of Texas citizens and to ensure that Texas communities remain safe, secure, and informed . . ."

The governor's action, which he later downplayed, attracted troubling responses from Texans, including some that would echo sentiments leading to the insurrection of January 6, 2021. One citizen wrote in typo-laden caps: "IT WOULDN'T SURPRISE ME IF OBAMA CALLED FOR MARSHALL LAW IN ORDER TO STOP THE NEXT ELECTION FROM TAKING PLACE. SO THANK, SIR FOR TAKING CARE OF TEXAS."

Abbott is not Trump. Though he's been described by political insiders as a bully, he lacks the bluster of Trump, and he's sharp enough to lob most of his barbs behind closed doors. For Texas, he's low-key compared to some of his predecessors. Therefore, back in his first year as governor, local pundits and academics were bewildered as to why such a smart and accomplished legal professional waded into the Jade Helm bog.

But the saga revealed a political style that would be less than amusing during a pandemic: He will always shoot for short-term political gain and minimum disruption within his Republican network. And he'll backtrack later, if necessary.

Time and again, Abbott has followed this playbook.

In 2017, Lieutenant Governor Dan Patrick, the most powerful politician in Texas, seized on a different hysteria and proposed a so-called bathroom bill that barred transgender students in schools from using bathrooms corresponding to their gender identity. This gave Patrick, a former conservative radio host, a huge spotlight that he knows well how to wear. But even the most conservative businesspeople and groups didn't want the bill to become law because it threatened to deter businesses, some of which had vowed to leave or change plans to relocate in Texas. This bill was such a hot potato that liberal advocacy groups found themselves bedfellows with the likes of Texas oil companies and powerful conservative business groups. The establishment, including Abbott, wanted the bill to die.

Abbott could have promised to veto the bill, saving his state the embarrassment and political backlash. But he instead tacitly endorsed it, hoping the measure would blow up before he was forced to make a decision—more specifically, a decision that could put him in the crosshairs of Patrick, the right-wing media, and constituents that consume it. He chose instead to leave it to the speaker of the House to kill the bill, a move that contributed to that longtime House leader's loss of favor within party ranks before he retired from public office.

Sarah Davis, a Republican and former state House member, says Abbott never forged relationships in the Texas Capitol to direct actual policy or diffuse such a hot-button issue before it could become a legitimate legislative effort. That's probably because, in seven years, he hadn't revealed much of a policy agenda at all. Other than staying in office, even Republican politicos strain to understand what Abbott actually wants to accomplish. Abbott has spent most of his attention on fundraising, campaigning, and putting Texas on Fox News chyrons—and he's good at it.

"I remember him being largely disengaged with the legislature," Davis, who represented a Houston suburb, told me.

With Abbott's carrot wanting, legislative members learned to fear his stick. That's what Davis got at the end of the 2017 legislative session, just before the start of a special session that Patrick had forced Abbott to call to keep the bathroom bill alive. During a sparsely attended press conference, Davis called the governor out for not adding "ethics reform" bills to the special session agenda. Davis oversaw a couple of committees but wasn't much of a power broker because she stood with Democrats on abortion. Abbott could have easily ignored the conference, but she had touched a nerve.

Abbott put Davis on his shit list. To kick her out of politics, he would eventually use his powerful endorsement, and money from his formidable campaign war chest, to support Davis's competition in the next Republican primary. Davis managed to win nonetheless.

"I thought, man, that escalated quickly," Davis joked. "I'm no threat to Greg Abbott, but the fact that he perceived me as a major threat—to expend so much time and energy? It tells you something."

Davis says the governor's decision making is driven by paranoia—of Patrick's ability to change the message, of dissent within his Republican ranks, of anyone who might challenge him in public. Perhaps most telling: In the next election cycle, when an anti-Trump wave threatened to hurt Republicans down ballot, casting the party's control of the state House in jeopardy and thereby threatening Abbott's best buffer against Patrick and his acolytes, Abbott endorsed Davis.

"He spends $250,000 to defeat me in one cycle. And then the very next cycle he endorses me. Why? Not because I asked for it. I didn't. It was because there was so much concern that he was going to lose the House, and he couldn't have that on his watch," she said.

"Greg Abbott cares about Greg Abbott."

Fast-forward to 2020, Abbott's second term.

As other states began to lock down, Patrick went on the offensive against lockdowns, essentially suggesting we ought to let elderly Americans die in order to keep the economy, Trump's best argument for re-election, running along.

"Those of us who are seventy-plus, we'll take care of ourselves. But don't sacrifice the country," Patrick, who was about to turn seventy, said during a conversation with Fox News' Tucker Carlson in late March.

"No one reached out to me and said, 'As a senior citizen, are you willing to take a chance on your survival in exchange for keeping the America that America loves—for its children and grandchildren?' And if that is the exchange, I'm all in," Patrick said.

Despite that painful grammatical syntax, the message was clear: Don't sacrifice commerce. Sacrifice grandma.

So, briefly, I and other Abbott observers were surprised in early April 2020 when Abbott ordered what amounted to a lockdown of all nonessential business in Texas. His was one of the last states to do it, but still, it was an act in the public interest, and one in which a huge chunk of the public wasn't interested. Ordering a Texan to stay at home would, on principle, require some die-hard Texans to leave home, I suppose. He instead referred to it as an "essential services and activities only" order, which caused instant confusion for residents and business owners who couldn't discern what his order did.

As local governments tried to wade through the order, reconciling it with, for instance, mask mandates already enacted in many cities, Abbott clarified: His order superseded any local ordinance. In effect, cities and counties couldn't require citizens to wear masks, the simplest and easiest way for individuals to slow the spread and save lives. Abbott was in charge, under emergency declaration orders, and the legislature, which is supposed to provide a check on his power but seldom does, was out of session. They meet only every two years, a convenient buffer for lawmakers who can escape the ire of a public that has the attention span for only the most recent Texas scandals, which occur with impressive frequency.

What Abbott didn't explain, among other things, was that his order did allow local governments to force businesses to require masks and endowed municipalities with the power to fine business for noncompliance, a loophole that took overwhelmed locals months to exploit for the benefit of their populace. When the top manager of Bexar County, which includes San Antonio, finally ordered mask wearing in private businesses, Abbott expressed amusement that the county judge "finally figured that out."

"Abbott was like, 'Welp, you finally figured it out!'" Davis remembers. "Like it's a fucking riddle."

The governor's office did not respond to my requests for an interview.

Still, the nonlockdown lockdown, despite its mealy-mouthed execution and subsequent confusion, was likely successful in tamping down the rise of confirmed cases and avoiding some of the terrors seen in the first waves in New York City and Seattle, for instance. Texas found itself in the same uneasy social contract as other states: asking individuals to make sacrifices to give the government time to get its shit together. But Abbott faced continuous pressure to rescind his orders from his right flank, especially from Patrick.

In late April, Patrick used the Fox News bullhorn to double down on his logic, telling Tucker Carlson, "I don't want to die. Nobody wants to die, but man, we've got to take some risks and get back in the game and get this country back up and running."

On April 29, the day before Abbott allowed restaurants, movie theaters, and stores to open at 25 percent capacity, Texas set a daily record for COVID-19 deaths, fifty dead in one day, and more than a thousand others testing positive. Those numbers would soon seem morbidly quaint.

In the first week of May, reporters at the *Daily Beast* and an Austin political newsletter got their hands on a recording that showed Abbott precisely understood the consequences of giving in to the pressure.

"How do we know reopening businesses won't result in faster spread of more cases of COVID-19?" Abbott rhetorically asked during a conference call with state lawmakers and members of Congress.

"Listen, the fact of the matter is pretty much every scientific and medical report shows that whenever you have a reopening—whether you want to call it a reopening of businesses or of just a reopening of society—in the aftermath of something like this, it actually will lead to an increase and spread. It's almost ipso facto."

Ipso facto.

The same day Abbott's eyes-open analysis was laid bare, a Dallas salon owner named Shelley Luther was sentenced to a week in jail and fined $7,000 for having defied the governor's order to close nonessential businesses. "If you think the law is more important than kids getting fed, then please go ahead," Luther told a state district judge, while omitting that her business had been a recipient of small business loans to keep her kids fed and businesses such as hers afloat.

The story blew up, and Luther became a Fox News folk hero. In a stroke of political genius, Patrick paid her fine.

Abbott had been embarrassed by the defiance of a constituent who personified the Texas spirit to which he panders. She had big hair, dances and sings, wears cowboy boots. She ripped up the judge's cease-and-desist order and dared police to come and take her. It was something to behold. Abbott had rocked the boat with something approaching decisive action, so to steady it, that same week, he nullified the enforcement provision in his order. Luther and a couple of other salon operators were set free.

"Throwing Texans in jail who have had their businesses shut down through no fault of their own is nonsensical, and I will not allow it to happen," Abbott said in a press release, announcing changes to his own executive order.

If Abbott had a dog in the fight against the virus, he'd just neutered it in public.

COVID-19 had not gone away. Cases were rising, and despite earlier proclamations that he'd wait to see if the first round of limited openings had led to a rise in cases, and following the embarrassment of the so-called Rebel Salon Queen, Abbott decided to speed up the reopening, to the pleasure of his far-right Republican critics. Luther, by now a famous and formidable critic of Abbott's handling of the pandemic, launched a campaign for the Texas Senate. (Abbott would endorse Luther's competition and spend hundreds of thousands of dollars from his own campaign funds to help defeat her.)

"I think that it affected Greg Abbott greatly," Davis said of the salon saga, and Patrick's handiwork. "I think that Abbott has very thin skin."

The mixed messaging, backtracking, obfuscation, and kowtowing belied the steady and sure aura of a governor who had shown strong leadership during Hurricane Harvey a couple of years before, when Texas gave an impressive display of tough and even—weirdly—common interest.

Chris Hooks, a *Texas Monthly* magazine writer who has dogged Abbott for years with trenchant writing and, in easier times, lots of sarcasm, offered the clearest indictment of Abbott's leadership that I've seen: "Texans are now discovering what lawmakers saw in Abbott during that first legislative session: an unwillingness to communicate clearly and a tendency to seek the most politically expedient position, particularly when confronted by the Republican Party's right wing. Neither of those qualities is a good match for a public health crisis."

By the first week of June, following a series of orders relaxing his earlier orders that limited public gatherings and business operations, his state had become a hotspot. Abbott opened the state ahead of infection rate goals he had publicly set for himself. Deaths had surpassed 1,700 and were rising at an alarming clip. Hospitals were filling up fast. The messaging, the rules for what is safe and what is not, remained fuzzy. Few people outside liberal city centers could be seen wearing masks. Abbott was still refusing to issue a mask mandate.

"I want to give the benefit of the doubt," said Davis, who lost her state House seat to a Democrat in 2020. "No governor wants the blood of their constituents on their hands. But we know he reopened before meeting those metrics—that's purely political."

As Abbott predicted in that phone call obtained by the *Daily Beast*, when lockdown restrictions eased, COVID cases increased. If he had finished the thought to its logical conclusion, it might have gone something like this:

As cases increase, more people will die.

Ipso facto.

CHAPTER **16**

"WHAT'S YOUR PROBLEM, MAN?"

THE STOCKY BALD MAN IN THE HOUSTON ASTROS SHIRT was rushing furiously toward me, his warehouse of startled workers behind him. He began to scream.

"What's your problem, man?" Paul Wexler, owner of Fillakit LLC, yelled as he approached like a schoolyard bully coming for my lunch money.

I was bigger than him, so I decided to hold my ground. It might have looked cool if I had not been simultaneously scrambling to pull my N95 respirator over my disheveled head while holding on to my notepad, pen, and phone. I was and remain terrified of being infected with any coronavirus. If one is to risk life and limb in the pursuit of journalism, as many intrepid war correspondents do, it ought to be for a worthwhile cause. This was not in the realm.

He got in my face, inches away, eye to eye, no mask, and screamed, "Get the fuck out of here!"

I pressed my pen to the notepad to be sure I documented what he'd just said, as is my custom and right. He slapped my notepad and continued to scream, "Get the fuck out of here!"

At this point, I felt obligated to inform him of something: "Whatever you choose to do next will end up in the story—either way," I said. "You decide."

What happened next involved a monocular, a speeding Enterprise rental truck, and a warning to public health officials in all fifty U.S. states and territories.

My visit to Fillakit's warehouse near Houston was a happy accident. It was one of those "great minds think alike" situations that had me and a colleague looking into the company, at first independently of one another. I had picked Fillakit LLC out of our "curious contractors" data set and ran the usual cross-references because the name just looked funny and their $10.5 million deal with FEMA was sizable enough to notice. My colleague Ryan Gabrielson, a Pulitzer Prize winner based in California, had noticed the company for much smarter reasons: They had been hired to supply test tubes and test media (tubes with a liquid solution to preserve samples) that were being distributed nationwide.

While I was the idiot chasing idiots chasing masks, Gabrielson had boned up on the science of testing and was, therefore, immediately skeptical that a company with no footprint in the medical space could provide reliable test kits. He'd gone deep to understand why the U.S. testing strategy was so woefully inadequate and plagued with delays, mistakes, and embarrassments. Based on the vague description that some poor contract officer entered into federal purchasing data, Gabrielson figured Fillakit's testing supplies were for PCR tests, the gold-standard laboratory-run tests that were more accurate and more complicated than the rapid tests.

Unlike those quick-turn antigen tests, the PCR tests require more science and greater care. As science goes, it's not all that complicated. Testers stick a long swab up a patient's nose and swirl around for brain boogers—a "nasopharyngeal swab," in nerd parlance. That sample of cells needs to be inserted into and preserved in some type of "media," a test tube with a solution, kept at a certain temperature, that can sustain the sample's life, so to speak. The sample can then be investigated for the presence of the virus. If this chain of events works correctly, the tests are usually accurate.

None of that cool science stuff can happen, however, if those media aren't done right. Quality control is paramount. So, Fillakit LLC had a big and important job. That job was yet more important given that the CDC had lost several precious weeks because the United States eschewed a well-established test created by the World Health Organization and instead deployed a flawed test that left public and private labs sitting on their hands, blinding us to the rapid spread of the virus during a critical time.

It was a fine mess. When historians look back, the failure to launch widespread testing earlier will be an important milestone along our country's winding track to near ruin. And beneath that milestone is a documented trail of stupidity and at least one angry Astros fan.

The lag in testing undercut the three-pronged approach that scientists hoped could slow the spread before we were completely screwed: test, trace, isolate. Without widespread testing, it's harder to trace the virus's trek from person to person, city to city, state to state. Without the ability to trace, local political leaders and public health officials are left reacting to outbreaks. Moreover, with the virus moving faster than the data needed to make decisions, isolation measures may come too late.

Put all that in the context of a global shortage of test tubes and swabs and—so we suspected—you're left with a very desperate federal government that's willing to buy test tubes from whomever.

Adding to our concern was the fact that Fillakit had formed only on May 1, 2020, in the state of Florida. That very same week, on May 6, FEMA hired the company to supply test tubes with a solution and swabs that were to be distributed to every U.S. state and territory as testing ramped up. The name of the company and the timing of its incorporation suggested that Fillakit was formed with the intention of profiting from the pandemic.

Then there was the owner, Paul Wexler, Astros fan.

In business filings, Fillakit's ownership was listed to a lawyer in St. Petersburg, Florida, but the contact information in the purchasing data linked back to Wexler, who was based in Conroe, Texas, a suburb north of Houston.

His life had an uncanny resemblance to that of Jason Cardiff, the guy in California with the dick pills. Wexler was also a telemarketer with

a history of fraud allegations. He too had been sued by the Federal
Trade Commission. He was also, as Gabrielson would later confirm, the
shadow owner of Fillakit.

From 2005 to 2012, Wexler operated a pseudo debt relief firm that
told consumers they could consolidate unsecured debt, such as a big
credit card balance, and pay off a new loan with as little as zero percent
interest, according to court records. This sounds-to-good-to-be-true
offer was marketed online and through telemarketing and robocalling,
including to those on the FTC's "do not call list."

Such a service would have been an enticing offer in this time, as
Florida was in many ways the epicenter of the Great Recession's assault
on the middle class, and heavy debt loads left many there struggling. As
it happens, I was working at a small Florida newspaper near Wexler's
company office when it was still in operation, and had benefited from a
legitimate consolidation loan to ease some crippling family debt. These
services can be helpful—unless they're a scam.

According to a 2012 FTC lawsuit filed against Wexler, the company
lured customers with a free consultation and collected customers' bank
information in order to repeatedly levy unauthorized charges on those
accounts. In the process, the company misrepresented itself as both a
credit counseling service and as a nonprofit, when it was neither. When
consumers noticed unauthorized charges, the company refused to issue
refunds, the FTC alleged.

Wexler denied the FTC's twelve charges of fraud and other violations but settled the case a year later. The settlement barred him from
offering debt relief services and imposed a $2.7 million judgment. That
publicly accessible judgment, however, did not ban him from becoming
a federal contractor with a key role in the country's response to the
worst pandemic in a century.

Gabrielson called Wexler, who confirmed he owned Fillakit but rebuffed questions, saying he was too busy to elaborate on how his company got a job so central to the nation's efforts to catch up to the virus.

Without much more to go on, we put what we knew about Fillakit
into a broader story that involved five reporters and catalogued how at
least 345 first-time federal contractors were awarded some $1.8 billion

in pandemic contracts by the Trump administration—and that was just in the first few months of a pandemic that would stretch well into the next year. Several of those bigger contracts were already being canceled for failure to deliver. The trend was becoming clear.

The story, the first to quantify this trend, was more smoke than fire, which is fine. We call this "priming the pump," in hopes that more details will emerge from reporting what we know. And it worked.

A couple of days after the story ran, I got a call from a state public health official who said he had come across the article while googling the company. He was at his computer to try to make sense of a strange bag of tubes he'd received from FEMA. Right away, he knew they couldn't be legitimate. First, they were made of a fragile sort of plastic he worried was too brittle to survive transport and the testing protocol. More obvious—they were too large to fit into standard lab equipment that he and countless other lab workers across the country use to test for the virus. Baffled, he shared the Fillakit tubes with a colleague who recognized what they were.

"They're not test tubes at all," the health worker told me. "They're soda bottle preforms. They're the most unusable tubes I've ever seen."

He explained that the tubes were tiny plastic "blanks" that with heat and pressure are blown up to become two-liter soda bottles found at the grocery store. What's more, he said, he had serious doubts that the solution inside the tubes was sterile. He was accustomed to test tubes coming individually and hermetically sealed with specific labels telling him the composition of the solution. These came in big plastic bags, dozens of them just thrown inside. He said state labs and local private labs were already rejecting them, and he'd decided not to distribute them to testing sites that were desperate to increase capacity. FEMA screwed up, and states were literally left holding the bag.

"They're going to sit in a warehouse, and no one can use them," he explained, saying it set his state back weeks. "We won't be able to do our full plan."

This government employee asked to remain anonymous because he had expensive medical bills he couldn't pay if he were fired. He was feeling political pressure from FEMA, where officials knew the tubes were junk and yet continued to urge states to find a use for them. It was CYA, he said.

I took the tip to Gabrielson, and we split up reporting tasks to get to the bottom of it. I worried I might have to travel to Florida, where the company was based, at least on paper. But I happened to be in Texas the very week Gabrielson learned from a source that these non-test-tube test tubes were still being processed in a warehouse in the Woodlands, a master-planned suburb south of Conroe and north of Houston. He called and asked if I was dumb enough to go scope it out. He didn't phrase it that way, of course, but in any case, I was.

———

It's pointless to say anything is off the highway in Houston, because the place feels like a slithering snake ball of highways, with people and tacos packed between the violent hiss of motors. But, sure enough, the industrial strip mall *was* just off the highway, and oddly located next to a residential neighborhood. It was quiet that day. I coasted around looking for the place, which wasn't easy to find because the only thing giving away the operation was a low-stock sheet of printer paper taped to a glass door and decorated with a blue and green clip-art volumetric flask, and beneath it the identifier "Fillakit."

I tried the front door, but it was locked. I pressed my hands and face to the glass to look through, and a woman approached and cracked open the door to ask what I wanted. I told her I was a reporter with ProPublica and was hoping to talk to Mr. Wexler. She said he wasn't around. I gave her my card and asked her to hand it to him.

Back in my car, I called Gabrielson, who said his source knew Wexler was in the warehouse. So I called the number listed on that printer paper taped to the door. The woman I'd spoken with answered, and I asked if she'd oblige my curiosity and provide a tour of the facility.

A static echo indicated I was on speakerphone. She was about to politely decline, before a man took over and snarled into it.

"There's no calls and no interviews!" Wexler said. "Don't ever call or be seen again."

Click.

It kind of hurt my feelings that they wouldn't give me a tour, though I certainly understood why. I had tried the front door, but their less-than-welcoming response inspired me to try the back one. I waited a few minutes and pulled my car around the back and down the parking lot, where, obscured by a large truck, I could see the rear warehouse door of Fillakit's makeshift office through my front windshield.

In my rush to investigate the mask repackaging ring in San Antonio a few days earlier, I had forgotten to pack my digital camera and tele-scoping lens, which I almost always bring along. More often than not, the real photographers reject my photos anyway, but I had stumbled into the exact ridiculous sort of stakeout situation where I could have used the damn thing. That's when I remembered that about six months before, on Christmas 2019, a family friend had given me a monocular as a gag gift, sort of ribbing me for being a meddling investigative re-porter. I was so tickled that I promised Aunt Lori that I'd pack the monocular in my go bag and would find a good use for it one day. And here we were.

So, peering through my monocular with 5X zoom, I watched the warehouse's large roll-up door and the rear entry door to the right of it. About a half hour had gone by when, finally, cartoonishly, Wexler peeked his head out of the entry and scanned left and right. He popped back in. A few seconds later, a large Enterprise rental truck passed and parked perpendicular to the door in a loading position. The driver went inside, and soon Wexler pulled on the chain that raised the door, and I could see the two talking as workers shuffled around behind them.

I set down the monocular, turned on the video feature on my phone, and held it behind my notepad, facing in front of me, so I could capture visuals while also taking notes. In my haste, I accidentally shot the video upside down. I approached from an angle, and as I neared the threshold, the driver and Wexler took notice.

"Can we help you?" Wexler said, according to my upside-down video.

"Yeah, I'm trying to talk to Mr. Wexler."

"You're trespassing," Wexler said, agitated. "Leave."

"I'm not on your property," I responded.

"You're trespassing," he said again. "Leave!"

"I'm not on your property," I repeated.

Behind him, I could see and catch on video large plastic bins containing plastic tubes in large piles. A worker had been using a snow shovel to load them into the bins from another larger plastic container. Some workers were wearing masks. Some weren't. A forklift beeped in the corner, apparently ready to load the latest shipment into the Enterprise rental truck, which was not refrigerated, as is needed for COVID-19 testing medium. Large industrial fans whipped the hot air around, along with whatever debris was in it.

"How are you sterilizing these vials, sir?" I asked. "Are these sterile?"

"Fuck you."

Wexler pulled the door down as I continued to ask questions.

I felt I should confirm that the company went ahead and shipped these particular tubes in that particular truck, and I had more questions, so I lingered a few yards back from the warehouse door, about halfway to my rental car. A minute passed. Wexler emerged from the back-entry door and steamed toward me yelling, "What's your problem, man?"

As he was in my face, hitting my notepad and suggesting he might punch me at any moment, I continued to ask questions.

"Fucking liberal media," he said. "All you do is attack, attack, attack."

Oddly, he screamed, "Get out of my face!"

I politely informed him that he was in my face. My face was here first.

In this exchange, he accidentally confirmed they were tiny soda bottles, not test tubes. It became clear he would not relent, and our interview, if you could call it that, was not productive. So I turned and walked slowly to my car, with Wexler marching closely behind until finally I got in, backed out, and drove away. I shuddered for a moment to think of how that accidental conflict might have gone if I were a woman. Still, there is a Zen quality to this type of confrontation. The angrier they get, and the calmer you stay, the more you're in charge of the conversation. Heated people spill the beans. Wexler had inadvertently added some rich texture to the story, for which I am grateful.

I still wanted my confirmation, so I just went around the corner and onto the street and parked along the sidewalk, where I could watch with my trusty monocular. I observed as he and his workers loaded large shipping crates onto the truck, and as the truck locked up and began to drive away, I could see that Wexler had spotted me again and started to march in my direction, a clipboard in his hand. I put the car in drive and drove to my extended stay hotel. I had seen enough.

———

After this encounter, we heard from three Fillakit employees who confirmed what I'd seen and offered some important specifics and, better yet, photographic evidence.

They confirmed that workers were using snow shovels to gather up the mini soda bottles from unsanitary surfaces and bins. Next, workers sitting at long tables added a saline solution to each tube, intended to preserve samples for analysis. The liquid, they said, was kept in trays exposed to the open air, which was being moved around by industrial fans.

"It wasn't even clean, let alone sterile," Teresa Green, a retired science teacher, told us. She had worked at Fillakit for just two weeks and walked out when she grew frustrated with what she'd witnessed. Before she left, she remembered shaking her head in disbelief, thinking, "*Surely what they're using this for is not, like, the real official tests for COVID?*"

It was.

In the company's first couple of weeks of operation, she and others weren't provided face masks, raising concerns that a sick person could be breathing right into saline or tubes that could infect others. More likely, it meant that millions of test kits central to FEMA's response could be contaminated. If workers were spitting microscopic particles into the tubes or the solution, the tests could produce widespread false positives, wreaking havoc on testing efforts nationwide.

Green and others said that Wexler and his business partner, the guy driving the Enterprise rental truck, ran the place like a sweatshop.

Wexler would come into the warehouse and "cuss and scream at everybody," Green said. The bosses "were telling us, 'Yeah, we gotta have four bins by lunch. We gotta have ten bins before you leave at five o'clock. Work faster, work faster.'"

My visit to the warehouse sent Wexler into a rage, workers said. He accused some workers of leaking the conditions inside the facility to the media and demanded to see their phones, she said. Wexler and his managers passed out masks and wrapped plastic over the solution trays and the pipettes used to squirt the solution into the tiny soda bottles. He drew the shades down on the doors and windows.

"At the end of the workday, Paul called everyone together for a big meeting," Green told us. "He told everyone that they were not allowed to talk to anyone outside the building—especially the little hippie guy reporter."

Look, I couldn't get a haircut at the time, okay. And I'm not little.

"Paul told the group that the left-wing communists are trying to intervene with Texans and keep them dependent on the government and keep him from making a living," Green said.

To round out the story, Gabrielson and I hit the phones, calling FEMA, about a dozen state health departments, a contract expert, and laboratory experts.

Officials in New York, New Jersey, Texas, and New Mexico confirmed that they had received and couldn't use their lot of the 4 million Fillakit tubes that had been sent along by FEMA. Already slow to roll out testing, Texas shelved 140,000 test tubes. At the same time, the number of confirmed COVID-19 cases there had risen by more than 30 percent in just two weeks.

Some labs rejected the testing media simply because of the solution being used. The U.S. Food and Drug Administration had only validated one solution, a so-called viral transport medium, as reliable enough to keep the RNA in the samples from being contaminated or decaying. But it was in short supply. Fillakit was using one of the potential alternatives green-lit by an emergency use authorization, phosphate-buffered saline.

There are many potential ways that a testing medium can be screwed up, and Fillakit had done just about all of them as the owners hastily turned around junk tubes to collect, in just a few weeks, more money than most people will see in their lifetimes.

One federal contract expert I spoke with expressed amazement that

FEMA not only accepted these suspect test kits but then also forwarded them to states. Because FEMA accepted them, it was not clear whether Wexler and his associates could be charged with a crime. FEMA hired them for a gig, they produced, and FEMA rubber-stamped the product.

Later, after the story ran, the *Wall Street Journal* published a story that confirmed much of what we had reported, as did others. As the Fillakit story gained momentum, in late June, FEMA sent out an advisory to all fifty states to not use the test kits. A FEMA spokeswoman said the agency would work with the FDA and the CDC to analyze the test kits.

In response, Democrats in Congress pressed for answers from FEMA and added the Fillakit contract to a growing stack of inquiries taken up by the House Select Subcommittee on the Coronavirus Response. The inspector general of homeland security launched its own inquiry. FEMA cited that ongoing investigation when it denied ProPublica's request for records through the Freedom of Information Act. Despite all of this, federal purchasing data shows Fillakit and Wexler still collected $10,507,988 for unusable test kits.

The ordeal wasted gobs of taxpayer money and, more important, it wasted time when time meant American lives.

That's my problem, man.

CHAPTER **17**

MONEY FOR NOTHING, CHECKS FOR FREE

FROM ORLANDO, HOP ON STATE ROAD 408 toward the Atlantic Ocean, pass Englewood Park and the airport, veer right as the highway becomes East Colonial Drive, and hang a left just beyond Zaxby's chicken fingers. Venture north fifteen minutes, past landscaped subdivisions, the Hitching Post Bar & Grill, and three large Christian churches. Two rights and a left will bring you to Kingfisher Point, on the northeast tip of Lake Mills. Enter the gated community, proceed to the property marked 3018, click open the gates, crawl up the circular brick drive, and behold a stolen American Dream.

A brilliant white facade, oak double doors, and thirty windows welcome visitors to a 13,000-square-foot mansion with multiple common areas, seven bedrooms, and a guesthouse facing the pool and submerged wet bar. Inside, a stone-floored atrium leads to a large living room and fireplace, a dining area, and a marbled kitchen with stainless-steel appliances. In the south wing is the two-story library, the British-style pub room, and the theater. Pass through any number of glass doors toward the pool, then head to the tennis courts beyond and the five-horse stable beyond that. Now take in all twelve acres of scorched, flat land surrounding the home's unnatural opulence. It could all be yours for just over $4.8 million.

Alternatively, you could get it for free with taxpayer money and a few hours of work. At least that's what federal investigators say Don Cisternino did before he was indicted on multiple fraud charges and fled to Croatia.

After the CARES Act passed in spring 2020, the federal government began issuing $800 billion in forgivable loans to support businesses that retained, rehired, and continued to pay employees through the pandemic. The Paycheck Protection Program loans were guaranteed by the Small Business Administration but processed and paid out through traditional banks and online lenders who had financial incentives to rush out as many loans as possible. The PPP and other relief programs were established overnight, with no initial transparency into who was getting paid and negligible vetting of those who applied. The SBA prioritized speed above all else. As a result, virtually anyone with a bank account could ask for millions and receive it in days.

It created a bonanza rife with fraud. Lots and lots of fraud. Really— just bonkers stuff.

After Congress approved the program, Cisternino, an actor and producer who played on an episode of the hit TV series *ER,* opened a bank account under a dormant marketing company. The company had no payroll and no employees except for Cisternino and his romantic partner, according to his indictment. But Cisternino told a small business lender in central Florida that he had an average monthly payroll of $2.9 million and 441 employees, a sizable company but just under the 500 maximum to qualify as a small business.

To get a loan, applicants had to fill out an application and provide evidence such as tax statements and bank records. Companies that showed the cash went to paychecks and expenses like rent could have some or all of the loan amount forgiven.

According to federal prosecutors in Florida, Cisternino lied on the SBA application when he submitted it to a commercial lender and fabricated bank and federal tax statements. He also submitted fake payroll records with names and Social Security numbers of employees who didn't work for his company, court records show. Cisternino submitted his application on May 5. Less than three weeks later, the government approved it and issued more than $7.2 million to the lender, which deposited the cash into Cisternino's account.

Cisternino, in his mid-forties and with few Hollywood credentials to his name, was apparently in significant debt. But he had now hit the jackpot. He behaved accordingly.

Two days after the money was wired, on May 30, Cisternino went to a dealership and dropped more than $89,000 on a Lincoln Navigator. A few weeks later, he went to a dealership in the sleepy beach community of Sarasota and dropped more than $251,000 on a Mercedes-Benz. He also paid off $48,000 still owed on his Maserati, $7,000 owed on his partner's Nissan, and another $1.4 million in personal debt. Cisternino paid another $41,000 to lawyers who represented him in an old lawsuit filed against him by a bank, and he paid $175,000 to GoDaddy.com to buy internet domains.

On July 6, the same day news outlets reported that 3,778 Floridians had died of COVID, and as the state had shut down bars for the second time, Cisternino bought his Seminole County mansion and twelve acres, paying more than $3.1 million in cash.

By the time he was indicted the next winter, federal agents seeking to seize his assets found that he had distributed about a million dollars in cash across various accounts. But he'd already spent most of it on his piece of the Florida myth.

After his indictment, Cisternino went on the lam. He was eventually arrested in the spring of 2021 on an international warrant near the border of Croatia and Slovenia. According to a Croatian news outlet, Cisternino would tell a judge there, "I was afraid that the new administration under President Joe Biden would prosecute me for this kind of business, even though it was allowed during the Trump administration. That is why I decided to flee to Europe after the election in the U.S. and seek asylum in Russia or some other country."

His was just one of hundreds of colorful schemes that erupted from the loose oversight and fast cash of the PPP program. Many people used inactive companies to get loans, while others bought shell companies with no operations to create the illusion of legitimate business activity. They bought luxury cars, homes, yachts, and jewelry. As Americans suffered, they flourished, while the FBI and Justice Department struggled to catch up to billions of dollars that had been clumsily scattered across the country.

On the Gulf Coast of Florida, in Fort Myers, the owner of a roofing and sheet metal company lied his way into getting more than $2 million in loans. Casey David Crowther didn't use those funds to keep his business afloat and pay his workers, which was the program's purpose. Instead, for just $700,000, he kept himself afloat in a new forty-foot catamaran. A conviction and three-year prison sentence would later take the wind out of his sails.

For a time, Florida was home to the largest known PPP fraud scheme. A network of nine people, seven of them in Florida and two in Ohio, worked together to defraud the program, according to the Justice Department. The scheme involved recruiting small business owners and submitting more than ninety fraudulent PPP applications on their behalf in exchange for kickbacks. Among the defendants were Joshua Bellamy, who at the time was a wide receiver for the New York Jets, and his talent manager, who prosecutors say concocted the plan after obtaining a fraudulent loan of his own. Prosecutors alleged that Bellamy got more than $1.2 million for his company, Drip Entertainment LLC, and that he purchased more than $104,000 in luxury fashion items from retailers such as Dior and Gucci. The co-conspirators applied for $24 million in forgivable loans, many of which were rejected by lenders. More than forty slipped through, however, resulting in payouts of about $17 million.

When a federal agent, posing as someone who could help Bellamy get another forgivable loan, asked how many employees Bellamy was paying, the NFL player said, "I got as many employees as I want."

Bellamy allegedly told the agent to seek out $1.2 million on the loan, which was more than the fifteen employees they had discussed would warrant.

"Put fifty, then," he told the agent, according to court records.

A man in the Dallas suburb of Coppell went bigger, as Texans do.

Dinesh Sah sought more than $24.8 million through fifteen fraudulent applications, on behalf of eleven companies, from eight different lenders. In those applications, Sah claimed the businesses had hundreds of thousands of dollars in payroll expenses. In all, he collected $17.3 million, which he used to buy multiple homes in Texas, pay off a mortgage in California, and buy a fleet of luxury cars, including a Corvette Stingray, a Porsche, and a Bentley convertible. Sah would later plead guilty to fraud charges and be sentenced to eleven years in prison.

In Georgia, a reality TV personality who starred on the show *Love & Hip Hop: Atlanta* was arrested and charged with fraud related to his $3.7 million PPP loan. Maurice Fayne, aka "Arkansas Mo," spent most of the loot in just days. His shopping spree included $85,000 in jewelry, including a Rolex Presidential watch, a diamond bracelet, and 5.7 carat diamond ring for himself. He used $40,000 to pay child support, which is nice but still illegal. Less impressive—he leased a Rolls-Royce with $136,000 and paid $50,000 in restitution for a previous fraud conviction. As FBI investigators dug into his finances, they learned he paid $230,000 to associates involved in a multistate Ponzi scheme in which he'd defrauded twenty people going back to 2013. He would later be sentenced to seventeen years in prison.

In the program's first year, including two waves of loans, more than 120 people would be criminally charged by the Justice Department. Counting PPP fraud and looting of similar relief programs, such as the Economic Injury Disaster Loan program, the Justice Department had charged more than 470 defendants, involving about $570 million in taxpayer-guaranteed and largely forgivable loans. The true accounting of fraud in those programs is likely much worse.

Many such schemes began or occurred in the first months of the pandemic, as many legitimate small businesses in dire need of a lifeline struggled to obtain loans. That struggle was especially pronounced among minority businesses and self-employed people who lacked existing relationships with traditional banks or otherwise got tangled in paperwork.

The program's design—rushing cash out through large and regional banks and their customers—favored the richest clients. Banks focused on providing fewer big loans to established businesses. Customers wealthy enough to enjoy the concierge service of Citi's private bank, with a minimum account balance of $25 million, were fast-tracked. The nation's largest bank, JPMorgan Chase, swiftly doled out loans to almost all of its private and commercial banking clients who applied, the *New York Times* reported in April 2020. But only one in fifteen customers who held traditional savings and checking accounts got loans in that initial phase. Chase wouldn't even consider loans of less than $1,000, which could go a long way for many struggling entrepreneurs.

By mid-April 2020, about two weeks into the program, the first gush of $349 billion in forgivable loans had run out. Yet the smallest and neediest companies were left in a lurch, forced to either close or lay off employees, who would file for unemployment benefits.

While the Trump administration tried to keep secret the details about which companies got loans, corporate filings and other disclosures began to show that much of the money hadn't gone to small businesses, as was intended by Congress and advertised to the public, but rather had flowed to large companies and publicly traded corporations. That included many companies that were awash in cash or could raise money on the stock market, unlike the small restaurateurs, bakers, salon owners, and others who needed loans.

The parent company of Ruth's Chris Steak House, a high-end dining chain with 5,000 employees, was among the first to disclose that it received $20 million through Chase, just four days after the SBA launched the program. Ruth's Hospitality Group Inc. had reported $42 million in profits the year before and distributed $41 million back to shareholders in stock buybacks and dividends. Potbelly Sandwich Shop got $10 million. Shake Shack, which had as much as $100 million in cash on hand, received $10 million. Large hotel companies, exploiting a loophole in the program, collected tens of millions in loans through subsidiaries and franchised properties. Following public scrutiny and warnings from lawmakers and the Treasury Department, many of the loans would be returned by companies, including Ruth's Chris, Potbelly, and Shake Shack.

Through spring 2020 and well into the summer, countless anecdotes of minority business owners who struggled to get loans spilled out across the country in local and national media. This unequal distribution of help at a critical time coalesced with decades of compounding disadvantages facing minority-owned businesses and highlighted the existing racial bias in the nation's banking system.

Several studies would show that banks favored wealthy white borrowers at the expense of minority companies in dire need of assistance. For instance, the National Community Reinvestment Coalition, a nonprofit in Washington, sent pairs of white and Black would-be PPP applicants to branches of seventeen banks. Each pair in the "mystery shopper" study had similar credit and wealth, though Black shoppers were given a slightly better financial profile to eliminate doubt. The study found that potential white borrowers were consistently treated better, while Black borrowers were offered different products and otherwise received worse treatment from bank employees in 43 percent of the tests.

The full extent of inequity in the PPP loan program may never be fully understood because the federal government made the inclusion of data on race and gender optional. But a *New York Times* analysis, using census and other data, found that 75 percent of loans released in the first phase went to businesses in areas where a majority of residents are white.

As ProPublica reported, while the number of Black-owned businesses was trending upward before the pandemic, the vast majority were sole proprietorships—for example, a self-employed hairstylist, accountant, freelancer, taxi driver, or musical artist. By July 2020, more than 18 percent fewer self-employed Black people were working than in the year before; compare that to just 6.2 percent fewer self-employed white people. The one-two punch of an economic crisis and the program's flawed design hit straight at the upward mobility of Black entrepreneurs and their families.

Some of that unequal relief would be addressed through millions of smaller loans churned out by financial tech companies, commonly referred to as "fintech." These online lenders aren't banks but rather work as intermediaries to connect applicants with lenders and investors. Fintech entered the mainstream with the advent of companies like SoFi,

which offered more favorable rates than banks for those looking to consolidate student loan debt. But the model found a niche—and billions
in easy profit—in servicing small and struggling businesses that banks
had overlooked or turned away.

Through automation, data, and statistical models that help determine if applicants will repay a loan, fintechs removed much of the
human work from the loan approval process. With less human involvement, it appears, came less racial bias. Researchers at New York University, for instance, found that businesses owned by Black people were
70 percent more likely to have gotten their PPP loan from fintech than
a small bank. The robots were more human than human.

While that was good for millions of small businesses eking by, it was
a multibillion-dollar boon for fintech companies, including two that
entered the fray during the pandemic.

The PPP program offered lenders a 5 percent cut on every loan they
approved that totaled less than $350,000, which was most loans. Be-
cause the federal government had guaranteed the loans, those lenders
had almost no risk and all upside to approve as many loans as possible.
The rules of the program incentivized speed and disincentivized basic
due diligence, which could have curtailed pervasive fraud.

Two companies, Blueacorn and Womply, came out of nowhere and
launched savvy marketing campaigns to attract sole proprietors, gig
workers such as Uber drivers, and small businesses to apply for loans
that paid out quickly. Together the two would account for a third of all
PPP loans approved, collecting as much as $3 billion in fees from the
federal government. Blueacorn was formed just as the loan program
presented the opportunity. Womply, which had been around for years
and sold marketing software, pivoted to focus on PPP loans.

The democratization of $800 billion in relief, spreading wealth to
where it was most needed, surely helped countless Americans. But it
also welcomed cheaters who are harder to track and will likely keep
federal investigators busy for years.

The SBA and the Trump administration tried to keep secret the
data detailing about 12 million PPP loans to 970,000 organizations,
which was a ludicrous violation of the Freedom of Information Act. So,

ProPublica and four other major new outlets banded together to sue for the release of the data, which a judge ruled should be made public in fall 2020.

Two of my colleagues, Lydia DePillis and Derek Willis, began crunching and looking for patterns and outliers. Like the federal contracting data we'd parsed months before, the inquiry led to a year of fruitful investigations that revealed rampant fraud and waste. Of all the wacky fraud stories to fall out of the pandemic relief funds, none were so outrageous and entertaining as theirs.

They grouped loans by lenders, ran a few filters, made dozens of calls, and found that one fintech company had awarded nearly 400 forgivable loans worth $7 million to fake companies. Kabbage, an Atlanta-based fintech, had awarded sizable loans to nonexistent farms, which should have raised red flags. "Ritter Wheat Club" and "Deely Nuts," one a wheat farm and the other a nut farm, were each awarded the maximum amount for sole proprietors, nearly $21,000. "Tomato Cramber" and "Seaweed Bleiman" also got sizable loans.

Loan applications listed these companies to residential addresses in Ocean County, New Jersey, a vacation hotspot that includes the Jersey Shore boardwalk, rows of summer homes, and ice cream shops, but no industrial farming. None of the companies existed in New Jersey business filings, which are the very first stop on any look into a business. When the reporters called the homes to which the companies were listed, their owners expressed shock. One supposed cattle ranch they checked up on, "Beefy King," traced to the home of Long Beach Township's mayor, who told Willis, "There's no farming here: We're a sandbar, for Christ's sake."

The two drilled down further on Kabbage's loans and found farms with funny names in improbable locales across the country. They found potato and strawberry farms in the same town in Nebraska, listed to a banker and anesthesiologist who had no idea why they were in the loan data as farmers. They found fake potato farms in sandy Palm Beach, Florida, and orange groves in freezing Minnesota. The reporters identified fake farm after fake farm and began to see a distinctive naming convention. Whoever applied for these loans took part of the name of someone who lived at the address and just placed it next to a random agricultural term.

Some examples: "Kittaneh Finfish" of Tempe, Arizona; "Tree Charles Patterson" of Panama City, Florida; "Rice Fields Deshong" of Pendleton, Indiana.

And Willis's personal favorite: "McDonald Not Burgers But Flowers" of Cornwall, New York.

All these nonexistent firms were awarded sizable loans.

Through numerous calls and cross-referencing with business filings and data, the reporting duo mapped out hundreds of fake businesses, most of them imaginary farms. Many traced back to dense clusters in Florida, Nebraska, Virginia, and New Jersey. After talking with unsuspecting people whose information was used to apply for the loans, the reporters found connections. In New Jersey, several people they called had hired the same financial accounting firm, which had notified its clients of a ransomware attack in which hackers obtained Social Security numbers and other financial information.

Seeing the common ties between the addresses of the phony farms, it appeared they may have been the result of synthetic identity theft, in which bits of personal information like birth dates, home addresses, and Social Security numbers can be stitched together by criminals to make a fake credit profile. Together that information can be used to take out loans and do incredible damage to people's credit.

Reporters dug further into Kabbage and found the company was a veritable PPP loan mill. In just the first round of loans, Kabbage had processed nearly 300,000 loans, second only to Bank of America. This was an astonishing total considering the relative invisibility of Kabbage compared to the nation's banking behemoths. By talking to former employees and scouring publicly available information such as court records, reporters found Kabbage was in dire financial straits when the pandemic hit. Its largest customer base, small businesses like coffee shops and yoga studios, were forced to shut down amid the lockdowns. With loan writing on hiatus, the company furloughed more than half of its nearly 600-person staff.

But government-backed loans with hefty fees offered a lifeline. By

August 2020, the company had completed $7 billion in loans and pock-
eted 5 percent of each loan it processed directly and an undisclosed
take on loans it processed for banks. What human review did happen
was perfunctory. Kabbage managers who held the most company stock
had personal financial incentives to push loans through, according to
former Kabbage employees. In one report detailing the company's PPP
blitz, the company boasted that it approved 75 percent of all its loans
without human review.

What I found most astonishing about this story is that, while it was
clear that millions in loans had been paid out to fake companies, some
apparently manufactured using stolen identities, it was unclear who got
that cash. It would take the resources of the federal government to track
down wire transfers and connect bank accounts to the apparent cul-
prits. The spend-first-and-ask-questions-later mentality would result in a
massive cleanup effort. According to the inspector general who looks
over the SBA, the government estimates it approved 55,000 loans for
ineligible businesses and that 43,000 businesses obtained more money
than they should have.

The release of the loan data led to dozens of other investigative
pieces by ProPublica and others, including several that detailed how
companies that collected hundreds of millions of dollars still laid off
employees and eliminated jobs the program was meant to protect. The
Center for Public Integrity, an investigative nonprofit in Washington,
reported that $1.8 billion in loans had been awarded to companies that
laid off 90,000 workers during the pandemic.

ProPublica data reporters set up a searchable and free public database that allowed anyone to comb through nearly 12 million loans the
government didn't want anyone to see. The database led to scores of
local media stories about those who had fleeced the program. Still,
more than $395 billion, almost half the total cost of the program, had
been forgiven by the federal government. Free money.

When the database went live, I wondered if any of the companies I
had encountered were in there. I typed in Robert Stewart Jr.'s company,
"Federal Government Experts," procurer of nonexistent N95s and
renter of private jets. The company popped up as having received

$805,000 in loans, which had been dispersed on May 1, the same week the federal government had canceled Stewart's deal and launched a fraud investigation into the company.

Stewart reported that all the money was devoted to payroll, saving thirty-seven jobs. I had gone to Stewart's tiny and empty office in Falls Church, Virginia, and I'd seen his operation up close. I knew for a fact he did not have thirty-seven employees.

It was a lie.

CHAPTER 18

DAZED AND CONFUSED

AS 2020 NEARED A CLOSE, the mask profiteering stories had pulled me west, southwest, south, and east on various reporting trips, some more successful than others. The chaos was winding down in the PPE space, though nitrile gloves had taken the place of the N95 mask for their extreme markups, rampant overuse, and reliance on Chinese factories. I was exploring new reporting lanes—stuff about nursing homes and blood banks.

Then a deus ex machina, like a floating piece of rubbish in a violent sea, reopened the hunt for the mysterious Juanita Ramos.

I received an email from a reader in Kansas, a biologist, who had come across my reporting and realized she'd been on a call with a Juanita Ramos in the spring of 2020 as her firm sought masks for healthcare workers in the Sunflower State. She provided a few emails, and one included a Seattle phone number for our mystery lady. I thanked her profusely.

I cross-referenced the number with the name. It didn't lead me to a stripper in Atlanta, unfortunately. Now, I'm no fan of the ecdysiast arts—it feels exploitative, and we Colorado boys are quick to blush. I am, however, a big fan of any story about a stripper with connections to the White House. Alas, no such luck.

But I did come upon a black-and-white photo of a woman dressed in a tribal-patterned woven sweater, a stone necklace draping from her neck, and stark white hair that shaded dark toward frizzled ends. She was holding a taxidermied eagle wing, which a blurb in a local magazine described as being bestowed upon her by elders of the Cherokee Nation, a symbol of the tribe's acceptance of her as a practitioner of Native American medicine.

She *was* a goddamn medicine woman. My friend back home was right all along. Damn you, Crizno.

She had spent years ambling about the American West guiding "two-leggeds" through spiritual detoxes, as the article described it, preaching the value of earth medicine. Earth medicine, naturally, intersected with her interests in marijuana and its legalization and sale.

I'd scoured LinkedIn, looked through lobbyist registrations, and searched political campaign contributions and more. But my bored friend had just gone down a late-night search engine frenzy months earlier and came upon this post and tried to inform me. I'm pretty good with Google, which I admit is not impressive, but I nonetheless couldn't figure out how his search terms led him to this obscure posting. Maybe he used Ask Jeeves? The guy is kind of old.

Thoroughly embarrassed, I called the number. She answered, and I told her I'm a reporter and that I had been looking for her.

"I have a story to share with you, Juanita," I told her.

"Okay?"

"I wish I had found you earlier. Your name is pretty common. And I was looking in sort of D.C. circles."

"D.C. circles?" she asked.

"Yeah, I'm in D.C. Anyway, so I am in D.C. here. I was working on a story about a contractor who got a deal with the VA for six million masks. And—okay—this contractor was fairly new. It was clear to me that they didn't have experience getting masks. I reached out and he says, you know, we're going to—we're going to close this deal in a day or two, why don't you tag along? So I tagged along and it was pretty clear the deal was falling through. . . ."

She sighed, knowingly.

"So the CEO I'm hanging out with," I rambled on. "He keeps saying he's got somebody named Juanita Ramos who has connections with the Mike Pence White House—"

"Mike Pence?" she said.

"Yeah."

"Oh, shit!" she said with a laugh. "I wish. Wait, no, actually, I don't wish. I take that back. I don't wish. The White House?"

"Yeah."

"Wow, that's really a trip."

It was becoming clear she knew as much about the White House Coronavirus Task Force as they knew of her—that is to say, not at all.

"Dude, I'm in the marijuana industry, okay?" the sixty-six-year-old woman explained. "I've helped write legislation. I help people with, you know, that kind of stuff—industrial hemp. I mean, I'm down for the farmer. And believe me, Mike Pence ain't gonna do shit for the marijuana industry or the farmer."

She was referring to her work with the Utah Association for Responsible Cannabis Legislation, and Sacred Roots Healing. The groups work to convince skeptics that non-THC cannabis products don't make children with autism, like, super high. She'd also worked for a major CBD company in Colorado, the first state to legalize recreational pot, a movement I covered as a cub reporter.

"I think you're right," I said. "I don't think Mike Pence is interested in that."

I emailed her what I'd already written and asked her to read what Stewart had told me, his colleagues, and the federal government. She pulled up the story and read along as I stayed on the line.

After a long pause, she spoke again.

"I'm reading this and I'm going, 'Holy hell!'" she said. "Like, what? Middlemen? Brokers? I never claimed to have a contact within the White House Coronavirus Task Force. First off, I don't even like Mike Pence. I shouldn't say I don't like him because I don't know the man. I really—I don't know the man. I don't know any of those guys, so I don't know how I became the mystery woman, but this was a great ha-ha."

But she said the story did jog her memory of a call she had, and it did involve Stewart, whose name she had forgotten until reading the story. She'd been on a phone call with Stewart and Troy King, who she erroneously thought was the attorney general of Arkansas, not Alabama. But she said she was only tangentially involved in the conversation. Some money guys in Boston had set it up. It came up because of her connections in the marijuana business. I asked if she'd be comfortable meeting. Seattle had calmed down from those terrifying months when the first large-scale outbreak tore through the city. I had my N95, and I could quarantine on either side of the jag, I explained.

She'd love to have me over for a visit, she said, and to potentially share some earth medicine. But she wasn't in Seattle anymore. She had just moved in with her daughter in—of all places—Texas.

This time, Austin.

The universe has jokes.

————

From her sunlit living room in a cookie-cutter subdivision in south Austin, Ramos, shoeless and comfortable in draping white linen, told the story of how she became a tangential player in a mess that would become the subject of investigations by the VA inspector general, the FBI and Congress.

In late April, amid the most stringent lockdowns, and just as states and the federal government were throwing money all over the place in search of PPE, Ramos got a call from a friend in the marijuana business.

This friend had launched a family business selling and marketing hemp products, which are made from the cannabis plant but won't get you high like recreational or medicinal marijuana. It's harmless, abundant, and useful. So the two proponents of earth medicine had come to know each other and would correspond, typically discussing marketing strategy, legalization, and each other's families.

But this time, the friend had reached out about a potentially huge payday. He had gotten wind that a group of guys were buzzing over a $34.5 million purchase order from the VA and a smaller FEMA contract worth about $3.5 million, awarded to Federal Government Experts.

This group of guys was prospecting far and wide in search of masks with hopes of taking a cut of the payoff from the master contractor, Robert Stewart, once the masks were delivered. None had any previous experience in sourcing this sort of medical garb. But, like all of us, they were grounded at home, and had decided to work their networks for a potential gold mine. What's there to lose?

It makes some sense that the VA and FEMA purchase orders made their way into the marijuana industry, where deals are often made quickly and in cash, due to the tenuous legal nature of the enterprise and the complications it presents with traditional banking and investment. Marijuana retailers, in limbo between state legalization and conflicting federal law, often get financing outside of traditional banks, from private-equity firms and wealthy individuals.

A famous example of the unsavory networks this burgeoning business creates was widely reported not long before the pandemic, in the Before Time, when two indicted Soviet-born businessmen working for President Donald Trump's personal attorney, Rudy Giuliani, tried to finance a pot business with cash from a Russian investor. This happened around the same time Lev Parnas and Igor Fruman conspired to violate campaign finance law, along with other colorful buffoonery.

It was in this context that the friend asked Ramos: Did she want in on the mask action?

Through her work and advocacy, Ramos had modest connections in the medical supply chain. She'd helped the Navajo tribe get hold of a few thousand masks, for instance. She figured she'd take a crack at the assignment because perhaps that network could be of some use to terrified healthcare workers and U.S. military veterans. A little extra cash wouldn't hurt, either. Ramos enlisted her fifty-year-old daughter, Dawn, and both hit the phones, calling moneyed folks they had encountered in the weed racket.

"I told my daughter, 'Hey, if we were to look at doing this, we would do like maybe a penny or two cents,'" Ramos said, referring to the potential commission on each mask. If they were successful at connecting Stewart and his new coterie of brokers on the VA deal alone, at two cents that would mean just $120,000 for maybe a week's work. Quite a payday, sure, but chump change to experienced government contractors and subcontractors.

In the marijuana space, Ramos thought, there were people with deep pockets who could move money around fast, avoiding the hangups that might slow such an urgent purchase.

"It's quick money," she told me. "And the broker game in the marijuana and industrial hemp industry—it's exactly the same."

What happened next was hauntingly stupid.

The elderly woman living with her daughter in a subdivision in south Austin found herself linked to a barrage of emails from people who claimed to possess obscene amounts of masks for sale to the highest bidder, or, if not that, they had a wealthy buyer in search of an obscene amount of masks. It depended on the day.

She saved her emails, ranging from the early days of the pandemic and well into its first summer. They provided the clearest documentation of the hidden greed and ludicrous behavior that the federal government and other buyers had spawned. The VA and FEMA deals had come to her and the friend via a real estate investor in New England who was freelancing for a firm by the name of Boston Capital Consultants. This is not to be confused with Boston Capital, the massive real estate development company founded in the 1970s.

No, this was a much smaller operation founded by Boston entrepreneur Aaron Marcy Sells. He founded Boston Capital Consultants in 2018 after doing years of marketing work for New England Patriots owner Robert Kraft, along with some real estate investing through firms branded with his initials. A serial entrepreneur, he'd also launched bars and liquor brands and, most recently, a holding company for cannabis ventures, which he dubbed AMSCAN Inc. It stood, ostensibly, for Aaron Marcy Sells Cannabis. It's a good name and good use of a name.

"They're all big marijuana guys," Ramos explained.

Ramos said alarming conversations with Boston Capital Consultants eventually led her to sever ties and, soon after, wipe her hands clean of the entire PPE effort.

They were "telling me that they put, like, $1.25 on top of a mask,"

Ramos alleged. That markup alone was about the retail cost of N95 masks before the pandemic.

"And I'm like: 'What are you talking about? People are dying, and you guys are ripping people off for a buck twenty-five?' It's like broker-broker-broker-broker for, like, fifteen people in the middle, right? And then that dollar mask turns into eight bucks, or seven bucks or whatever.

"I don't want to get caught up in ripping people off," she added. "That's blood money to me."

Emails show that various representatives of Boston Capital Consultants were aggressively marketing PPE to a growing list of private buyers, including international investors linked, allegedly, back to the United Kingdom, Switzerland, and Australia. And then there was Ramos, somehow in the mix. And Stewart, who thought she was working in the White House.

"DEAL OF THE DAY: 5.87 million KN95 Masks (FDA)—.95 cents per mask on the ground in L.A. PO/POF gets POL . . ," one email from Boston Capital Consultants read, illustrating the parlance of the PPE trade.

A PO meant purchase order. POF is proof of funds. And POL is the proof of life.

"THESE WILL MOVE FAST SO PLEASE DO SO AS WELL," the email ends.

Ramos shared emails that included several letters of intent, commonly referred to as LOIs, which illustrated how secret investors were trying to profit off Stewart's ill-fated VA deal. In these pitch documents, prospective buyers outline how much they'll pay for masks that are either sitting in a warehouse or dropping off a manufacturer's production line.

In late April, as Stewart was working to fulfill contracts with both the VA and FEMA, Ramos received an LOI showing that a Zurich-based investor who runs a dietary supplement company hoped to buy 100 million N95 respirators a week from 3M. He offered to pay $3.71 each and explicitly stated he would resell them to FEMA and other agencies. The document was fascinating in that it detailed an investor buying in for masks destined for FEMA, which had awarded Stewart a contract paying out about $7 per mask. That's a markup of roughly $3.29 per mask, or nearly 89 percent, to be split among the investor and brokers.

There were some obvious, eye-roll-worthy problems with this proposal, however. First, masks are light and small, but they're not weightless and minute. A shipment of 100 million masks would take up an enormous amount of space, and the weight would require a sophisticated freight and distribution process. Not to mention that 3M's deal with the entire U.S. government called for the delivery of just 35 million masks per month. In a press release in May 2020, the company had said it doubled its N95 production to reach about 1.1 billion masks a year, or about 92 million masks a month for both the government and the private sector. The LOI was on its face impossible, yet it was obvious those sharing these records either believed in the deal or believed they could get someone else to believe enough to wire money.

Still, figures included in that LOI illustrated how inexperienced investors sought to feast on the fat between the cost of an actual mask and the prices arbitrarily set by the federal government's publicly disclosed contract amounts. Imagine a rich guy coming into an auto dealership and saying, "Yes, hello, I'd like to buy this Corvette for $120,000." Would it behoove the salesman to divulge that the manufacturer's suggested retail price is about $60,000? This is not a rational way to do business, yet taxpayers were by proxy an idiot rich guy at a dealership.

In this way, the federal government was inadvertently fueling the mask bonanza at the same time it sought salvation through the free market. America was screwing itself over, and the brokers were playing their part. At the very least, these absurd offers were obscuring and perhaps amplifying the market price of a mask. These were the buccaneers to which Stewart was referring on our journey to Chicago.

When I reached out to the Boston marijuana guys about their foray into the mask business, Marcy Sells provided possibly the best quote I've pulled out of a subject: "If you asked me under oath what happened, I couldn't tell you."

Sells lobbied hard for me not to include his name in any reporting on the PPE trade.

"I am not involved in this Ramos and Troy King nightmare," he said. I asked him multiple times if Boston Capital Consultants was as involved in the PPE game as emails sent out by his employees clearly showed. He dodged the questions.

"We do a lot of different business," he said.

Massachusetts business filings show that on July 14, 2020, Sells founded a new venture: Safe and Clean Protection LLC. Its stated business purpose is to "manufacture and sell personal protective equipment (PPE)." So, cleared that up.

Ramos also shared several transaction records that turned out to be forgeries, all apparently provided by anonymous investors. Over time, Ramos said she would just roll her eyes and send the emails to the trash folder. But I asked to see them.

One exchange perfectly illustrated the magical thinking that pervaded the PPE trade. Remember, most of the country was stuck at home, and international travel was not an option.

In the late spring, a potentially existent English investor, using an obscure international charity, was working with a London-based consulting firm to establish that he was a reasonable distributor for 3M products. In his proposal, he included a letter with HSBC Bank letterhead that stated he had more than $2 billion in available funds. This letter of assurance from a bank constituted a "proof of funds," or POF, if, in fact, it was real. The package also came with a letter of support from a California-based energy company that, he claimed, was vouching for his business as a client.

The proposal floated between Boston Capital Consultants, including its owner, and a guy named Joseph Ingarra, of Palm Beach Gardens, Florida. In his email signature, Ingarra identifies himself as "head rainmaker" for Apex Growth Solutions LLC. The company appears to do some sort of marketing and claims to use "cutting-edge technology with strategies based on the world's leading science of how people make choices." Its website is one static page with a twelve-second video with no words or narration, but with an illustration that shows a red liquid being poured from a laboratory beaker into an Excel data filter funnel icon. The images then transform into a cell phone with a bar graph on the screen. The cell phone somehow shoots an arrow at a target—bull's-eye. The video ends with a jingle.

In other words, I have no idea what the hell this company does.

"I'm aware of a huge fckn [*sic*] lot 1-2B range in the UK," Ingarra wrote to the Boston guys in early May, referring to a large mask transaction.

"Get this shipped in one big shot and get paid quickly," he wrote in bold letters.

This proposed deal and accompanying documents were curious. First, they came via a company in Palm Beach County, Florida, which is home to a host of colorful vulture capitalists and cons.

Second, the Delaware address the billionaire investor listed as his U.S. office connected to a residential home valued below $200,000. Third, around this time in the pandemic's first spring, brokers say it's improbable, if not impossible, that such a large stock of masks ever existed. They just weren't being manufactured and stored in great surpluses beyond pre-pandemic demand.

Then there's the letter vouching for the buyer on letterhead from UDECM, a California firm that designs and builds solar energy rigs for governments and hospitals, primarily overseas. I would later send the letter to the firm's owner, who said it was a forgery like dozens of others that he'd batted away in recent months.

"The letter is one hundred percent fake," he said.

Why pick his firm? He didn't know, but they had been involved in some small PPE deals early in the pandemic; he said his firm was leveraging its international supply chain connections to help some nonprofits find masks. But after UDECM dipped its toes into the sea of brokers, "it went viral," he said.

"Everybody's got documents out there being forged now," he said.

Ingarra, the Florida rainmaker, said he didn't know the document he shared wasn't real.

"I have zero idea of who drafted that letter," he said in an email. "I hope they catch the scumbag."

It was this smoke-and-mirrors clusterfuck that brought Ramos and I together, sitting on a large brown leather sectional, in an unremarkable house inside a master-planned maze of sneeze-inducing cedar trees and stone facades southwest of downtown Austin, whose bustling weirdness of music and art and free-flowing booze had given way to silence.

Ramos loved the new neighborhood, where residents enjoy a golf course, meandering bike trails, and an Olympic-sized pool that is, inexplicably, heated. It was a good, quiet, and peaceful life.

Ramos was far from the shrewd, White House–connected capitalist I had been led to expect. Between expressions of disgust at the mask market into which she had delved and soon escaped, she described her higher being as "creator." In the bathrooms and kitchen, she had placed colorful stones in the sinks, so when the two-leggeds washed their hands, bad energy would wash off and return to the earth.

In the end, after all this, Ramos said she and her daughter only pocketed about $200. She had no idea how much the other cast of characters may have profited.

As I took notes on everything she explained, I felt like one of the less fortunate characters in a Coen Brothers movie. Like, *What the fuck did we learn here? That maybe we shouldn't trust the safety of American healthcare workers to weed dealers?*

This seemed self-evident, but I guess I had the goods to prove it. The emails and stories she shared that day were artifacts of what political leaders should expect when they throw chum into shark-infested waters with no greater strategy: madness.

"So what . . ." I asked Ramos, "what . . . is the point of all this?"

In thought, she scratched the ears of her two aging white fluffy dogs, Sherlock and Inspector Clouseau, whose longevity she credited to CBD oil.

History was about to repeat itself, she finally said. She worried that hospitals, schools, and governments would waste their time and money with middlemen and profiteers as the virus returned in the coming waves.

"It's coming," Ramos said. "It's going to be repeated."

As the interview that took us from D.C., to Boston, to Kentucky, to Texas, to Alabama, and to Europe wound down, we devolved into pleasant small talk of a maternal nature. This shit happens to me all the time.

She expressed concern that I had not yet been married. My aura was good, she said, and I'd benefit from such a union. I asked about her husband, and she said they were divorced.

I told her I couldn't think of any more lines of questioning, though I'd follow up. The complete lack of tourists to Austin's once-buzzing Congress Avenue had afforded me a great deal in a luxury hotel I had eyed for years. It beckoned. But I shouldn't leave just yet, she said.

"You should stay," she said cheerfully. "Smoke a little."

I declined but nonetheless left dazed and confused.

CHAPTER **19**

LUCRATIVE LIES

IN A FAINT AND RUSTY VIBRATO, Robert F. Kennedy Jr. began as any skilled pitchman might—with a sympathetic story.

"I apologize for my voice," he began, his strained speech diminutive compared to the oratory might of his father, Robert "Bobby" Kennedy, and that of his uncle, President John F. Kennedy.

". . . I had a very, very strong voice until I was forty-two years old, in 1996," he said. He was speaking to thousands of people tuned into a virtual anti-vaccine conference, a couple of months ahead of the expected deployment of the COVID-19 vaccines.

"And then I got this. It's an injury called spasmodic dysphonia, which has mystified doctors for many, many years."

His use of the word *injury* was curious. Spasmodic dysphonia is a neurological disorder, likely genetic, that affects the muscles in the larynx and inhibits speech. While it is true the disorder is something of a medical mystery, researchers believe it is inherited and typically not the result of a particular trauma.

Kennedy continued the story in a cleverly nonlinear way, jumping to and from points in his life decades apart, touching on his credentials,

217

thereby condensing time and space to insinuate a cause and effect together: *He got a flu vaccine in the mid-1990s, and around that time he began
showing symptoms of a neurological disorder. Isn't that weird?*

It wasn't until recently that he'd connected the dots between his
condition and an immunization he'd received twenty-five years before.
The revelation came to him as he was doing research for a "large" lawsuit related to vaccines, though he did not specify the defendant. As he
dug into the case, he said, "I was surprised to see that spasmodic dysphonia was one of the injuries, one of the side effects that was listed for
the flu vaccine. That gave me the first clue, that I never even suspected,
that my injury to my throat may be a vaccine injury."

It was but one of countless unproven, false, or misleading claims
shared during a virtual three-day conference in October 2020. There,
in plain view, a small group of internet celebrities who profit from dis-
seminating lies and misinformation presented their strategies for stok-
ing distrust and fear of COVID-19 vaccines.

As long as vaccines have existed, there have been enclaves of resistance, though nothing anywhere near as damaging as this. The event
was organized by the National Vaccine Information Center, which since
the 1980s has promoted debunked claims about vaccines causing autism in children, among other claims. But now they were motivated, and
legitimated, by politicians and even some irresponsible media outlets.

Kennedy, wearing a thin blue tie and crisp white shirt, and with
hundreds of books stacked to the ceiling in his background, leaned into
this computer's camera and his audience.

"We're seeing an inflection of events that is bringing our issue to
the forefront," he said. "Vaccines are talked about every day, on all the
news shows—very unusual for us because we've been encountering cen-
sorship from the beginning and not allowed to have this discussion.
The discussion is still heavily, heavily censored, and the point of view
that people are getting is really the industry orthodoxy. But for the first
time, you have newscasters and smart people and leading members of
the intelligentsia who are actually asking tough questions about vaccine
development."

The message, once fringe, was now mainstream. Next, Kennedy conflated disparate anxieties to suggest a broad conspiracy to control free-thinking Americans.

"We're seeing an onslaught of authoritarian clampdown and a giant shift of wealth from the middle class, which is just being obliterated by the quarantine, to the wealthiest people, the people like [Bill] Gates and Elon Musk and [Mark] Zuckerberg and all of the people who kind of own Silicon Valley and own 5G, and many of them also own vaccines."

In one breath, Kennedy managed to evoke our deepest societal fears and resentments and associate them with outlandish fantasies such as that Microsoft founder Bill Gates had sneaked microchips into the vaccine or that COVID-19 was actually caused by the advent of 5G cellular infrastructure. He offered both problems and imagined reasons for the existence of those problems. This jumbling of a visceral sense of powerlessness and a little bit of fact—yawning wealth inequality is real—with an overload of nonsense serves to create a more general distrust of institutions such as the news media and the CDC, which are cast as agents of authoritarianism. This is a tried-and-true strategy not limited to vaccines.

It is no coincidence that there is substantial crossover between anti-vaxxers and conspiracy theorists who believe a global cabal of Satan-worshipping pedophiles have taken over the government and the media, elections are being stolen, the 9/11 terrorist attacks were an inside job, and the first Black U.S. president was born on foreign soil. These worlds are intertwined. Conspiracy theories further proliferate in times of crisis to explain complex and threatening situations. As a recent study out of Europe found, for instance, those who already espoused conspiracist ideologies were more likely to believe hydroxychloroquine was a useful preventative against COVID-19.

This phenomenon was pronounced during the Trump administration, but it is not exclusive to the right wing of the Republican Party. Vaccine hesitancy is something of a bridge between the far left and the far right, where similar characteristics of feeling under attack and needing to defend one's individualism manifest in sentiments of "that's my truth" and "don't tread on me," respectively. Kennedy, for instance, is a

Democrat and has been a staunch critic of Republican policies, especially those of former president George W. Bush. Yet Trump invited Kennedy to be chairman of a White House task force to review vaccine safety. Their common ground: Both men gain from promoting vaccine hesitancy, one politically, the other financially.

When people are scared and distrustful of establishment sources, complicated science, and evolving medicine, those offering answers, however convoluted, stand to make a fortune, and they do.

Aside from being a member of a fabled political dynasty, Kennedy is a Harvard-educated environmental lawyer with a storied track record of taking on industrial polluters. He's written many books, including a couple of bestsellers and children's books. But he is also the founder and chairman of Children's Health Defense, which is one of the leading drivers of misinformation about vaccines, delivered through content and advertising on Facebook and other social media. In that role, Kennedy collects a $255,000 a year salary, according to the nonprofit's most recently available tax filings. That's on top of whatever he makes from his various other endeavors, including books devoted to dubious claims about vaccines and attacks on prominent scientists such as Dr. Anthony Fauci.

With millions a year in donations, Children's Health Defense ramped up its advertising and produced videos and films spreading innuendo and misinformation from the onset of the COVID pandemic, sometimes targeting minority communities. Before social media companies began to crack down on vaccine misinformation in 2021, Kennedy and the nonprofit boasted almost 2 million followers across platforms including Facebook, Twitter, and YouTube, according to an analysis by the Center for Countering Digital Hate, an international nonprofit that tracks the online spread of racist propaganda and medical misinformation.

As the pandemic hit, Kennedy, with his famous surname and organization, became arguably the leading voice of the anti-vaccine movement. He helped spread, in addition to the Bill Gates computer chip and 5G conspiracies, the dangerous lie that "the flu shot is 2.4x more deadly than COVID-19."

The CCDH analyzed the pandemic activities of Kennedy and other members of the group they dubbed "the disinformation dozen" in a 2021 report: "Pandemic Profiteers: The Business of Antivaxx." The group found that this dirty dozen account for about 65 percent of all anti-vaccine propaganda spread on Facebook and Twitter. Kennedy's far from the biggest beneficiary of commoditized lies.

That designation falls to an osteopath named Joseph Mercola. Based in Cape Coral, Florida, Mercola runs the world's most popular "alternative health" news site, which urges visitors to reject consensus medical advice and treatments in lieu of megadoses of vitamins, unproven supplements, or equipment, which he conveniently sells on his "Mercola Marketplace." His website is the fulcrum of a larger network of businesses and subsidiary websites that sell books, health foods, marketing services, hemp oil for dogs, and more. He oversees about 159 employees in the United States and in the Philippines, according to news reports. This network of private companies has given Mercola a net worth in excess of $100 million. In the fifteen years leading up to COVID-19, federal regulators had cited or sued Mercola for false health claims numerous times.

Yet nothing stopped Mercola from using COVID-19 to further grow his empire. He set up StopCovidCold.com to market vitamin D supplements as a COVID-19 preventative. Vitamin D, which our bodies make for free with sunlight, has long been a profit driver for Mercola, who marketed and sold expensive tanning beds as a solution to address vitamin D deficiency. Customers who tanned more, he claimed, could "slash the risk of cancer" and attain a clearer skin tone and a more youthful appearance. Tanning beds increase the risk of cancer, according to science and reason. The Federal Trade Commission sued Mercola for those claims and accused him of paying an organization called the Vitamin D Council to promote his tanning beds and systems. In 2016, Mercola settled the case and agreed to pay back $2.6 million to more than a thousand customers who bought his tanning systems.

In April 2020, Mercola promoted the at-home inhalation of small amounts of hydrogen peroxide as a treatment for COVID-19. In a testament to his reach and knack for going "viral," the hydrogen peroxide nebulizer treatment became an alarming trend on social media sites well into 2021. Many months after his first articles and videos promoting the treatment appeared, the Asthma and Allergy Foundation of America deployed its own meme-oriented social media campaign warning against the treatment, which can damage the lungs.

Mercola's reach is difficult to discern, but the CCDH estimated he directly reached about 4 million people through social media during the worst of the pandemic. From there, content is shared online and word of mouth spreads like, well, a virus. Pulling from available records, that group estimated his empire brought in about $7 million during that time, though it's probably more.

Despite loads of reporting discrediting his claims and pointing to Mercola's history, his book titled *The Truth About COVID-19* would become a bestseller, recommended by Amazon.com's algorithm, as the virus continued to take American lives.

Mercola also spoke at that October 2020 convent of anti-vaxxers, just before Kennedy, though he spent his two hours talking less about conspiracies and more about supplements and products, referring viewers to websites where they could learn more and potentially buy stuff. His presentation hinted at the symbiotic relationships that exist among those who get rich peddling pseudoscience and misinformation. They collaborate, feed off each other, and share revenue. Many of the big players in the misinformation racket collect fees by referring susceptible people to each other's products and propaganda, just as Instagram influencers get a cut when people click through to products they endorse.

Their interconnectivity goes well beyond business. Mercola's partner, Erin Elizabeth, is also among the "disinformation dozen." She's responsible for spreading memes targeting worried mothers with claims such as "Hydroxychloroquine was more thoroughly tested than the vaccines they want to mandate on your baby."

Married couple Ty and Charlene Bollinger have made millions by producing and selling multipart documentaries directly to consumers. For $199 to $499, depending on the package, customers can absorb hours of anti-vaccination propaganda as part of the Bollingers' "The Truth About Vaccines 2020" series. According to the couple, people ate it up. The couple claims to have sold tens of millions of dollars of prod-ucts and paid out $12 million to affiliates. By fall 2020, the couple boasted nearly 2 million direct followers on social media, where among other lies they spread a debunked story that the COVID vaccine was responsible for several deaths in the West African country of Senegal.

Another couple, Sayer Ji and Kelly Brogan, each manage their own branded misinformation operations. Brogan claims to be a practitioner of "holistic psychiatry" and has contributed to and been featured by Goop, actress Gwyneth Paltrow's cultishly confounding new-age life-style brand. Through videos and posts on her website, Brogan promotes the notion that diseases are not caused by infectious agents but rather—it's all in our heads.

In the first weeks of the pandemic, Brogan denied the existence of COVID-19 altogether, stating "there is potentially no such thing." She was among the first to raise the specter that requiring proof of a vaccine to travel or engage in other social activities was part of a U.S. govern-ment conspiracy to gain "totalitarian governmental control not unlike the divide-and-conquer dehumanization agendas that preceded the Holocaust." It is a small comfort that she acknowledges the Holocaust happened, I suppose.

The CCDH estimated the anti-vaccine industry brings in about $36 million a year; that figure, based on a small window into the finances of private companies that pop up in court filings and other rare disclo-sures, is almost certainly an underestimate. By the center's count, the anti-vaccine industry employed at least 266 people. What's more, using publicly available data and industry benchmarks, the center estimates that the anti-vaccine industry's social media following of 62 million ac-counts equates to about a billion dollars a year in revenue to companies like Facebook and Twitter.

The social media celebrities picked out in that report are but a few who participated in the spread of misinformation related to the corona-virus and vaccines. None responded to my requests for comment. It is impossible to reliably account for the personal riches wrought by such betrayals of fact and reason, and its damage to the nation's pandemic response is immeasurable.

But we can measure how much taxpayers spent to help screw ourselves.

Several of the leading misinformation peddlers took advantage of small business loans, many of them forgivable, offered by the federal government as part of the CARES Act. The Paycheck Protection Program gave out at least $1.5 million to the cottage industry, according to federal data.

Kennedy's Children's Health Defense received more than $145,000, all of which was forgiven by the federal government. In other words, it was free money, a gift from the American people.

Mercola's businesses alone collected $617,000 in taxpayer money, according to federal data. More than half of that—$335,000 granted to his Mercola.com website—was forgiven.

The Bollingers applied for loans through TTAC Publishing, which stands for "The Truth About Cancer," which spreads dubious claims about cancer treatment. They got nearly $474,000. More than half of it was forgiven, according to a ProPublica database tracking PPP loans.

Brogan and her husband were granted about $56,000 and $48,000, respectively. All of it was forgiven.

The federal government has the power to forgive such monetary debt. Moral debt—that rests with a higher power.

CHAPTER 20

UNDERLYING CONDITIONS

JUST BEFORE THE 2020 HOLIDAYS, Colorado State University asked me to join a virtual discussion with fellow alumni who were "on the political front lines." I had been in D.C. just eight months before COVID took over my attention, so I was as much on the political front lines as Juanita Ramos. I accepted nonetheless, because I caused that school many headaches in my time there. The discussion was fine—Eugene Daniels, a *Politico* reporter and MSNBC commentator, stole the show—as we attempted to distill what we'd observed in 2020, which were varying vantages of the same horror. Nearing the hour-and-a-half mark, the mediator, hoping to end on a positive note, asked what we might do to encourage civil dialogue and disagreement in this age of division.

One by one, the others offered optimism that we might find a way to speak to one another in good faith and in recognition of our common interests. I wish I could have added to the chorus, but I was the party pooper. The week before, I had wandered through a massive and raucous crowd that formed outside Walter Reed National Military Medical Center, where President Trump received treatment for COVID-19, benefiting from expensive therapeutics that were not afforded to hundreds of thousands of Americans who had been infected before him. Few in the crowd wore masks. Of the dozen or so I spoke with, none believed the president could have saved us the suspense by wearing a mask. Several trashed science; others trashed my profession. Some said COVID was a hoax. It was not altogether unexpected.

I was drawn there because, when Trump left the White House for the hospital, he looked as we had never seen him. It was the look of someone who believed he could die. Someone who understood the reality he willfully denied at the peril of his own countrymen and women. His bluster was at bay, if for a day, because the only thing he cared about more than his image was his corporeal ability to control it. I thought maybe some of his supporters had seen it, too, and perhaps concluded they should do what they could to stop the spread. I saw the opposite.

When the moderator finally came to me for thoughts on how we might improve our national discourse, I shared what was weighing on me and answered, "I have no idea. . . . We've really lost something." I wish I were wrong.

———

It was an unforgettable year in the worst way. To hasten its demise, I took a road trip just after Christmas to Vermont, to ski icy slopes, eat cheese, and ring in the new year with drunk friends. Fuck 2020, we declared with justification and feigned optimism. There wasn't enough booze in Burlington to rid our memories of that shit show, but we gave it our best. The first vaccines were on their way, so there was reason to blow off some steam, to entertain hope.

I happened to return to D.C. just after noon on Wednesday, January 6. The news alerts hit like successive body blows. I looked to Twitter, then CNN. Congress was besieged by a mob waving Trump flags. Police were being overpowered, beaten, one with a pole draping an American flag. The rioters had breached the building. Congress was in lockdown. Journalists, interns, lawmakers, and custodial staff were inside. Shots had been fired.

They had come to disrupt the perfunctory validation of Joe Biden's legitimate electoral win and to terrorize those adhering to the Constitution and a peaceful transition of power. A vast majority were white, and male, an average age of forty. Some came with weapons. Some donned insignia of white supremacist hate groups and far-right militias like the Proud Boys and Three Percenters. Some wore funny hats and war paint. But most had no obvious ties to such groups. They were CEOs, salon owners, lawyers, doctors, and accountants. Of those that would be arrested for their part in the political violence, one in five served in the U.S. military.

Whatever the demographics, January 6 was the worst of us. Thousands of people gathered without wearing masks, risking the health and lives of everyone they hold dear, at the behest of an immunized, departing president who watched the violence on television. Confederate flags, a literal symbol of treason against the United States, flapped alongside the U.S. flag. Cops were beaten relentlessly by a crowd that included off-duty law enforcement officers and several flapping "thin blue line" pro-police flags. Military veterans who had once pledged their lives to protect American democracy were caught on video defiling it. The display of ideological confusion and rejection of even self-serving rationality revealed what January 6 really was: obstinacy and hatred masquerading as individual liberty and patriotism.

In high definition, we saw that America was sickened by far more than a coronavirus.

Many who perpetuated the "Stop the Steal" movement, alleging the 2020 election had been stolen from Trump, were also prominent beneficiaries of the anti-vaxxer movement. Del Bigtree, Alex Jones, and married couple Ty and Charlene Bollinger helped organize rallies that day, stirring together two pernicious lies.

As messy as it was, the images of that day efficiently synthesized our current state of discourse. The consequences of demagoguery, politically useful lies, and willful ignorance were laid bare. All it took to inspire a mob to storm the capitol of the most powerful nation in the world was Trump doing what he does—deflection. Blindly and without evidence, he simply claimed the election had been stolen. His sycophants, his favorite cable news channel, and his party contributed to the doubt. The message amplified through an existing ecosphere of people

and institutions who profit financially and politically from misinformation. A lie so provably false could not spark such a reaction alone. No, it
metastasized in an ever-growing morass of conspiracy theories, innuen-
dos, and outright lies that serve the few who've monetized it at the expense of those who fall for it. Ideas spun from this echo chamber can
neither be logically explained nor rationally debated, but adherents
believe them still, and with fervor. In the end, a mind saturated with
incoherent outrage, false narratives, and indefensible ideas knows no
language but violence. And Trump had beckoned them to speak their
minds.

It was a a vulgar display of our nation's underlying conditions. The
celebration of overconfident ignorance, the denigration of expertise
and science, systemic and blatant racism, the failure to heed warnings,
the unwillingness to adapt to modest inconveniences, the inability to
listen in good faith, the refusal to place strangers' lives above our own
pride—all are symptoms of a pernicious cultural disease. I do not know
the remedy, but if I had to guess a prognosis, I'd bet the violence will
continue.

Violence is not always physical. We kill with brutality and action but
also with passivity and inaction. The violence of willful ignorance didn't
destroy democracy that day. But it would kill us slowly in the months to
come, as millions of Americans rejected COVID-19 vaccines.

CHAPTER **21**

"CAPITALISM, BABY"

I HATE NEEDLES. THEY ARE INVASIVE, unnatural, stabby. I usually look away, but this time I watched. I wanted to remember.

As the nurse jabbed that second woman-made miracle in my left arm on April 22, 2021, I felt a relief I had no idea I'd ever need. I sat at the end of a long row of plastic tables inside the Veterans of Foreign Wars outpost in Luray, Virginia, where rural nurses ambled about and masked strangers in flannel and trucker hats sat in wait for cooking timers to ding. After fifteen minutes, those who showed no adverse reactions were allowed to exit into a world with renewed possibility.

I might have cried, if I weren't so angry. As of that morning, the United States had confirmed about 32 million infections, and 570,082 Americans had perished. The 600,000-death milestone was fast approaching. But the injection soothed, for a moment, the grief of knowing it didn't have to be this way. Despite ourselves, there was hope. I spent my fifteen minutes thinking about the dark year and of the sincerely beautiful and patently opportunistic things that had to happen to get that concoction inside me. I thought about how I didn't deserve it. Hell, most of us didn't. There I was, receiving salvation well before most of the world, for no special reason other than the fact that I was an American. For all our blundering and self-imposed heartache, we had accomplished at least this. And we did it the American way: We threw money at that sumbitch. Lots of it.

"Capitalism, baby," I whispered to no one in particular.

The United States did in months what would have previously taken years. It was a true industrial feat, helped along by innovation that proponents will say capitalism fosters. The efficiency with which it was done is largely a credit to the capacity, investment, and knowledge base of the private sector and publicly traded companies. And, yes, greed was a factor. Government scientists, to the Trump administration's credit, overcame bureaucratic barriers to balance expedience and safety.

But the success of the vaccine in the United States is not without nuance. It was only through decades of government investment and publicly funded research that the bedrocks upon which the vaccines were built came to be. A guaranteed payday and the promise of perpetual income also spurred pharmaceutical companies to develop, test, and deploy vaccines. We paid for the research that made them possible, then for their development, and we'll continue to pay for the products themselves to the enrichment of pharmaceutical corporations and their shareholders in perpetuity.

The Pfizer-BioNtech shot I'd just received, as well as the vaccine by Moderna, was designed to trick human cells into copying and producing a harmless piece of the virus to trigger an immune response. By emulating spike proteins unique to SARS-CoV-2, the vaccines teach the body to attack it. Should the real virus show up, the body would be ready with our own custom antibodies to knock it out before it could take over.

Traditional vaccines introduce the body to a safe amount of a virus, often a partial or inert version, which is just enough to trigger the body's immune response, but typically not enough to sicken the patient. This is how we inoculate against chickenpox, measles, and influenza. They work. But producing and testing a new vaccine this way is tricky and can take years.

Instead, the Pfizer-BioNtech and Moderna vaccines breezed through human testing and FDA approvals by exploiting a biological end run that a few scientists had eyed for decades, but which hadn't been brought to market until COVID-19 mobilized scientists across the globe.

Those vaccines were built using messenger ribonucleic acid: mRNA. A single strand of genetic material, mRNA delivers instructions to cells about how to produce proteins. mRNA has one job, and that is to pop into a cell, drop off some blueprints, and then disappear.

In the 1990s, scientists began exploring whether these genetic couriers could be tweaked to instruct cells to pump out designer proteins, so to speak. If scientists could tell cells which proteins to make, the body could create its own defenses to treat any number of ailments ranging from the flu to cancer. The potential application of such a technology seemed boundless, and the upside for humanity immeasurable. Whoever figured it out, one would think, would be an instant billionaire.

But nothing is so easy. The story of how modified mRNA grew from a fantasy to a global vaccine worth many billions of dollars, and the scientists who toiled through poverty and obscurity to make it happen, is worthy of its own book.

Its protagonist would be Dr. Katalin Karikó, a Hungarian-born biochemist who spent much of her career on the fringe of academia, navigating a male-dominated field, struggling to secure research funding for an obsession the larger scientific community dismissed. After she landed a low-level research professor job at the University of Pennsylvania in 1989, she and a few colleagues tried for years to show mRNA could patch up blood vessels ahead of surgery, for instance, or maybe help treat stroke patients. They tested on lab tissue samples, mice, and rabbits. By the mid-1990s she could instruct cells to produce the proteins she wanted in a petri dish, but in lab tests the mice injected with synthetic mRNA got sick. Their immune systems were sensing treachery early and were killing the messenger before it could reach their destination cells.

Karikó's many appeals for grant funding were rejected, and without money to support her job, the university essentially demoted her to a researcher without a lab or financial support, an academic no-man's-land. She pressed on and in the late 1990s partnered with a fellow

UPenn scientist, an immunologist named Dr. Drew Weissman. Together the two secured about $2.3 million in grants from the National Institute of Allergy and Infectious Diseases, Dr. Anthony Fauci's agency. That public money helped support nearly a decade of trial and error. Finally, in 2004, they cracked the code.

They realized that their synthetic mRNA was missing a key modification that wraps naturally produced mRNA in a kind of invisibility cloak. Once they introduced that modification, they were able to send in their synthetic mRNA to work its magic without setting off any immune system alarm bells. It worked, and in fact the additional molecule greatly amplified the strain's ability to synthesize proteins. They now had a reproducible method for altering cell protein development without wreaking havoc on the immune system.

Still, few cared. The two struggled to secure substantial funding. They submitted findings to scientific journals, which were equally indifferent. They continued with better experiments nevertheless. Eventually they proved they could induce a monkey's body to make proteins that elevated red blood cells, a major discovery that raised other possibilities. Could the same process be used to create protein hormones like insulin, as a potential treatment for diabetes? Or even to instruct cells to copy parts of a virus and induce an immune response?

They patented their method, hoping to find a way to bring the technology to market, following other scientists who parlayed publicly funded innovations into riches. They pitched their work to pharmaceutical companies and venture capital firms, but none would bite. In 2005, they published the bedrock paper that illustrated how to successfully sneak synthetic mRNA past the immune system to, in essence, hijack a cell's protein production.

That pioneering 2005 paper caught the attention of Derrick Rossi, a Canadian biologist who saw the potential for the technology to create stem cells, bypassing the ethically sticky issue of working with stem cells derived from human embryos. In 2007, working as an assistant professor at Harvard Medical School, Rossi and his lab found success. Rossi knew the market potential and reached out to another Harvard scientist and another biomedical rock star named Dr. Robert Langer, whose lab was down the street at the Massachusetts Institute of Technology. Langer's résumé boasts more than 220 "major awards" and hundreds of patents licensed to many pharmaceutical and other medical companies. He knew how to get it done.

The three ambitious scientists managed, with some colorful hype, to attract deep-pocketed investors and in 2010 formed Moderna, a portmanteau of "Modified RNA." The company began building on Karikó's discovery, and with some savvy executive hiring and bullish marketing, the founders' wealth grew by billions of dollars before Moderna even brought a product to market.

As Moderna made headlines, a scientist couple in Germany launched a quieter foray into the cottage industry Karikó and Weissman had set off. In 2008, Ugur Sahin and his wife, Özlem Türeci, founded BioNtech, shorthand for Biopharmaceutical New Technologies. They would make their U.S. headquarters in Cambridge, Massachusetts, home to both Harvard and MIT. While Moderna exhibited the spectacle and glitz of a tech startup, BioNtech's proprietors stuck to science, avoiding public relations while at the same time publishing for the world's benefit research mostly focused on cancer treatments. In 2013, the company hired Karikó as an executive, finally offering her financial remuneration for her groundbreaking work, which she technically didn't own.

In 2016, the University of Pennsylvania licensed Karikó and Weissman's key patent to a Wisconsin company called Cellscript. The next year, that Wisconsin company would make easy money by sublicensing the patent to Moderna and BioNtech for $75 million each, according to *Scientific American* magazine. Neither of the two companies was initially working toward vaccines as its primary business, according to news reports.

After raising more than $2 billion, Moderna hauled in another $600 million in its initial public stock offering. In January 2020, before announcing it was working on a COVID vaccine, the company was worth around $6 billion. BioNtech also went public in the fall of 2019, raising a more modest $150 million, for a total valuation of about $3.4 billion.

The two companies couldn't have had better timing. As soon as scientists in China shared the novel coronavirus's genetic sequence in January 2020, the companies got to work. BioNtech partnered with Pfizer to create and distribute a vaccine. Unlike other companies, Pfizer chose not to accept seed money through Operation Warp Speed, the Trump administration's "Manhattan Project" to develop the vaccine, envisioned by Dr. Rick Bright, Peter Navarro, and others. Pfizer's CEO said the decision kept the company free of political influence. Democrats may want to forget this, but then senator and vice presidential candidate Kamala Harris and others had raised concerns about any vaccine the Trump administration rushed through. Trump, after all, was a well-documented liar, but the message did not help to bolster public confidence in the legitimate scientific work being done behind Operation Warp Speed.

Moderna managed to design its vaccine, built from the virus's genetic information, in just two days and shipped the first dose to the National Institutes of Health by February 24 to begin testing, a marvelous turnaround. Moderna had already designed its vaccine and was flush with cash, yet it would become one of the top beneficiaries of Operation Warp Speed. After Congress approved the CARES Act in spring 2020, the administration began a roughly $18 billion funding spree with private companies to develop a vaccine.

In mid-April, Moderna was given about $483 million in federal money, sending the company's stock price on an upward trajectory that would continue well into the next year. Less than two weeks later, the company awarded board member and longtime pharma executive Moncef Slaoui options to buy more than 18,000 company shares at $46.37, according to filings with the Securities and Exchange Commission. This meant that, depending on the timing, if Moderna's stock skyrocketed, he could buy up shares at a discount not made available to the public. That added to about 137,000 options he already had.

On May 15, Trump announced that Slaoui would be one of two czars in charge of Operation Warp Speed; facing public scrutiny, Slaoui resigned from Moderna's board, forfeiting his most recent options, which had not yet vested. But because the Trump administration labeled Slaoui a contractor, he was allowed to otherwise keep his existing stake and vested options at the same time he helped direct billions that would go to that very company. That day, Slaoui's Moderna portfolio was worth about $7 million, according to an analysis by Kaiser Health News. Three days after his appointment, Moderna announced positive results from its first clinical trials. The company's stock price jumped, and Slaoui's value in the company reached $9.1 million, Kaiser Health News reported, though HHS told the news outlet that he sold them at around the $8 million mark.

From January 1 to late May 2020, the company's stock price soared about 300 percent, from less than $20 a share to a peak of about $80 a share. In that time, Moderna executives made a mint, selling off $89 million in stock. Moderna's CEO, Stéphane Bancel, pocketed $13.6 million, selling just a sliver of his 9 percent stake in the company. The company's chief financial officer, Lorence Kim, made a $37 million profit in the same time frame.

Damien Garde, a reporter for STAT News, a respected science news outlet, bird-dogged this trend over many months. In July, BARDA gave Moderna another $472 million for vaccine development. By October 2020, Moderna's chief medical officer, Tal Zaks, was growing a million dollars richer every week through stock sales, STAT News reported.

On December 18, the FDA gave emergency use authorization to the Moderna vaccine, which boasted an astounding efficacy of 94.1 percent, sending its stock soaring. The federal government would order 300 million doses of the vaccine for about $4.94 billion. By February 2021, roughly a year into the pandemic, Moderna executives had sold more than $321 million of stock in hundreds of transactions, far more than any other company associated with Operation Warp Speed.

Because of COVID and enormous buy-in from the federal government, the company's valuation ballooned from less than $6 billion in 2019 to nearly $129 billion by the fall of 2021. From the beginning of 2020 to the middle of August 2021, when it peaked at about $484 a share, Moderna's stock price increased a whopping 2,419 percent. Just before the stock peaked, the company announced a $1 billion stock buyback program, cashing investors out at a stock price some analysts believed to be overhyped. This maneuver extracted cash almost entirely attributable to taxpayer money and rewarded it to company executives and shareholders.

Moderna also benefited from other public investments besides the mRNA innovation, including from direct partnership with the National Institutes of Health. One advocacy group, Knowledge Ecology International, reviewed Moderna's patent portfolio and estimated the company benefited from $20 million in federal grants, which the group alleged were not properly disclosed. That group argued that the federal government, therefore, had a stake in nearly a dozen patents used to make Moderna vaccines. For its part, the National Institutes of Health has claimed partial ownership of a key patent behind the mRNA vaccine, for which Moderna hadn't paid royalties. The NIH did not enforce its rights over that patent as part of Operation Warp Speed, and advocates for low-cost drugs have urged the U.S. government to leverage its stake to deploy cheaper vaccines in the United States and around the world. Had the government enforced its rights, one study from New York University researchers pointed out, Moderna would have owed taxpayers $1.8 billion and counting.

Moderna did not respond to my request for comment.

Moderna isn't the only company to hit pay dirt thanks to COVID and taxpayer money. By the spring of 2021, the federal government would pay about $6 billion for 300 million doses of the Pfizer-BioNtech vaccine, $1.2 billion for 300 million doses of the vaccine developed by British company AstraZeneca, and nearly $1.5 billion for development and purchase of just 100 million doses of the Johnson & Johnson vaccine.

While Pfizer declined seed money through Operation Warp Speed, that didn't stop the Trump administration from taking credit for the company's success. Pfizer took on its own risk in developing the vaccine, though its development was aided by $455 million from the German government through BioNtech. It did help that the U.S. government promised to buy the vaccine once it passed scientific muster, however.

The boom in biotech and healthcare stocks created at least forty new billionaires who had ties to companies that gained from COVID-19, *Forbes* magazine would report in April 2021. But by all accounts, those with ties to Moderna fared best. One Cambridge venture capital firm, Flagship Pioneering, sold more than $1.5 billion in stock during the pandemic's first year. That firm was helmed by Moderna's own co-founder and chairman, Noubar Afeyan. At the same time, executives at Moderna, Pfizer, Novavax, and others sold shares for a total of $1.9 billion, *Forbes* reported.

None of it could have happened without public money.

Accounting for the billions that were profiteered by corporations and rich investors from public investment, and tracing who may be owed what, will likely take years, maybe even some litigation. Still, the fact that the government paid for the research, owned some of the intellectual property behind the vaccine but didn't cash in, then proceeded to pay billions for the development of the vaccines based on stuff it had already funded, and then proceeded to pay through the nose to give the vaccines to every American free of charge, illustrates both the benefits and perils of public-private partnerships. At least, the perils as they pertain to publicly traded companies who ideologically place shareholder profit above all else.

Still, from the vantage of a worn-out nobody in the VFW hall in rural Virginia, I almost didn't care about the machinations that led to this moment. We got the vaccine. It worked, and it worked well. Some rich guys got richer, and the federal government got left holding the bag, but this is nothing new. America was built by pirates, and so too was our deliverance from COVID. There is probably a better way, a more equitable way, but this is how we did it.

My kitchen timer dinged. I went outside, ready for what I sincerely believed would be my generation's Summer of Love. Deliverance, however expensive, seemed near.

We blew it.

CHAPTER **22**

THE DEATH PITS

GLENN OSCAR GILL WAS POPULAR with the ladies.

The numbers were on his side, of course. But it wasn't just that he was one of few men in the Grove wing of the Brighton Rehabilitation and Wellness Center, outside Pittsburgh. His daughter attributed his many "girlfriends" to his brilliant blue eyes and charm that endured despite the dementia that had him lost in time, slipping through broken memories of a life in decline.

Jodi Gill got to know the women on her weekly trips to the massive for-profit facility in Beaver, Pennsylvania, and brought them cookies and gifts. She knew they did not receive visitors. Then COVID hit, and the center blocked visitors. When it finally came time to reunite with her dad in spring 2021, she thought of him, and then them.

It had been more than a year since she'd been inside the site of one of the worst nursing home outbreaks in the country, a year since she'd held his hand, hugged him in his wheelchair, and humored such imaginings by him as "I had to work this morning. And it was a pain!"

"I know you did," she would lie.

She was the only living person he remembered with any consistency, though he remembered vividly the ancient details. He knew the two loved to go to Steelers games. Every November 2, he asked Jodi to send birthday flowers to his grandmother, who had died many decades before.

Easter 2021 was around the corner, so Jodi, a festive person, procured a bundle of white and pink rabbit ear headbands, which she planned to share with the residents and staff.

As she finally embraced him, she sobbed. Her father hadn't a clue as to why. He just smiled. She placed a pair of ears on his head and handed some out to the young female nurses who had managed to keep him alive. Four of them huddled around the old man for a photo, and he joked, "I'm like Hugh Hefner. I have my bunnies!"

Jodi looked around.

"Where are your girlfriends?" she asked her dad.

"I don't know," he replied. "They must have gone to the store."

Jodi looked to one of the nurses, whose eyes confirmed it. They were not coming back.

In this moment, she was grateful her father could not remember the ordeal they'd just endured. More than 80 of his fellow residents had been killed by the virus. More than 400 of them, including Gill, had been sickened, as had more than 200 staff members. As he sat alone in oblivion, her year, just as countless others with loved ones locked in nursing homes, had been one of anxious fear and impossible patience.

He was lucky to be alive.

Almost one in every three Americans who died of COVID was a resident or worker in a long-term care facility. That figure may change over time, but the trend remains. There are some obvious reasons for this, including that elderly people are especially susceptible to the virus and are more likely to have compounding health issues. Still, more than 30 percent of our dead were supposed to be in the safe hands of medical professionals but were captive in buildings where the virus was allowed to spread like wildfire. In April 2020, amid the first of many devastating nursing home outbreaks, a headline in the *New York Times* labeled America's nursing homes "death pits."

Horrific as the numbers are, they are not surprising. Nursing homes are a highly profitable business in which a growing number of secretive companies and private equity firms have incentives to lower costs as they also take in medically fragile people whose needs yield a higher reimbursement from the federal government. The more needs a patient has, based on "acuity level," the more programs like Medicare pay to nursing homes.

More high acuity patients + less spending on actual care = profit.

Taxpayers fuel these enterprises through billions of dollars in Medicare and Medicaid payments. It can get complicated, but in general, whatever companies don't spend on care and upkeep can be realized as profit or absorbed through some perfectly legal accounting tricks. The mechanics of nursing homes and federal spending are so attractive that total investment by private equity firms in the space jumped from less than $5 billion in 2000 to more than $100 billion in 2018. Total nursing home spending is expected to exceed $240 billion a year by 2025, according to one estimate.

————

Numerous studies have shown for-profit nursing homes are more likely than government-run or nonprofit facilities to be flagged by regulators for issues such as infection control failures or thin ratios of medical staff to patients who need them. About 70 percent of all U.S. nursing homes are for-profit. With an eye on profits, such facilities often curb full-time employee hours or employ lower-wage vocational nurses rather than more expensive, and better trained, registered nurses. With low pay comes increased turnover and fewer healthcare workers per patient. As with so much in the American health system, it is patients who suffer so the bottom line does not.

One 2020 study examined more than 18,000 nursing homes, about 10 percent of them owned by private equity, and found nonprofit versus profit could mean the difference between life and death. Those researchers discovered that short-term mortality, people dying not long after being placed in a nursing home, was 10 percent higher at facilities owned by private equity. That study, commissioned by the federal government, estimated that meant more than 21,000 deaths over a dozen years. The sample predated COVID.

Jodi Gill knew none of this when she came to the painful conclusion, in fall 2019, that her father needed to be placed in a home. He'd suffered a serious fall, and the doctors said he now needed 24/7 care.

The youngest of three girls, Jodi was the kid he had worked most to make in his image, the one who became his copilot through loving indoctrination. In his old age, she was the natural pick to be his caregiver. Despite his cognitive decline, they did everything together—NASCAR races, football games, museums. She still practiced immigration law and taught full-time at the Penn State extension in Beaver County, on the western edge of the state. For as long as she could, she would bring him to her office. Every day, she joked with colleagues, was "bring your father to work day." But he was now running off and getting into trouble.

She could not do it alone, so she picked the nearest place that could take him, Brighton, a sprawling campus with more than five hundred patient beds that a corporation had purchased from the county in 2014.

Even before the virus came, Jodi had problems with the facility. She'd show up to find her dad was unclean and unkempt; his nails had grown too long and his eyeglasses were either missing or so dirty he couldn't see through them. She remembers the facility itself was often dirty, observing, for instance, feces in the bathroom, stains on the walls, and food on the floor. Her father's linens were soiled or dirty, as were his clothes. She took it upon herself to manage his laundry and bought clippers to cut his hair after many weeks of requesting he be scheduled for a trim. She began to work the nurses, developing personal relationships with as many as she could with the hope that they would take extra care of her father.

Federal and state regulators had noticed problems, too.

In early 2019, federal inspectors with the Centers for Medicare & Medicaid Services arrived to find Brighton residents bundled up in coats, hats, and multiple layers of blankets because the heat was off. That placed "87 residents on three nursing units in an immediate jeopardy situation," CMS wrote. This went on for days.

A few months later, CMS cited the facility for a litany of other failures, including infection control blunders such as failing to supply soap for nurses to wash their hands in rooms where they work with patients and

handle medication. Inspectors watched staff violate numerous proce-
dures designed specifically to prevent the spread of disease in such tight
quarters. In all, CMS had cited fifty-three deficiencies in just a few years.

In December 2019, just weeks before COVID hit the United States,
the Pennsylvania Department of Health cited Brighton again for failing
to keep clean and sanitary conditions in guest rooms. They noted multiple soiled curtains, dirty pillowcases, leaky pipes, sticky floors, and
broken soap dispensers. The facility had received dozens of citations
over many years, records show.

This was not a place that was ready for a novel coronavirus—though
few nursing homes were.

Just a few months after those warnings, in March 2020, Jodi learned
that a wound on her father's back had tested positive for MRSA, a su-
perbug that spreads easily and can devastate entire hospitals and nursing homes. The spread of MRSA is often a major indication that a
hospital needs to literally clean up its act.

Six days later, though she couldn't have known, she'd have her last
face-to-face visit with her dad before the facility went into lockdown.

By March 11, the news of a novel coronavirus was impossible to ignore, and she had watched enough to feel terror. But she was shocked
to see that day that nothing had seemed to change in Brighton. It was
business as usual, people coming in and out, no one wearing masks,
though the toilet paper had run out in the solarium.

Something changed overnight. The next day, Jodi got a call from a
nurse, informing her that the facility was locking down and visitors
were barred. She felt blindsided.

Unlike some of the other patients, her father couldn't use a cell
phone. She relied on the one landline that served the entire floor where
he lived. Over and over, for two weeks, she tried to reach him by phone
but could not get through to a nurse who could connect them. She began
to write to him, though she doubted he could still read, so she searched
for colorful greeting cards that could at least convey some brightness to
his day, the details of which she could only imagine.

On March 22, Brighton's medical director made a plea for more
masks in an interview with the *Washington Post*. Several patients were

showing symptoms, and they had no idea how to treat them. If he was worried, Jodi thought, it must be bad. She went into full panic mode.

The last week of March, she and other family members received a phone call: The facility had confirmed its first case of COVID-19. By the weekend, there were more. Many more. As elsewhere, the numbers the facility released conflicted with the Department of Health and news reports. She kept calling. On the rare occasion she could get through, she was told the infections were contained to a separate wing. But by now she had connected with other families whose loved ones were sick, and they were not isolated to one wing. She believed the facility had lied to her.

By the first week of April, the exponential growth of cases and deaths was a dominant news story. She tried other nursing homes to see if she could transfer her dad. No way, she was told, would someone from Brighton be accepted.

Jodi put on her lawyer hat and began filing complaints with the state health department, local police, and the county. She had no idea what was happening inside, and it kept her up most nights.

On April 9, she received a call that her father had a low fever. Luckily, the test would come back negative. She pleaded with a nurse to connect her to her dad using FaceTime. She did. It was the first time she'd seen his face in nearly a month.

That Friday, the facility called again, this time asking her to sign off, in case her father fell ill, on the use of an experimental drug, hydroxychloroquine, which the president had been touting and responsible doctors and scientists had been warning against in Washington.

Someone on staff said the only "scary" part of using the drug was the potential heart issues, she remembers. Her father had a weak heart. She called friends who worked in medicine, and they told her to ask if he'd be tethered to an EKG to follow his heart rhythms. No, she was told. She remembers being pressured to decide, on the spot, "whether I was going to help my dad or not." He had a Do Not Resuscitate order in place, so if he got sick and his heart gave out, that was it. Finally, through tears and feeling trapped in a sort of Solomonic dilemma, she gave permission to use the drug.

Over the next few weeks, she called the Grove wing several times a day, unable to get through. It wasn't until she threatened a receptionist with calling the police to report a kidnapping that she was finally patched through to check on her dad. A sympathetic nurse gave Jodi her personal cell and promised to connect her in the future, a lifeline.

On April 16, local news outlets reported that the county coroner had ordered a community ice rink be refrozen to work as a contingency morgue. They expected the bodies to pile up, and Brighton was the source of most of them.

As family members struggled to glean any information from the facility, the numbers alluded to the nightmare within. By the second week of May, 71 patients had died and 319 patients and 22 staff members had tested positive. The Pennsylvania National Guard was called in to provide support, and nurses from Texas were coming in to help. Somehow her father was just one of about 20 patients at the time who had not yet been sickened, Jodi was told.

Around the same time, Jodi was told that her father was being moved to a new ward designated for patients who had tested negative. A separate ward would house those who were infected. She was relieved to hear the facility was finally following guidelines to isolate sick patients, but this also meant she lost her lifeline, the nurse with the phone, to keep tabs.

The new ward, however, had a low window where Jodi could at least try to shout at him. That week, she climbed through bushes and stretched high on her tiptoes and was, at last, able to see him.

With the National Guard, some new management, and the intense scrutiny from the state and local media, Jodi's anxiety ebbed for a few days. That was until May 28, when she got the call that her father had COVID-19.

He was being moved to the positive ward. The moving around—the pokes and prods and x-rays and tests—had begun to take a toll on her father. His hallucinations were getting worse and the corresponding aggression had heightened. Miraculously, however, he was not showing the worst symptoms of the disease.

"It was when he got moved to Grove One, where everybody was supposed to be negative—the people who had never tested positive and who were not positive," Jodi told me. "That's when my dad got COVID. He got COVID when they moved him."

"They still had staff moving throughout the entire building," she said. "And obviously, we weren't in there, so the only place that they could get it from was from staff."

The facility, seeing how thoroughly overrun it was, decided to presume all 800 residents and workers inside were sick.

Through all the chaos, Jodi spent late nights researching the company that owned the facility—Comprehensive Healthcare Management Services LLC. The company had very little footprint online. She searched secretary of state records and tracked the entity to a New Jersey parent company. From there she pored over the Westlaw legal filings database, following a string of civil lawsuits filed against the company and its subsidiaries. She gathered up what she could find, including the addresses and phone numbers of the parent company's individual owners, and relayed it to local reporters.

She also filed a lawsuit of her own against the Department of Health and began to stir up criticism in the local media and connect with a handful of other families who had agonized in complete ignorance of what was happening to their family members inside Brighton. She called her state representatives, members of Congress, county commissioners.

She and a dozen other families bound together to file a class-action lawsuit against the facility's owners. Most of them had lost people to the virus in the early months of the pandemic. The lawsuit alleges, among many failures, that the facility's management was slow to follow infection protocols. Nurses weren't wearing masks early enough, they weren't trained, patients weren't separated, and dangerous remedies were administered, the lawsuit claims.

One litigant I talked to said he found out his mother was dead from COVID when he got a sympathetic call from her financial guardian. He called the facility, he says, and the nurses on staff said she was just busy and couldn't come to the phone. Even after burying his mother, he never received confirmation from Brighton staff of his mother's death and the circumstances surrounding it.

Bob Daley, the Pennsylvania lawyer arguing the case on behalf of families, says his plaintiffs have ample evidence that the facility and its owners were negligent and that led to catastrophic loss of lives.

"They weren't given adequate training with PPE," he said of the staff inside. "They weren't wearing it because they didn't have access to it."

When the facility did finally procure masks and other protective garb, he says, "No one was trained on how to use it. They're not using PPE appropriately. For example, not changing gloves between patients. They're not wearing masks the proper way. . . . I think it's really just kind of a training issue. And I think there was a sense at Brighton that things are out of control. And we cannot ask anyone for help. And they just spiraled."

The case will likely take years to resolve. The company did not respond to a request for comment but has argued it is immune from civil liability because of protections that kick in for healthcare providers when an emergency disaster declaration is called.

A five-month investigation by the *Pittsburgh Post-Gazette*, following up on the torturous experiences of Jodi's family and others, found that Brighton's owners failed to enforce even the most basic infection control measures that might have saved lives. The newspaper also found that, long before COVID, the company had significantly cut its full-time staff at the facility, setting the stage for the nightmare that would befall its inhabitants.

After the company bought the facility from the county for $37.5 million, the company made upgrades so that it could house more complex patients who rely on Medicare, the federal program that covers the elderly and disabled and pays out more than Medicaid.

Before the facility was sold, the county received about $1 million a year from Medicare. By 2018, the company had increased that haul to more than $9.5 million, the newspaper found. Profits from Brighton soared.

The company pockets yet more money by renting to itself. A Comprehensive company manages the building and pays rent to another company, a subsidiary of the same eventual owner. The rent, naturally, keeps going up, from $3.9 million in 2014 to $6.8 million in 2019, the newspaper reported. The company also pays itself a "management fee" of more than a million dollars a year.

This arrangement is not uncommon. In this space, as in the larger Medicare/Medicaid insurance space, it's all about finding legal ways to suck money out that would otherwise go to caring for needy people.

Two criminal investigations, by the Pennsylvania attorney general and the FBI, were launched to look into the company.

For their infection control deficiencies, the federal government fined Comprehensive Healthcare Management Services LLC about $62,000. The Brighton facility alone takes in about $55 million a year. When the Trump administration set up financial bonuses for nursing homes that had low death counts in the later months of 2020, Brighton was awarded $145,000. The facility qualified because its more than 80 deaths occurred before the program began.

CHAPTER **23**

A PIRATE WALKS THE PLANK

THE YEAR HAD NOT BEEN KIND to Robert Stewart Jr.

His sturdy build had softened, filling out a pale and wrinkled gray suit. Even behind the mask, his countenance seemed to have dimmed. He had grayed, several prime years lost in the span of one. So had I.

In the cold and austere confines of the U.S. district courthouse in Arlington, Virginia, Stewart's cunning and colorful caper had come to its end. He had come to accept his sentence, as many as thirty-five years in prison. He had already pleaded guilty to three counts of felony fraud, all of which were uncovered when investigators followed up on what ProPublica had reported the previous year.

It had been more than a year since his invite aboard that jet set me off on a meandering quest through unsavory networks of profiteers and other riffraff. On that mid-June day in 2021, I sat in the courtroom with a familiar weight. A story I'd written was the catalyst to a man's ruin, which reporters do not take lightly. I reminded myself this was his doing and that what prosecutors unearthed after the reporting eradicated curiosity. I no longer wondered whether Stewart was a deliberate fraud or just a befuddled victim of his own ambition and circumstance. He was the very pirate he protested all along. And I was his confessor.

249

He sat two oak pews behind, no family or friends with him, pretend-ing not to notice my backward glances and scribbles. He watched the criminals before him on the docket as they faced Judge Rossie Alston Jr., presiding on a high wooden perch behind Plexiglas. A U.S. marshal with tired eyes, wearing a mask stitched with Marine Corps insignia, brought the criminals in and out. They were convicted brawlers, sexual assaulters, and thieves, cuffed as their lawyers pushed court dates and entered guilty pleas. Stewart did not belong with these men, but he would soon be among them.

Because he had cooperated with federal prosecutors and had no previous criminal record, Stewart had been allowed to remain free in the four months since he pleaded guilty. He had gone home to Alabama to be with family and sell off possessions to repay his substantial debts.

The first count, making false statements to the federal government, stemmed from what I reported along our hapless journey in late April 2020. The U.S. prosecutor discovered Stewart had explicitly stated in emails to FEMA and the VA that he had millions of N95 masks in his possession. As a result of those lies, he was awarded two no-bid con-tracts, together worth $38.5 million. Had the federal government done a shred of meaningful vetting, neither the contracts themselves nor this charge would have come to pass. As one of Stewart's friends would note in a letter to the judge, had he not invited me along for the ride, it might all have gone unnoticed.

But Stewart had sealed his fate in other ways.

The second count, wire fraud, stemmed from his gaming of the Paycheck Protection Program. As I had suspected, Stewart had grossly exaggerated the number of employees on his payroll to enrich himself, probably the most common scam perpetrated against the $800 billion program. Stewart created fake tax records showing he employed 37 peo-ple for a monthly payroll of $322,000, when his actual monthly payroll totaled less than $14,000. On that false information, Celtic Bank ap-proved a $805,000 loan to Federal Government Experts LLC. He also defrauded the Economic Injury Disaster Loan Program for another $260,000, which he used for personal expenses.

It was this million-dollar-plus pot of cash that Stewart used to pay for the private jet on which he'd taken me, his family, the VA, and the American people for a ride. Taxpayers had paid for it all, theatrics included. These were mad times, and Stewart was far from the only person to cave to the temptation of quick and easy government money. As the judge had wondered aloud during the plea hearing earlier that year, anyone with a shred of empathy could see how a man with big dreams could dip his toe into the bog, only to fall deeper and deeper until his lies buried him alive. This could be assumed of Stewart, if it were not for the third charge, theft of government funds.

After federal watchdogs referred Stewart's case to criminal investigators, the U.S. attorney's Financial Crimes and Public Corruption unit pored over a decade of his personal finances. They found Stewart had been bilking the VA since 2013, seven years before he'd been awarded that life-changing contract for masks. Stewart was an honorably discharged veteran of the Air Force Reserve, which entitled him to VA benefits and an edge in competing for government contracts. But that was apparently not enough. From September 2013 to October 2020, he collected $74,000 in additional medical and education support from the VA by lying on paperwork. He claimed to have also been a decorated veteran of the Marine Corps, discharging at the rank of corporal. He supplied the VA with false paperwork in which he claimed to have attained, among many accolades, the National Defense Service Medal, the Sea Service Deployment Ribbon, and a Kuwaiti Liberation Medal.

That chunk of ill-gotten change paled compared to the value of his other schemes, but the charge alone carried a maximum ten years in prison. It was the first I had ever heard of a military veteran impersonating a military veteran.

Stewart stood up and walked out just before his case was about to be called. I followed and stopped in front of the entrance to Judge Alston's courtroom to head him off on his return. He soon exited the bathroom down the hall and walked toward me, his head down.

"Rob, I gotta ask," I said, "is there anything you want to say before this?"

He walked past without a word and took his seat.

I understood. There was little else to say.

He had pleaded guilty to all three charges in February 2021 and in the intervening months, before this day's sentencing, had done what he could to establish contrition in the eyes of the court. He liquidated his assets and paid his entire restitution—a rare occurrence before sentencing—of more than $1 million to the Small Business Administration, $13,000 to a bank, and $74,000 to the VA. Ahead of the sentencing, his lawyer asked for leniency, and a sentence of probation or house arrest, noting that Stewart's infant son needed those precious years with his father. In the defense's sentencing position package were photos of Stewart with his boy and copies of his real military certifications and achievements, including a letter of commendation from the undersecretary of defense related to his work as a contract specialist. Despite knowing he'd likely never be admitted to a state bar, Stewart had enrolled in law school in fall 2020 and was receiving decent grades. He wanted to use it to steer others from the slippery slope of white-collar criminality, his lawyer argued.

Longtime friends of Stewart, including two I had encountered, wrote character references on his behalf. The letters, though effusive in their praise, hinted that even Stewart's closest allies struggled to discern truth from fantasy in Stewart's life.

Dawn Lockhart, his human resources manager, wrote that she had known "Stevie Turtle" since the two were in the seventh grade. He earned the name because he wore thick eyeglasses, and when he removed them, he resembled a turtle in Disney cartoons. From her letter, it was clear she did not know the finer points of the case, of his documented mendacity, and seemed to think this whole ordeal was related to a payroll glitch. Nonetheless, she argued he "has always been regarded as a person of character."

An older friend who had known Stewart since he was twelve recounted the time, during a long road trip, when a cat urinated all over Robert's bag, soiling souvenirs he was carting back to his family in Alabama. The young Stewart didn't get upset, the friend said, and explained that it was no one's fault. More recently, the friend said, Stewart, through kindness and patience, had helped him become a more informed citizen on issues of race in the South.

Another friend, the attorney who had advised him not to bring a reporter along on the private jet to Chicago, wrote that Stewart had helped him get a job as a consultant at the Department of Defense years before and became a friend and mentor. "Rising from a disadvantaged background in Alabama, he had spent his formative years as a soldier deployed in Iraq and he had really internalized the U.S. Army's values," the friend wrote. However, Stewart was never an Army soldier deployed in Iraq. He was an Air Force reservist who managed procurement and small business programs at the Defense Department in Virginia.

Stewart had helped him during a difficult time, the friend said, after he received a shocking medical diagnosis and ended up bankrupt, unemployed, and homeless. "Mr. Stewart treated me as if I was a member of his own family," the friend said. As to the charges, the friend wrote, "Mr. Stewart is not responsible for the catastrophe surrounding the federal government's efforts to secure PPE. . . . What Mr. Stewart's real crime here is appallingly bad optics. . . .

"Mr. Stewart made the mistake of inviting a journalist from Pro[Publica] along on the flight," the friend told the judge.

Finally, the judge called Stewart's case. Judge Alston had read all of the materials submitted by the prosecution and the defense, and he had questions, but first each side would speak.

U.S. Attorney William Fitzpatrick took the lectern, surrounded by Plexiglas on three sides, facing the judge. He began by pointing out that, often, multiple charges are applied as part of one criminal act, but in this case, Stewart had committed three distinct crimes.

"Each time, he chose to make a decision to commit a crime," Fitzpatrick said.

"This is not a single error of judgment," the judge agreed.

"The communications demonstrated, in each of these schemes, outrageous and fundamental lies . . ." the prosecutor continued.

He had taken advantage of a national emergency, he told the judge, and duped our government in its time of need.

"The lie was direct. The lie was clear. The lie was impactful," the prosecutor said.

"The question you have to answer is—" the judge said. "Is this a person with malice in his heart?"

"Your honor, I think there was gross negligence, gross recklessness," the prosecutor responded. "The fact that this was in a national emergency. This was not for the [federal government] to acquire paper. This was for the medical supplies we needed."

"When people are desperate," the judge said, nodding, "he does these things."

Stewart must be made an example of, the prosecutor argued.

"There is an impactful deterrence factor," Fitzpatrick said.

When he fraudulently obtained more than a million dollars in pandemic relief loans, Stewart was not destitute, he continued. He had $400,000 in equity in a house, $20,000 in a retirement fund, three cars, and more.

As for the long-running scam against the VA for heightened benefits, the prosecutor continued, "That conduct is particularly aggravating. To make stuff up, to lie, about being a Marine, about being a decorated Marine—it's brazen, and it's shameless."

Alston added, "He knew what he was doing was wrong, and it's *that* that makes it more suspicious as to what his heart is."

Stewart sat silent and still. It did not look good. Stewart had become the poster child of greed in the COVID-19 era. He'd come to represent something big, something ugly, about our country, our time, about ourselves. Yet, he is only a man. And can we ever truly know what's in a man's heart? And does it matter?

For all his crimes, the prosecution concluded, Stewart had accepted responsibility in "a full-throated manner," which should be considered in sentencing.

Stewart's attorney took the lectern to offer the rebuttal.

Stewart was a man who "went down a bad road and then spiraled out of control," the defense attorney told the judge. "Mr. Stewart isn't an evil person with bad stuff in his heart."

"I'm almost willing to give him the benefit of the doubt," the judge responded. The mask deals with the plane and the VA and the brokers, he said, "I can see how someone could get caught up in that." But the premeditation of the other crimes, "that has to be balanced with the argument he was over his skis."

What kind of message would the court be sending, the judge asked, if he didn't send Stewart to prison for a couple of decades?

The defense attorney rattled off all the reasons: He's a new father, he's paid the money back, he's back in school, his friends have attested to his character, he did serve his country.

After a long moment, Judge Alston's eyes darted to Stewart. In a fatherly cadence, the judge instructed him that whatever he said next would have a profound impact on the rest of his life. Stewart stood and faced him.

"What I want to know is why you, as an intelligent man, thought you could get away with this?" the judge said. "Why the court should think that you're not just a slick guy who is taking advantage of vulnerable people?"

Finally, it was Stewart's turn to explain.

"First and foremost, I would like to apologize to you, everyone in this courtroom, and the American people," he began. "My conduct was repulsive, really repugnant."

He told the story of how his son was born on April 14, 2020, perhaps the most frightening time to have a child in recent memory. "Back then I was a pretty selfish guy," he said. "I had a business, and I sort of had this 'I can do' mentality. I saw an opportunity, not to hurt people, but maybe to help people. I can't change anything about the past, and I am a shitty person, but that does not mean I can't be a fath—"

At the word *father*, Stewart choked into a cry, stopping himself short of sobbing.

"I got into a situation, and I just messed up. My dad was a decorated war hero," he managed to say next. "I was in the Chair Force, so to speak. . . . I didn't do the things which I thought would make me great. I did the thing that made me a villain, made me somebody I never wanted to be. I grew up in a pretty poor and desperate place, and I have a fear of dying poor and dying alone. I saw my parents struggling, and I didn't want to do that."

"It was greed. It was fear," Judge Alston responded. "You not only achieved, you overcame, but you got greedy."

"I hold my son," Stewart struggled to say. "I don't like myself. I hold my son, and I hope he doesn't grow up anything like his father."

His own father, Stewart said, was ashamed of him. But he had a chance with his son. Stewart asked to read aloud a letter he'd written to the one-year-old.

"Dre," he read, "I'm going to pray extra hard and hope that God places his hands over you and your mom and gives you strength to forgive me . . . last year your daddy made some big mistakes. I hurt a lot of people and got into a lot of trouble. . . ."

When Stewart finished, Judge Alston offered an anecdote about his own father, a tough man of an older generation who withheld affirmation from his children for nearly his entire life. Yet, on the day his father died, the judge said, he grabbed his son's hand and finally said, "I know you did your best."

The point was, the judge told Stewart, "You can still do things that make your dad proud."

The time had come for Stewart's judgment.

"You're either the best manipulator I've ever met," the judge said, "or you're a man who has changed in his heart."

"I'm not going to sentence you to a long time of incarceration," he continued. "But I do believe you need to see the inside of prison."

In what the judge acknowledged was a huge break for Stewart, he was sentenced to just one year and nine months in prison with three years of probation.

It is not for me to say what Stewart did or did not deserve, and I don't know what's in his heart. But I would be lying if I said I wasn't relieved he'd have a chance to know and raise his son and, maybe, if time is kind, make his father proud. I hope he's not too hard on himself, or the boy, for if we were destined to repeat the sins of our fathers, this country would not be worth saving. I believe it is.

EPILOGUE

WE WERE FREE TO EMERGE from our caves for a time. Some stumbled out grayer, fatter, socially awkward, with worrisome alcohol tolerances. Some had procreated for some reason. Others popped out in the best shape of their lives, ready to mingle and share whatever hobbies they'd acquired, to enjoy the fruits of sacrifice and solitude. Those people were the worst.

President Joe Biden's administration fell short of its goal—70 percent of eligible Americans jabbed at least once—but the numbers weren't bad. Cases were dropping and, ipso facto, so were hospitalizations and deaths. Hospitals and their inhabitants felt some breathing room. Some called it "hot vax summer." The bars and clubs were crowded again. Tableaus of strangers meeting at parties without masks were no longer nightmare fodder but photos in newspapers. Dating was in full swing, maybe too much swing. As one July 2021 headline reminded us, nature is a buzzkill: "Post-pandemic rise in sexually transmitted diseases imminent."

I remained captive to this book but took a break to catch a Colorado Rockies game at Coors Field, always a beautiful place to enjoy a loss. Afterward, the crowd waited for the sun to hide behind the mountains and for the fireworks overhead to display in banging exuberance our American independence.

Free we were, but not of ourselves.

In Washington, D.C., Republicans united against a Democratic administration's spending agenda had again leveraged the debt ceiling to manufacture a crisis. At the worst time, the ability for America to pay its bills, and the health of the broader economy, were placed at risk. Vaccination rates were dropping. Fights over patents and profit were stalling the deployment of vaccines to poorer countries, despite knowing viruses care not of such human distinctions. Nature's punishment for such shortsightedness would manifest in variants of the virus we'd not yet conquered.

Increased unemployment benefits were going away amid worker shortages at restaurants and fast-food joints. Conservatives argued the support disincentivized people from returning to work. Anecdotes from waiters and cooks and cashiers and other "essential workers"—the subjects of low pay, insane hours, and harassment throughout our dark era—told a different story. Unemployment and free healthcare had afforded them a mental pause in which they realized their jobs were killing them; they had decided, instead, to live, to take the time to find something that afforded self-actualization and nourishment of the soul. Implicit in the debate, regardless of one's political leanings, was the recognition that the stigma of being out of work and collecting paltry checks was preferable to returning to American working conditions.

Workers were responding to the market, as rational actors. But few dared to ask the question: Shouldn't we want to live in a country where employment is more attractive than unemployment?

From Denver, I flew down to Dallas to see a guy about masks. I'd talked at length with Mike Bowen but felt he, like me, was an acquired taste best absorbed in person. We met before the start of the workday in the cracking and empty parking lot of Prestige Ameritech. Neither of us wore masks, as was allowed for vaccinated people under current CDC guidelines, which in hindsight might have been a lousy guide. He guided me through the building, first to his office, and then the wing where custom-made machines unspooled fabric and sent it spinning along a serpentine trajectory like a miniature printing press, dumping out on the other side the simple devices over which we'd all lost our damn minds.

Workers snatched them up and took them to their next destination, stitching on ear band loops and branding, depending on the order. That day, it was the standard surgical mask. It all felt too easy. The machines were spitting out millions of masks with clockwork efficiency. But dormant, in one corner were the bigger, shinier and more complicated N95 machines the federal government failed to wake up. The company bought them for a steal but never saw the demand to invest the money to get the machines running—a point some politicians in Washington ignored.

"The machines could have made 7 million respirators a month," Bowen told me through the din of pneumatic hisses and clunks and chatter.

In the massive warehouse around the corner, the final batch of FEMA's order was shrink-wrapped on a pallet and ready to be shipped. The orders, the chaos, the machines, were dying down. It felt like an ending, I wrote in my notepad. We returned to his office to chat. After a few minutes, Bowen's daughter popped through the door and, at the sight of me, slightly back out of it. She was wearing a mask. Bowen introduced us.

"Oh, I'm vaccinated," I said, assuredly.

"Yeah, but this whole Delta variant is terrifying," she responded.

Bowen's daughter was far ahead of the curve. At this point, little was known about the new variant, and it would be weeks before the CDC updated its guidelines to reinstate mask wearing indoors. More contagious and more capable of causing severe illness, the Delta variant was first identified in India but was quietly marching through the United States, propelled by a hot vax summer and needlessly low vaccination rates. Those who'd not been immunized were at greater risk than before. More alarming, though, was the news that even vaccinated people could be infected by the virus and transmit it. It heralded to the public what scientists already knew—freedom from COVID was a long way away. The fall would not bring the salvation we had imagined.

Just more than 40 percent of Texans were fully vaccinated, lagging the national picture of nearly 50 percent, and the rate of new vaccinations was slowing. Because testing was still lousy, there was no definitive data on Delta's spread in Texas, though it had already popped up in

Houston and Dallas. As we spoke, Delta was putting on a show, ripping through a Texas prison with shocking efficiency. Of the 233 federal inmates there, 185 inmates were fully vaccinated, yet nearly 74 percent of the entire population had been sickened.

Our hope that the vaccines alone would deliver us was a false one. Not long after my tour of the mask factory, I would get an ominous text from Bowen: "The Delta variant combined with irresponsibility caused us to have to ramp up again."

The story of COVID-19 was not done with us.

Four hundred miles north of Dallas, in Hutchinson, Kansas, a 75-year-old woman who devoted her life to children had gotten the vaccine and her life back. The lockdowns had made Jacqueline Crossman feel like a caged bird, unable to give hugs or to host family gatherings. These were everything to her. She had taught many children through an after-school program she started decades before, as well with the Hutchinson Boys and Girls Club, where she taught baking and arts and crafts. Without the after-school work, she had grown depressed and angry.

As a single mother, Crossman had raised seven of her own children—two girls and five boys—the most famous of whom is Dr. Rick Bright.

As her son made national headlines through the pandemic, she snapped all the newspaper clippings she could find and stuffed them in her purse. She kept them with her wherever she went, to show them off. As with all mothers, his successes were also hers.

"She was so proud," Bright told me. "At one point, she told me, 'You know, why don't they ever mention me in these stories? I mean, I'm your mother. They read all the stories about you. But no one knows I'm your mother.'"

When a Kansas newspaper named Bright one of its Kansans of the Year, he insisted that her name be included in the story, and to her delight, it was.

Right after she got the vaccine, she called Bright and jubilantly explained her plans to go outside and be with people again. He warned her that she should still wear a mask, which frustrated her. Life was calling.

Despite their famous native son, leaders of Reno County, whose seat is Hutchinson, resisted mask mandates and overrode the recommendations of their increasingly concerned health director. Some citizens protested mask mandates. By late July 2021, the county had a comparably low vaccination rate, just 38 percent of total eligible residents, despite exponentially rising infections.

Among the unvaccinated was one of Bright's relatives. Around this time, their mother had a pacemaker placed in her chest and stayed with them to recover. After two days together, the relative tested positive, and she left the house.

She came down with an apparent respiratory infection. The doctors wouldn't test her, she told family, because she was fully vaccinated, so she couldn't have the virus, which Bright knew to be untrue. He tried talking with doctors via phone. They refused and instead gave her an antibiotic.

Two weeks later, before a trip to Iceland, Bright talked with his mother, who said she was feeling better, that maybe the antibiotic was working. But two days later, on August 17—574 days since Bright received that first panicked email from Bowen about an uptick in mask orders—Bright got the call that his mother was dead. She had deteriorated quickly.

Anger washed over him. It was everything he'd tried to stop, for the country and humanity, yet the virus was allowed to fester and strengthen until finally it came for the most important person in his life. Anger always seeks a direction. Bright thought of aiming it at the unvaccinated, of those in his own family who, even after her death, scoffed at masks and doubted the science. He found no comfort there.

"I thought about it long and hard," Bright told me. "And I don't blame the unvaccinated people because they've gotten so much misinformation, and I can see where it can be extremely confusing on what is the right thing to do. Politics are playing a role, misinformation about public health officials, unclear guidance from the CDC and others the last few years.

"I can see why people would be confused," he said, "and even a little skeptical."

He choked down the anger and returned home.

In those final days, Bright's mother behaved as tough people do, not burdening anyone with her own feelings. Bright wanted to know what he had missed. He began rummaging through her things, communing with the tangibles that proved she was once among us. In doing so, he came upon her phone. He tapped into her search history.

Over her final two weeks, day and night, all alone, she had been looking into one thing: The signs and symptoms of COVID-19.

ACKNOWLEDGMENTS

I WOULD LIKE TO THANK the many people who shared their stories and time to make this book happen. Among them: Robert Stewart, Denny Rehberg, Sarah Davis, Mike Bowen, Dr. Rick Bright, John Polowczyk, Juanita Ramos, Jaime Rivera, Jackie Bray, Dan Symon, and Jodi Gill. For research and feedback, thanks to Brittney Martin, aka B dot. For the journey, I thank my agent, Becky Sweren; my editor, Julia Cheiffetz; her assistant, Amara Balan; and the folks at One Signal.

I am grateful to many people at ProPublica who offered support and expertise, especially my editor during most of this reporting, the legendary Marilyn Thompson. When I came to her with a crazy idea and an even crazier way of telling it, she trusted her reporter to see it through and advocated, and for that I am forever in her debt. Many thanks to Stephen Engelberg, Robin Fields, and Eric Umansky for entertaining an unexpected answer to the daunting question of "What is a ProPublica story?" For the backup, ideas, and for reading over my shoulder, I thank my current and former colleagues: Yeganeh Torbati, Lydia DePillis, Derek Willis, Doug Sword, Isaac Arnsdorf, Sean "Old Pig Bones" Walsh, Jonathan Tilove, Ryan Gabrielson, and Jack Gillum. For helping me through new territory and for the mentorship, I am grateful for Ken Armstrong and Pamela Colloff, both rock stars in my mind. For giving me first and sometimes second chances, editors Leslie Eaton,

Mike Wilson, Ryan Rusack, Debbie Hiott, and Scott Carroll. For keeping me in the game, I'm thankful to the Investigative Reporters and Editors tribe, namely, mentors Alison Young and Matt Apuzzo.

I wouldn't be a journalist at all if it were not for my strange network of adopted family: Cindi and Rick Costa, Candi and Brittany, Alan and Cory Rieck, Lori and Rob McKinney, and the many stray kids who seem to stick to these people. As well, some influential and big-hearted teachers: Jack Martin, Casey Hawk, John Calderazzo, Pamela Jackson, Donna Rouner, Michelle Wellman, and Anne Marie Merline. For teaching me to never be afraid of life, thank you, Bill Baker. For lifting me up, to the chagrin of some, I am eternally grateful for Barb Musslewhite and the First Generation Award at Colorado State University.

For the critiques, jibes, and devotion to our craft, I'm thankful for the Writebros: Sean Reed and Luke Johnson. Your turn, guys. To the people who keep me going, through pandemics and life, the best group of friends a guy could ask for, my people, in a random order that you should totally read into: Kevin Bock, Kali and Carley Janda, Swan, Christoper "Crizno" Noel, Hailey McDonald, Johnny Hart, Aaron Hedge, Andrea Ball, Anita Hassan, Sam and Kate Spillane, Matt Minich, Nikki Anderson, SoJo. For talking me out of some bad ideas, I owe thanks to Jim Sojourner and Yasmin Hilpert. Thanks for having my back, more than once, Kristopher Hite.

I remain thankful for my sister, Victoria, and pray we find a way back to each other.

For filling me with big dreams, grit, empathy, and for that pretentious byline "J. David," because it made me sound smarter than I am— I am most thankful for my late mother, Shelly. I wish you could see the trouble I've gotten into now.

NOTES

1. The Private Jet

2 **serving 9 million military veterans** Veterans Health Administration, "About VHA," June 10, 2009, https://www.va.gov/health/aboutvha.asp.

2 **his attorney had a late night** J. David McSwane, "How Profit and Incompetence Delayed N95 Masks While People Died at the VA," ProPublica, May 1, 2020, https://www.propublica.org/article/how-profit-and-incompetence-delayed-n95-masks-while-people-died-at-the-va.

4 **yet he had zero experience** Ibid.

5 **But Stewart had gotten the VA** Ibid.

6 **Within the VA hospital system** J. David McSwane, "'Those of Us Who Don't Die Are Going to Quit': A Crush of Patients, Dwindling Supplies and the Nurse Who Lost Hope," ProPublica, December 30, 2020, https://www.propublica.org/article/those-of-us-who-dont-die-are-going-to-quit-a-crush-of-patients-dwindling-supplies-and-the-nurse-who-lost-hope.

6 **Nurses with whom I exchanged** Ibid.

7 **One company leveraged its monopoly** Chris Hamby and Sheryl Gay Stolberg, "How One Firm Put an 'Extraordinary Burden' on the U.S.'s Troubled Stockpile," *New York Times*, March 6, 2021, https://www.nytimes.com/2021/03/06/us/emergent-biosolutions-anthrax-coronavirus.html.

7 **but because of poor oversight** Patricia Callahan and Sebastian Rotella, "Taxpayers Paid Millions to Design a Low-Cost Ventilator for a Pandemic. Instead, the Company Is Selling Versions of It Overseas," ProPublica, March 30, 2020, https://www.propublica.org/article/taxpayers-paid-millions-to-design-a-low-cost-ventilator-for-a-pandemic-instead-the-company-is-selling-versions-of-it-overseas-.

7 **The small company the government hired** William Lazonick and Matt Hopkins, "How 'Maximizing Shareholder Value' Minimized the Strategic National Stockpile: The $5.3 Trillion Question for Pandemic Preparedness Raised by the Ventilator Fiasco," Institute for New Economic Thinking, Working Paper Series, 2020, 1–64, https://doi.org/10.36687/inetwp127.

8 **issued the first of nearly $40 billion** Moiz Syed and Derek Willis, "Coronavirus Contracts: Tracking Federal Purchases to Fight the Coronavirus," ProPublica, May 27, 2020, https://projects.propublica.org/coronavirus-contracts/.

8 **contracts were handed out to anyone** Ryan Gabrielson and Lydia DePillis, "A Closer Look at Federal Covid Contractors Reveals Inexperience, Fraud Accusations and a Weapons Dealer Operating out of Someone's House," ProPublica, May 27, 2020, https://www.propublica.org/article/a-closer-look-at-federal-covid-contractors-reveals-inexperience-fraud-accusations-and-a-weapons-dealer-operating-out-of-someones-house.

8 **Trump lieutenants steered contracts** J. David McSwane, "Documents Show Trump Officials Skirted Rules to Reward Politically Connected and Untested Firms with Huge Pandemic Contracts," ProPublica, March 31, 2020, https://www.propublica.org/article/trump-covid-pandemic-contracts.

8 **What barriers did exist were overcome** J. David McSwane, "He Removed Labels That Said 'Medical Use Prohibited,' Then Tried to Sell Thousands of Masks to Officials Who Distribute to Hospitals," ProPublica, June 25, 2020, https://www.propublica.org/article/he-removed-labels-that-said-medical-use-prohibited-then-tried-to-sell-thousands-of-masks-to-officials-who-distribute-to-hospitals.

9 **FEMA hired a company** J. David McSwane and Ryan Gabrielson, "The Trump Administration Paid Millions for Test Tubes—and Got Unusable Mini Soda Bottles," ProPublica, June 18, 2020, https://www.propublica.org/article/the-trump-administration-paid-millions-for-test-tubes-and-got-unusable-mini-soda-bottles.

9 **buy themselves sports cars** Arnold & Porter, "Cares Act Fraud Tracker," https://www.arnoldporter.com/en/general/cares-act-fraud-tracker, accessed December 2, 2021.

9 **One man took taxpayers for more than $7 million** "Seminole County Man Charged with Covid Relief Fraud," United States Department of Justice, February 8, 2021, https://www.justice.gov/usao-mdfl/pr/seminole-county-man-charged-covid-relief-fraud.

9 **the result of massive investments** Hussain S. Lalani, Jerry Avorn, and Aaron S. Kesselheim, "US Taxpayers Heavily Funded the Discovery of Covid-19 Vaccines," *Clinical Pharmacology & Therapeutics*, 2021, https://doi.org/10.1002/cpt.2344.

10 **all to the enrichment of shareholders** Inti Pacheco, "Insiders at Covid-19 Vaccine Makers Sold Nearly $500 Million of Stock Last Year," *Wall Street Journal*, February 17, 2021, https://www.wsj.com/articles/insiders-at-covid-19-vaccine-makers-sold-nearly-500-million-of-stock-last-year-11613557801.

10   **undermined by the preexisting and profitable machinery** *The Disinformation Dozen* (London: Center for Countering Digital Hate, 2021).

10   **the pandemic economy created** Chase Peterson-Withorn, "Nearly 500 People Became Billionaires during the Pandemic Year," *Forbes,* April 6, 2021, https://www.forbes.com/sites/chasewithorn/2021/04/06/nearly-500-people-have-become-billionaires-during-the-pandemic-year/?sh=774874025c08.

10   **Overall, U.S. billionaires saw their wealth** Chuck Collins and Sarah Anderson, "Updates: Billionaire Wealth, U.S. Job Losses and Pandemic Profiteers," Inequality.org, October 20, 2021, https://inequality.org/great-divide/updates-billionaire-pandemic/.

10   **"The food supply chain is breaking"** Katie Shepherd, " 'The Food Supply Chain Is Breaking': Tyson Foods Raises Coronavirus Alarm in Full-Page Ads, Defends Safety Efforts," *Washington Post,* May 7, 2020, https://www.washingtonpost.com/nation/2020/04/27/tyson-food-supply-coronavirus/.

10   **At the same time** Katie Shepherd, "Tyson Foods Managers Had a 'Winner-Take-All' Bet on How Many Workers Would Get Covid-19, Lawsuit Alleges," *Washington Post,* November 19, 2020, https://www.washingtonpost.com/nation/2020/11/19/tyson-foods-waterloo-bets-covid/.

10   **Across the country, hundreds of meatpacking** Bernice Yeung and Michael Grabell, "After Hundreds of Meatpacking Workers Died from Covid-19, Congress Wants Answers," ProPublica, February 4, 2021, https://www.propublica.org/article/after-hundreds-of-meatpacking-workers-died-from-covid-19-congress-wants-answers.

2. "Hindsight Just Isn't What It Used to Be"

13   **about the Tea Party budget battles** Yeganeh Torbati and Isaac Arnsdorf, "How Tea Party Budget Battles Left the National Emergency Medical Stockpile Unprepared for Coronavirus," ProPublica, April 3, 2020, https://www.propublica.org/article/us-emergency-medical-stockpile-funding-unprepared-coronavirus.

14   **Even though Obamacare** Congressional Budget Office, "CBO's Analysis of the Major Health Care Legislation Enacted in March 2010 before the Subcommittee on Health Committee on Energy and Commerce U.S. House of Representatives," statement of Douglas W. Elmedorf, director, March 30, 2011.

14   **They resolved to use** Sarah A. Binder and Molly E Reynolds, "20 Years Later: The Lasting Impact of 9/11 on Congress," Brookings Institution, August 27, 2021, https://www.brookings.edu/blog/fixgov/2021/08/27/20-years-later-the-lasting-impact-of-9-11-on-congress/.

14   **decrease the national deficit** "CBO Releases Updated Estimates for the Insurance Coverage Provisions of the Affordable Care Act," Congressional Budget Office blog, March 12, 2012, https://www.cbo.gov/publication/43080.

14   **They could, however, hold the entire government** William G. Gale, Sophia Campbell, and Bill Whyman, "The Debt Ceiling: An Artificial Crisis," edited by

Paul E. Peterson and Gary Burtless, Brookings Institution, July 28, 2016, https://www.brookings.edu/on-the-record/the-debt-ceiling-an-artificial-crisis/.

15   **Originally housed under the CDC** Katherine McIntire Peters, "An Ounce of Prevention," *Government Executive,* January 17, 2012, https://www.govexec.com/magazine-2005-service-to-america-medals/magazine-2005-service-to-america-medals-homeland-s/2005/10/an-ounce-of-prevention/20318/.

15   **inspired at least in part** Judith Miller and William J. Broad, "Exercise Finds U.S. Unable to Handle Germ War Threat," *New York Times,* April 26, 1998, https://www.nytimes.com/1998/04/26/world/exercise-finds-us-unable-to-handle-germ-war-threat.html.

15   **The stockpile's earliest work** Peters, "An Ounce of Prevention."

16   **The stockpile played a small role** "How Effectively Are Federal State and Local Governments Working Together to Prepare for a Biological, Chemical or Nuclear Attack?" Hearing before the Subcommittee on Government Efficiency, Financial Management and Intergovernmental Relations, March 22, 2002.

16   **The stockpile's role would expand** Matthew Mosk, "George W. Bush in 2005: 'If We Wait for a Pandemic to Appear, It Will Be Too Late to Prepare,'" ABC News, April 5, 2005, https://abcnews.go.com/Politics/george-bush-2005-wait-pandemic-late-prepare/story?id=69979013.

16   **A fifth-generation rancher** "Congressman Danny Rehberg," House.gov, U.S. House of Representatives, n.d., http://rehberg.house.gov/index.cfm?sectionid=12¬ßiontree=3,12.

16   **he argued inside all fifty-six Montana counties** Charles S. Johnson, "Rehberg Remains True to Views," *Montana Standard,* September 27, 2010, https://mtstandard.com/news/state-and-regional/rehberg-remains-true-to-views/article_942af186-c9f5-11df-ba26-001cc4c002e0.html.

17   **"The problem with AIDS is"** Bob Anez, "Rehberg: Revival of AIDS Comment Dirty Campaigning," Associated Press, May 24, 2020.

17   **He also targeted Pell Grants** Amanda Terkel, "GOP Congressman: Pell Grants Are Becoming 'the Welfare of the 21st Century,'" *HuffPost,* December 7, 2017, https://www.huffpost.com/entry/denny-rehberg-pell-grants-welfare-21st-century_n_843712.

17   **and the free school lunch program** Evan McMorris-Santoro, "Montana GOPer Fears School Lunch Fraud Is Eating Taxpayer Money," *Talking Points Memo,* October 1, 2011, https://web.archive.org/web/20120104223550/http:/2012.talkingpointsmemo.com/2011/10/montana-gop-rep-worries-poor-people-are-bilking-the-school-lunch-program.php.

17   **The administration asked for $892 billion** *Advancing the Health, Safety, and Well-Being of Our People* (Washington, DC: U.S. Department of Health and Human Services, 2012).

17   **Tucked in there was a request** Ibid.

17   **That was about $59 million more** Ibid.

17   **Rehberg authored legislation** Yeganeh Torbati and Isaac Arnsdorf, "How Tea

Party Budget Battles Left the National Emergency Medical Stockpile Unprepared for Coronavirus," ProPublica, April 3, 2020, https://www.propublica
.org/article/us-emergency-medical-stockpile-funding-unprepared-coronavirus.

18 **The Senate offered more** Ibid.

18 **It was the first substantial cut** "National Stockpiles: Background and Issues
for Congress," 2020.

18 **the administration proposed deeper cuts** Departments of Labor, Health
and Human Services, Education, and Related Agencies Appropriations for
2013.

18 **"The budget request will allow"** Ibid.

18 **In the years to come** Chris Hamby and Sheryl Gay Stolberg, "How One Firm
Put an 'Extraordinary Burden' on the U.S.'s Troubled Stockpile," *New York
Times*, March 6, 2021, https://www.nytimes.com/2021/03/06/us/emergent
-biosolutions-anthrax-coronavirus.html.

19 **"Reduction could result in fewer people"** "Departments of Labor, Health
and Human Services, Education, and Related Agencies Appropriations for
2014," Hearings Before a Subcommittee of the Committee on Appropriations (Washington, DC: Government Printing Office, 2014).

19 **Starting in 2003** *Bioterrorism: Preparedness Varied across State and Local Jurisdictions* (Washington, DC: U.S. Government Accountability Office, 2003).

19 **In 2005, then President George W. Bush** Mosk, "George W. Bush in 2005: 'If
We Wait for a Pandemic to Appear, It Will Be Too Late to Prepare.'"

19 **His administration soon drafted** *National Strategy for Pandemic Influenza: Im-
plementation Plan* (Washington, DC: Homeland Security Council, 2006),
https://lccn.loc.gov/2006360985.

20 **called for $7.1 billion** Timothy Williams, "Bush Announces $7.1 Billion Bird
Flu Plan," *New York Times*, November 1, 2005, https://www.nytimes.com/2005
/11/01/world/americas/bush-announces-71-billion-bird-flu-plan.html.

20 **the nonpartisan Congressional Budget Office** Donald B. Marron, *A Potential
Influenza Pandemic: An Update on Possible Macroeconomic Effects and Policy Issues*
(Washington, DC: Congressional Budget Office, 2006).

20 **That report foretold** Ibid.

20 **The administration had doled out** Anna Nicholson, Scott Wollek, Benjamin
Kahn, and Jack Herrmann, *The Nation's Medical Countermeasure Stockpile: Op-
portunities to Improve the Efficiency, Effectiveness, and Sustainability of the CDC
Strategic National Stockpile: Workshop Summary* (Washington, DC: National
Academies Press, 2016).

20 **The CDC commissioned a study** *Assessing Policy Barriers to Effective Public
Health Response in the H1N1 Influenza Pandemic* (Washington, DC: ASTHO,
2010).

20 **"Delays and conflicts in federal guidance"** Ibid.

21 **"States experienced significant challenges"** Ibid.

21 **"There should be a central repository"** Ibid.

3. "We're in Deep Shit"

24 **To his left stood the dusty glass** "Surgical Mask Maker Prestige Ameritech Reborn in North Richland Hills," Prestige Ameritech, March 29, 2010, https://www.prestigeameritech.com/archived-articles.

24 **First, it belonged to Tecnol Medical Products** Ibid.

24 **On January 22, 2020, in the dim** Aaron C. Davis, "In the Early Days of the Pandemic, the U.S. Government Turned Down an Offer to Manufacture Millions of N95 Masks in America," *Washington Post,* May 11, 2020, https://www.washingtonpost.com/investigations/in-the-early-days-of-the-pandemic-the-us-government-turned-down-an-offer-to-manufacture-millions-of-n95-masks-in-america/2020/05/09/f76a821e-908a-11ea-a9c0-73b93422d691_story.html.

25 **with about a billion and a half** "Fiscal Year 2021 Budget-in-Brief," phe.gov, June 8, 2021, https://www.phe.gov/about/aspr/Pages/aspr-fy2021-bib.aspx.

27 **Later that day, January 22** Rick Bright, *Complaint of Prohibited Personnel Practice and Other Prohibited Activity by the Department of Health and Human Services Submitted by Dr. Rick Bright* (Washington, DC: Katz, Marshall & Banks LLP, 2020).

27 **He had been pleading** Ibid.

28 **He'd requested funding** Ibid.

28 **His relationship with his boss** Ibid.

28 **Kadlec, and the resources** Ibid.

28 **The virus was already hopping the globe** "Archived: WHO Timeline—Covid-19," World Health Organization, April 27, 2020, https://www.who.int/news/item/27-04-2020-who-timeline--covid-19.

28 **Bright had nudged Kadlec** Bright, *Complaint.*

28 **But Kadlec wanted to slow-play it** Ibid.

29 **He CC'd a bunch of people** Ibid.

29 **Laura Wolf, director of Critical Infrastructure** Ibid.

31 **HHS told the news site Axios** Jennifer A. Kingson, "Sparked by Coronavirus Fears, Stores Sell Out of Face Masks in Cities like Chicago and New York," Axios, January 27, 2020, https://www.axios.com/coronavirus-surgical-face-masks-america-2cdae7d0-edf4-4d29-b24e-b10f16cbcd84.html.

31 **On January 29, Navarro dispersed** Maggie Haberman, "Trade Adviser Warned White House in January of Risks of a Pandemic," *New York Times,* April 7, 2020, https://www.nytimes.com/2020/04/06/us/politics/navarro-warning-trump-coronavirus.html.

31 **Trump announced a White House task force** Rebecca Ballhaus, "Trump Announces Coronavirus Task Force," *Wall Street Journal,* January 30, 2020, https://www.wsj.com/articles/trump-announces-coronavirus-task-force-11580359187.

31 **the White House announced it would bar** "Proclamation on Suspension of Entry as Immigrants and Nonimmigrants of Persons Who Pose a Risk of Transmitting 2019 Novel Coronavirus," White House, January 31, 2020, https://trumpwhitehouse.archives.gov/presidential-actions/proclamation

-suspension-entry-immigrants-nonimmigrants-persons-pose-risk-transmitting
-2019-novel-coronavirus/.

32 **"like an eleven-year-old child"** Gabriel Sherman, " 'I Have Power': Is Steve
Bannon Running for President?" *Vanity Fair,* December 21, 2017, https://www
.vanityfair.com/news/2017/12/bannon-for-president-trump-kushner-ivanka.

33 **Bright presented to HHS and CDC officials** Bright, *Complaint.*

35 **gained fame for being wrongly suspected** Eric Lichtblau, "Scientist Officially Exonerated in Anthrax Attacks," *New York Times,* August 8, 2008, https://
www.nytimes.com/2008/08/09/washington/09anthrax.html.

36 **Bright and Navarro worked together** Bright, *Complaint.*

36 **Halt the export of N95 masks** Ibid.

4. Into a Gunfight with a Box of Tissues

39 **He downplayed the virus** Katie Cox, "President Trump Thinks Coronavirus
Will 'Miraculously' Go Away When the Weather Warms Up," WRTV, February 12, 2020, https://www.wrtv.com/news/national-politics/president-trump
-thinks-coronavirus-will-miraculously-go-away-when-the-weather-warms-up.

39 **the World Health Organization coined the name** "Naming the Coronavirus
Disease (COVID-19) and the Virus That Causes It," World Health Organization, February 11, 2020, https://www.who.int/emergencies/diseases/novel
-coronavirus-2019/technical-guidance/naming-the-coronavirus-disease
-(covid-2019)-and-the-virus-that-causes-it.

39 **He said the risk was "relatively low"** "Straight from the Source: Experts Discuss Novel Coronavirus: Aspen Ideas," Aspen Ideas Festival, February 12, 2020,
https://www.aspenideas.org/podcasts/straight-from-the-source-experts-discuss
-novel-coronavirus.

40 **"Your credibility is gone"** Ibid.

40 **"the virus is not spreading"** "CDC Update on Novel Coronavirus," Centers
for Disease Control and Prevention, February 12, 2020, https://www.cdc.gov
/media/releases/2020/t0212-cdc-telebriefing-transcript.html.

40 **had died of the disease** Erin Allday and Matt Kawahara, "First Known U.S.
Coronavirus Death Occurred on Feb. 6 in Santa Clara County," *San Francisco
Chronicle,* April 22, 2020, https://www.sfchronicle.com/health/article/First
-known-U-S-coronavirus-death-occurred-on-15217316.php.

40 **killing Americans in January** Harriet Blair Rowan and Emily DeRuy, "Exclusive:
How Did a Kansas Grandmother Just Become the First U.S. Covid Death? Not
Even Her Family Knew until This Week," *Mercury News,* September 4, 2021,
https://www.mercurynews.com/2021/09/02/exclusive-how-did-a-kansas
-grandmother-just-become-the-first-u-s-covid-death-not-even-her-family-knew
-until-this-week/.

40 **Meanwhile, HHS leaders continued to stall** Rick Bright, *Complaint of Prohib-
ited Personnel Practice and Other Prohibited Activity by the Department of Health and
Human Services Submitted by Dr. Rick Bright* (Washington, DC: Katz, Marshall
& Banks LLP, 2020).

40 **Throughout January and February** Juliet Eilperin, Jeff Stein, Desmond Butler, and Tom Hamburger, "U.S. Sent Millions of Face Masks to China Early This Year, Ignoring Pandemic Warning Signs," *Washington Post,* April 19, 2020, https://www.washingtonpost.com/health/us-sent-millions-of-face-masks-to -china-early-this-year-ignoring-pandemic-warning-signs/2020/04/18/aaccf54a -7ff5-11ea-8013-1b6da0e4a2b7_story.html.

41 **In Italy, just weeks after** Angelo Amante, "Update 2—Italy Declares Corona- virus Emergency after First Two Cases Confirmed," Reuters, January 31, 2020, https://www.reuters.com/article/china-health-italy/update-2-italy-declares -coronavirus-emergency-after-first-two-cases-confirmed-idUSL8N2A02S1.

41 **On February 23, just after 9 a.m.** "In His Own Words: Trump and the Coro- navirus," Reuters, October 2, 2020, https://www.reuters.com/article/uk -health-coronavirus-usa-trump-comments/in-his-own-words-trump-and-the -coronavirus-idUKKBN26N0VF.

41 **"The Coronavirus is very much under control"** Morgan Chalfant, "Trump Asserts Coronavirus 'Under Control' as Stocks Plunge," *The Hill,* February 24, 2020, https://thehill.com/homenews/administration/484408-trump -asserts-coronavirus-under-control-as-stocks-plunge.

41 **She warned many Americans** Tim Dickinson, "Rolling Stone Timeline: Coro- navirus in America," *Rolling Stone,* May 8, 2020, https://www.rollingstone.com /politics/politics-news/rolling-stone-timeline-coronavirus-america-982944/.

41 **the Dow Jones Industrial Average** Aimee Picchi, "Dow Drops More than 800 Points on CDC Warnings of Coronavirus Spread in U.S.," CBS News, Febru- ary 26, 2020, https://www.cbsnews.com/news/stocks-down-dow-plunges-after -mondays-rout-on-coronavirus-fears/.

41 **Trump announced he was replacing HHS secretary Azar** Adam Cancryn, Quint Forgey, and Dan Diamond, "After Fumbled Messaging, Trump Gets a Coronavirus Czar by Another Name," *Politico,* February 27, 2020, https://www .politico.com/news/2020/02/27/white-house-coronavirus-response-debbie -birx-117893.

42 **a ten-pack of the gold-standard** Megan Cerullo, "Face Mask Prices Surge as Coronavirus Fears Grow," CBS News, February 27, 2020, https://www.cbsnews .com/news/amazon-coronavirus-face-mask-price-gouging-shortages/.

42 **HHS secretary Azar told the House** Morgan Winsor and Ivan Pereira, "Coronavirus Has 'Pandemic Potential,' WHO Warns as US Ramps up Test- ing," ABC News, February 27, 2020, https://abcnews.go.com/International /latest-american-infected-coronavirus-1st-case-community-spread/story?id =69251035.

42 **Washington State announced the first known death** "CDC, Washington State Report First COVID-19 Death," Centers for Disease Control and Prevention, February 29, 2020, https://www.cdc.gov/media/releases/2020/s0229-COVID-19 -first-death.html.

42 **the federal government was working** Dan Browning, "3M Can't Confirm

Pence Comments about Making More Masks," *Star Tribune*, March 1, 2020, https://www.startribune.com/3m-can-t-confirm-pence-comments-about-making -more-masks/568354132/.

43 **The study examined more than 72,000** "The Epidemiological Characteristics of an Outbreak of 2019 Novel Coronavirus Diseases (COVID-19)—China, 2020," *China CDC Weekly* 2, no. 8 (February 17, 2020): 113–22, https://doi.org /10.46234/ccdcw2020,032.

43 **flu's overall mortality rate** Anthony S. Fauci, H. Clifford Lane, and Robert R. Redfield, "Covid-19—Navigating the Uncharted," *New England Journal of Medicine* 382, no. 13 (2020): 1268–69, https://doi.org/10.1056/nejme2002387.

43 **As of that morning** Dawn Kopecki and Berkeley Lovelace Jr., "US Coronavirus Death Toll Rises to 9, Mortality Rate of COVID-19 Rises," CNBC, March 4, 2020, https://www.cnbc.com/2020/03/03/coronavirus-latest-updates-outbreak.html.

43 **nine people and counting** "Coronavirus Daily Update, March 3: What We Know So Far about Covid-19 in the Seattle Area, Washington State and the Nation," *Seattle Times*, June 11, 2020, https://www.seattletimes.com/seattle-news /health/coronavirus-kirkland-seattle-updates-tuesday/.

43 **fifty residents and staff showing symptoms** Oscar Jimenez and Julia Jones, "A Nursing Home in the Seattle Area Is at the Center of the US Coronavirus Outbreak," CNN, March 3, 2020, https://www.cnn.com/2020/03/03/health /life-care-center-nursing-home-coronavirus/index.html.

44 **"While I am profoundly grateful"** "An Emerging Disease Threat: How the U.S. Is Responding to Covid-19, the Novel Coronavirus: The U.S. Senate Committee on Health, Education, Labor & Pensions," March 3, 2020, https://www.help.senate.gov/hearings/an-emerging-disease-threat-how-the -us-is-responding-to-covid-19-the-novel-coronavirus.

44 **Burr was something of a pandemic expert** "President Signs Into Law Senator Burr's Legislation to Defend Nation from Pandemics and Bioterrorism," Richard Burr for North Carolina, June 24, 2019, https://www.burr.senate.gov /2019/6/pahpai-signed-into-law.

44 **Long before the public knew much** Robert Faturechi and Derek Willis, "Senator Dumped up to $1.7 Million of Stock after Reassuring Public about Coronavirus Preparedness," ProPublica, March 19, 2020, https://www.propublica .org/article/senator-dumped-up-to-1-7-million-of-stock-after-reassuring-public -about-coronavirus-preparedness.

44 **But Burr had sold off** Ibid.

44 **Those holdings would have lost** Ibid.

45 **An investigation by the Securities and Exchange Commission** Robert Faturechi, "Burr's Brother-in-Law Called Stock Broker, One Minute after Getting off Phone with Senator," ProPublica, October 28, 2021, https://www.propublica .org/article/burrs-brother-in-law-called-stock-broker-one-minute-after-getting -off-phone-with-senator.

45 **According to a secret recording** Tim Mak, "Weeks before Virus Panic, Intel-

ligence Chairman Privately Raised Alarm, Sold Stocks," NPR, March 19, 2020, https://www.npr.org/2020/03/19/818192535/burr-recording-sparks-questions-about-private-comments-on-covid-19.

45 **She and her husband** Chris Joyner and Tia Mitchell, "Loeffler Reports More Stock Sales, Denies Wrongdoing," *Atlanta Journal-Constitution*, April 1, 2020, https://www.ajc.com/news/state—regional-govt—politics/loeffler-reports-more-stock-sales-amid-insider-trading-allegations/YFPDT3pChO873nuzNKa44K/.

45 **Dianne Feinstein, a Democrat** "Richard Burr and Other Senators Sold Lots of Stock as Virus Fears Started," CBS News, March 20, 2020, https://www.cbsnews.com/news/richard-burr-coronavirus-kelly-loeffler-dianne-feinstein-james-inhofe-sold-lots-of-stock-virus-fears-started/.

45 **Senator Mitt Romney, Republican of Utah** "An Emerging Disease Threat: How the U.S. Is Responding to Covid-19, the Novel Coronavirus: The U.S. Senate Committee on Health, Education, Labor & Pensions," March 3, 2020, https://www.help.senate.gov/hearings/an-emerging-disease-threat-how-the-us-is-responding-to-covid-19-the-novel-coronavirus.

46 **"Ten percent of what we need"** Ibid.

46 **The day after the hearing, Kadlec corrected** Berkeley Lovelace, "HHS Clarifies US Has about 1% of Face Masks Needed for 'Full-Blown' Coronavirus Pandemic," CNBC, March 4, 2020, https://www.cnbc.com/2020/03/04/hhs-clarifies-us-has-about-1percent-of-face-masks-needed-for-full-blown-pandemic.html.

46 **A day after the hearing** Juliet Eilperin, Jeff Stein, Desmond Butler, and Tom Hamburger, "U.S. Sent Millions of Face Masks to China Early This Year, Ignoring Pandemic Warning Signs," *Washington Post*, April 19, 2020, https://www.washingtonpost.com/health/us-sent-millions-of-face-masks-to-china-early-this-year-ignoring-pandemic-warning-signs/2020/04/18/aaccf54a-7ff5-11ea-8013-1b6da0e4a2b7_story.html.

46 **On March 11, the WHO made it official** "WHO Director-General's Opening Remarks at the Media Briefing on COVID-19—11 March 2020," World Health Organization, March 11, 2020, https://www.who.int/director-general/speeches/detail/who-director-general-s-opening-remarks-at-the-media-briefing-on-covid-19—11-march-2020.

47 **On March 13, Trump declared a national emergency** "Proclamation on Declaring a National Emergency Concerning the Novel Coronavirus Disease (COVID-19) Outbreak," White House, March 13, 2020, https://trumpwhitehouse.archives.gov/presidential-actions/proclamation-declaring-national-emergency-concerning-novel-coronavirus-disease-covid-19-outbreak/

47 **"I don't take responsibility at all"** Caitlin Oprysko, "'I Don't Take Responsibility at All': Trump Deflects Blame for Coronavirus Testing Fumble," *Politico*, March 13, 2020, https://www.politico.com/news/2020/03/13/trump-coronavirus-testing-128971.

5. "It's Like Being on eBay with Fifty Other States"

49   **the same day the CDC warned** Emma Bowman, "CDC Recommends against Gatherings of 50 or More; States Close Bars and Restaurants," NPR, March 16, 2020, https://www.npr.org/2020/03/15/816245252/cdc-recommends-suspending-gatherings-of-50-or-more-people-for-the-next-8-weeks.

50   **According to a recording** Jonathan Martin, "Trump to Governors on Ventilators: 'Try Getting It Yourselves,'" *New York Times,* March 16, 2020, https://www.nytimes.com/2020/03/16/us/politics/trump-coronavirus-respirators.html.

52   **That very day, emails show, the commissioner** Texas Department of State Health Services, "DSHS Urges Providers to Order Additional COVID-19 Vaccine as Needed," May 1, 2021, https://www.dshs.state.tx.us/news/releases/2021/20210501.aspx.

52   **the response is tiered** National Response Framework, 2019, https://www.fema.gov/sites/default/files/2020-04/NRF_FINALApproved_2011028.pdf.

54   **his own "shadow task force"** "Ethics Review Needed into Kushner Shadow Task Force," CREW: Citizens for Responsibility and Ethics in Washington, September 16, 2020, https://www.citizensforethics.org/news/press-releases/news-ethics-corruption-ethics-review-needed-kushner-shadow-task-force/.

54   **It was composed of a small network** Nicholas Confessore, Andrew Jacobs, Jodi Kantor, Zolan Kanno-youngs, and Luis Ferré-sadurní, "How Kushner's Volunteer Force Led a Fumbling Hunt for Medical Supplies," *New York Times,* May 6, 2020, https://www.nytimes.com/2020/05/05/us/jared-kushner-fema-coronavirus.html.

56   **Trump spoke first** "President Trump with Coronavirus Task Force Briefing," C-SPAN, March 23, 2020, https://www.c-span.org/video/?470599-1/president-trump-coronavirus-task-force-hold-briefing-white-house.

56   **their fumbling and the chaos** Yasmeen Abutaleb and Ashley Parker, "Kushner Coronavirus Effort Said to Be Hampered by Inexperienced Volunteers," *Washington Post,* May 5, 2020, https://www.washingtonpost.com/politics/kushner-coronavirus-effort-said-to-be-hampered-by-inexperienced-volunteers/2020/05/05/6166ef0c-8e1c-11ea-9e23-6914ee410a5f_story.html.

58   **The Kushner kids had sat on a promising lead** Confessore, Jacobs, Kantor, Kanno-youngs, and Ferré-sadurní, "How Kushner's Volunteer Force Led a Fumbling Hunt for Medical Supplies."

59   **The *New York Times*' front page carried the headline** Ben Casselman, Patricia Cohen, and Tiffany Hsu, "Job Losses Soar; U.S. Virus Cases Top World," *New York Times,* March 26, 2020, https://www.nytimes.com/2020/03/26/business/economy/coronavirus-unemployment-claims.html.

59   **Trump posted a shame tweet** Rosalind Adams, "After One Tweet to President Trump, This Man Got $69 Million from New York for Ventilators," *BuzzFeed News,* May 3, 2020, https://www.buzzfeednews.com/article/rosalindadams/after-one-tweet-to-president-trump-this-man-got-69-million.

59   **There was nothing to indicate** Ibid.

60   **Instead of waiting** "FEMA Phasing Out Project Airbridge," Federal Emergency

Management Agency, June 18, 2020, https://www.fema.gov/press-release/20210318/fema-phasing-out-project-airbridge.

61 **the project's first commercial carrier** Steve Holland, "White House–Led Airlift of Urgently Needed Medical Supplies Arrives in New York," Reuters, March 29, 2020, https://www.reuters.com/article/us-health-coronavirus-trump-airlift/white-house-led-airlift-of-urgently-needed-medical-supplies-arrives-in-new-york-idUSKBN21G0LB.

61 **"At President Trump's direction"** Ibid.

61 **states with governors loyal to Trump** Toluse Olorunnipa, Josh Dawsey, Chelsea Janes, and Isaac Stanley-Becker, "Governors Plead for Medical Equipment from Federal Stockpile Plagued by Shortages and Confusion," *Washington Post*, April 1, 2020, https://www.washingtonpost.com/politics/governors-plead-for-medical-equipment-from-federal-stockpile-plagued-by-shortages-and-confusion/2020/03/31/18aadda0-728d-11ea-87da-77a8136c1a6d_story.html.

61 **The program would be beset with allegations** Amy Brittain, Isaac Stanley-Becker, and Nick Miroff, "White House's Pandemic Relief Effort Project Airbridge Is Swathed in Secrecy and Exaggerations," *Washington Post*, May 10, 2020, https://www.washingtonpost.com/investigations/white-house-pandemic-supply-project-swathed-in-secrecy-and-exaggerations/2020/05/08/9c77efb2-8d52-11ea-a9c0-73b93422d691_story.html.

61 **New York had become the epicenter** "New York Governor Cuomo Coronavirus News Conference," C-SPAN, March 31, 2020, https://www.c-span.org/video/?470848-1/governor-cuomo-brother-chris-coronavirus.

61 **Cuomo sat down at a dais** Ibid.

61 **his state was "flying blind"** Gregory S. Schneider, Rebecca Tan, Rachel Chason, and Erin Cox, "Hogan Calls Trump Testing Claims 'Just Not True' as Region's Virus Cases Continue Surge," *Washington Post*, April 1, 2020, https://www.washingtonpost.com/local/hogan-trump-testing-claims-not-true/2020/03/31/fa9950ba-735b-11ea-87da-77a8136c1a6d_story.html.

63 **"The notion of the federal stockpile"** Aaron Blake, "Analysis: The Trump Administration Just Changed Its Description of the National Stockpile to Jibe with Jared Kushner's Controversial Claim," *Washington Post*, April 3, 2020, https://www.washingtonpost.com/politics/2020/04/03/jared-kushner-stands-trump-proceeds-offer-very-trumpian-claim-about-stockpiles/.

63 **It was a flagrant and verifiable lie** Amy Sherman, "Fact-Checking Jared Kushner's Comments on the National Stockpile," PolitiFact, April 3, 2020, https://www.politifact.com/article/2020/apr/03/fact-checking-jared-kushners-comments-national-sto/.

63 **those words were deleted** Ibid.

63 **Kushner went on to say** Allyson Chiu, "Jared Kushner's Coronavirus Briefing Debut Sparks Outcry, Confusion," *Washington Post*, April 3, 2020, https://www.washingtonpost.com/nation/2020/04/03/jared-kushner-coronavirus-briefing/.

63 **Connecticut governor Ned Lamont** Sarah Mervosh and Katie Rogers, "Governors Fight Back against Coronavirus Chaos: 'It's Like Being on eBay With

50 Other States,'" *New York Times,* March 31, 2020, https://www.nytimes.com/2020/03/31/us/governors-trump-coronavirus.html.

6. "You Might Be Buying a Ferrari"

65 **It was 5:58 p.m. on March 22** *United States of America v. Ronald Romano,* 2020.

65 **"I think we are finally at a point"** Ibid.

65 **"I want to assure the American people"** "President Trump with Coronavirus Task Force Briefing," C-SPAN, March 22, 2020, https://www.c-span.org/video/?470588-1/president-trump-coronavirus-task-force-briefing.

66 **Romano had elucidated his ambitions** *United States of America v. Ronald Romano,* 2020.

67 **"The Defense Production Act, sir"** "President Trump with Coronavirus Task Force Briefing."

67 **(While companies like General Motors)** Dartunorro Clark, "Trump Invokes Defense Production Act to Force GM to Make Ventilators for Coronavirus Fight," NBC News, March 28, 2020, https://www.nbcnews.com/politics/donald-trump/trump-invokes-defense-production-act-force-gm-make-ventilators-coronavirus-n1170746.

68 **"Trump press conference not promising"** *United States of America v. Ronald Romano,* 2020,

68 **Romano had fabricated a document** Ibid.

68 **Though the concept of using masks** Mark Wilson, "The Untold Origin Story of the N95 Mask," *Fast Company,* April 24, 2021, https://www.fastcompany.com/90479846/the-untold-origin-story-of-the-n95-mask?partner=rss&utm_source=twitter.com&utm_medium=social&utm_campaign=rss%2Bfastcompany&utm_content=rss.

68 **The female inventor of 3M's N95** Ibid.

69 **The company would begin suing** Mike Hughlett, "3M Has Investigated 4,000 Reports of N95 Fraud, Filed 18 Lawsuits," *Star Tribune,* July 17, 2020, https://www.startribune.com/3m-has-investigated-4-000-reports-of-n95-fraud-filed-18-lawsuits/571790002/.

70 **The story of his arrest** William K. Rashbaum, "A Car Salesman, a Macedonian Ex-Minister and a $45 Million Mask Scheme," *New York Times,* May 26, 2020, https://www.nytimes.com/2020/05/26/nyregion/coronavirus-fraud-masks-new-york.html.

73 **The city's first COVID death** "A COVID-19 Day of Remembrance," NYC.gov, March 14, 2021, https://www1.nyc.gov/assets/covidmemorial/.

73 **And in just two weeks** Kif Leswing, "New York City Death Toll Passes 1,000, Coronavirus Expected to Cripple US Auto Sales," CNBC, April 1, 2020, https://www.cnbc.com/2020/03/31/coronavirus-latest-updates.html.

73 **In a press briefing that day** PIX11 Web Team, "Latest Coronavirus Updates in New York: Wednesday, April 1, 2020," PIX11, April 1, 2020, https://pix11.com/news/coronavirus/latest-coronavirus-updates-in-new-york-wednesday-april-1-2020/.

74 **prompting a lawsuit from the comptroller** Luis Ferré-Sadurní, "New York's Fiscal Watchdog Sues to End Mayor's Pandemic Spending Powers," *New York Times,* July 6, 2021, https://www.nytimes.com/2021/07/06/nyregion/coronavirus-spending -nyc.html.

76 **One was a $162 million deal** Andrea Fuller and Joe Palazzolo, "Overwhelmed by Coronavirus, New York City Awards Contracts to Unproven Vendors," *Wall Street Journal,* May 6, 2020, https://www.wsj.com/articles/overwhelmed-by -coronavirus-new-york-city-awards-contracts-to-unproven-vendors-11588762803.

77 **The city's deals included an $8.3 million deal** Ibid.

7. Release the Billions

80 **Trump called him "my Peter"** David J. Lynch, Carol D. Leonnig, Jeff Stein, and Josh Dawsey, "Tactics of Fiery White House Trade Adviser Draw New Scrutiny as Some of His Pandemic Moves Unravel," *Washington Post,* September 2, 2020, https://www.washingtonpost.com/us-policy/2020/09/02/navarro -pandemic-coronavirus/.

80 **He's been described** Alan Rappeport, "Peter Navarro Invented an Expert for His Books, Based on Himself," *New York Times,* October 16, 2019. https://www .nytimes.com/2019/10/16/us/politics/peter-navarro-ron-vara.html.

80 **Navarro ran as a liberal Democrat** Carla Marinucci, "Navarro Left a Trail of Political Wreckage in California," *Politico,* April 8, 2020, https://www.politico .com/news/2020/04/08/trump-adviser-peter-navarro-california-170105.

80 **"the biggest asshole I've ever known"** Ibid.

80 **He's written thirteen "academic" books** Rappeport, "Peter Navarro In-vented an Expert for His Books, Based on Himself."

80 **When academics and reporters called him out** Ibid.

80 **He once got in an f-bomb laden screaming match** Lachlan Markay and Asawin Suebsaeng, "Trump Advisers Steve Mnuchin and Peter Navarro Got into a Profanity-Laced 'Screaming Match' on the China Trip," *Daily Beast,* May 17, 2018, https://www.thedailybeast.com/trump-advisers-steve-mnuchin -and-peter-navarro-got-into-a-profanity-laced-screaming-match-on-the-china -trip.

80 **the MIT Center for Transportation and Logistics** Stephanie Mencimer, "Peter Navarro Is the Worst Possible Person to Be in Charge of Pandemic Supplies," *Mother Jones,* April 9, 2020, https://www.motherjones.com/politics /2020/04/peter-navarro-is-the-worst-possible-person-to-be-in-charge-of -pandemic-supplies/.

81 **Navarro was waging his brand** Letter to John Polowczyk, *COVID-19 Essential Medicine Briefing Update,* March 26, 2020.

82 **He urged the president** Ibid.

82 **Throughout the month of March** J. David McSwane, "Documents Show Trump Officials Skirted Rules to Reward Politically Connected and Untested Firms with Huge Pandemic Contracts," ProPublica, March 31, 2021, https: //www.propublica.org/article/trump-covid-pandemic-contracts.

83 **Navarro used his position** James E. Clyburn, Carolyn B Maloney, Bill Foster, Raja Krishnamoorthi, Maxine Waters, Nydia M. Velázquez, and Jamie Raskin, letter to Xavier Becerra, Congress of the United States, March 30, 2021.

83 **The company, Phlow, had incorporated** McSwane, "Documents Show Trump Officials Skirted Rules to Reward Politically Connected and Untested Firms with Huge Pandemic Contracts."

83 **But its CEO, Eric Edwards** Clyburn et al., letter to Xavier Becerra.

83 **Kaleo's first epinephrine delivery device** Susan Scutti, "EpiPen Competitor Alternative Auvi-Q Returning Soon," CNN, October 27, 2016, https://www.cnn.com/2016/10/26/health/auvi-q-epinephrine-autoinjector-returns/index.html.

83 **Kaleo was also known for price gouging** Ed Silverman, "Drug Maker Upped Opioid-Overdose Antidote Price 600 Percent. Taxpayers Paid," *STAT,* November 19, 2018, https://www.statnews.com/pharmalot/2018/11/19/kaleo-opioid-antidote-price-probe/.

83 **Navarro wrote to BARDA** McSwane, "Documents Show Trump Officials Skirted Rules to Reward Politically Connected and Untested Firms with Huge Pandemic Contracts."

84 **"Phlow needs to get greenlit"** Clyburn et al., letter to Xavier Becerra.

84 **a consultant helping Phlow** Ibid.

84 **Hatfill was given office space** "Clyburn Issues Subpoena to Trump White House Advisor Dr. Steven Hatfill on Coronavirus Response," House Committee on Oversight and Reform, September 23, 2021, https://oversight.house.gov/news/press-releases/clyburn-issues-subpoena-to-trump-white-house-advisor-dr-steven-hatfill-on.

84 **He was a force** McSwane, "Documents Show Trump Officials Skirted Rules to Reward Politically Connected and Untested Firms with Huge Pandemic Contracts."

84 **At the same time Navarro and Hatfill** Clyburn et al., letter to Xavier Becerra.

88 **The single largest no-bid contract** J. David McSwane and Yeganeh Torbati, "The White House Pushed FEMA to Give Its Biggest Coronavirus Contract to a Company That Never Had to Bid," ProPublica, April 10, 2020, https://www.propublica.org/article/the-white-house-pushed-fema-to-give-its-biggest-coronavirus-contract-to-a-company-that-never-had-to-bid.

88 **the White House had taken the extraordinary step** Ibid.

89 **Navarro, who had no authority** McSwane, "Documents Show Trump Officials Skirted Rules to Reward Politically Connected and Untested Firms with Huge Pandemic Contracts."

89 **When the company announced its deal** "AirBoss Defense Group Selected by FEMA to Support the US National COVID-19 Response," GlobeNewswire News Room, AirBoss Defense Group, April 1, 2020, https://www.globenewswire.com/news-release/2020/04/01/2010317/0/en/AirBoss-Defense-Group-Selected-by-FEMA-to-Support-the-US-National-COVID-19-Response.html.

89 **The next week, the parent company's stock price** McSwane and Torbati, "The White House Pushed FEMA to Give Its Biggest Coronavirus Contract to a Company That Never Had to Bid."

89 **The company would almost triple** McSwane, "Documents Show Trump Officials Skirted Rules to Reward Politically Connected and Untested Firms with Huge Pandemic Contracts."

8. Buccaneers and Pirates

92 **another peculiar deal awarded to Zach Fuentes** Derek Willis and Yeganeh Torbati, "The Feds Gave a Former White House Official $3 Million to Supply Masks to Navajo Hospitals. Some May Not Work," ProPublica, May 22, 2020, https://www.propublica.org/article/the-feds-gave-a-former-white-house-official-3-million-to-supply-masks-to-navajo-hospitals-some-may-not-work.

92 **the company was in bankruptcy** Mark Maremont, "FEMA Cancels $55.5 Million Mask Contract with Panthera," *Wall Street Journal,* May 13, 2020, https://www.wsj.com/articles/fema-cancels-55-5-million-mask-contract-with-panthera-11589330231.

93 **The department had denied news reports** Zachary Cohen, "Veterans Affairs Denies Reports of Face Mask Shortages at Hospitals," CNN, April 11, 2020, https://www.cnn.com/2020/04/11/politics/veterans-affairs-denies-mask-shortages/index.html.

93 **In late April** Lydia DePillis, Ryan Gabrielson, J. David McSwane, Derek Willis, and Connor Sheets, "A Closer Look at Federal Covid Contractors Reveals Inexperience, Fraud Accusations and a Weapons Dealer Operating out of Someone's House," ProPublica, May 27, 2020, https://www.propublica.org/article/a-closer-look-at-federal-covid-contractors-reveals-inexperience-fraud-accusations-and-a-weapons-dealer-operating-out-of-someones-house.

95 **The *Journal* had quoted Stewart** Mark Maremont, Austen Hufford, and Tom McGinty, "U.S. Pays High Prices for Masks from Unproven Vendors in Coronavirus Fight," *Wall Street Journal,* April 18, 2020, https://www.wsj.com/articles/u-s-pays-high-prices-for-masks-from-unproven-vendors-in-coronavirus-fight-11587218400.

96 **a 1982 article** Arthur N. Turner, "Consulting Is More than Giving Advice," *Harvard Business Review,* August 1, 2014, https://hbr.org/1982/09/consulting-is-more-than-giving-advice.

97 **Famously, Robert Kraft** Kaitlin McKinley Becker, "'No Days off': Patriots' Plane Delivering over 1.7 Million N95 Masks," NBC10 Boston, April 2, 2020, https://www.nbcboston.com/news/sports/patriots/patriots-plane-bringing-medical-supplies-to-massachusetts-report/2101163/.

9. Airborne

106 **Troy King, a Republican lawyer** Kyle Whitmire, "The Immutable Weirdness of Troy King," AL.com, May 9, 2020, https://www.al.com/news/2020/05/the-immutable-weirdness-of-troy-king.html.

108 **Stewart was building his company** J. David McSwane, "How Profit and Incom-

petence Delayed N95 Masks While People Died at the VA," ProPublica, May 1, 2020, https://www.propublica.org/article/how-profit-and-incompetence -delayed-n95-masks-while-people-died-at-the-va.

109 **The grainy cell phone video** Ibid.

111 **The letter read** Ibid.

116 **he ignored my calls** Ibid.

10. History Rhymes

120 **A Brooklyn pharmacist named Joseph M. G. Tukay** "Messages for the New Year," *Democrat and Chronicle,* December 31, 1918.

120 **An advertisement printed** Ad for Miller's Antiseptic Oil, *Kansas City Times,* December 10, 1918.

120 **To the left of the snake oil** Ibid.

121 **Grove was a self-made pharmaceutical** K. C. Cronin, "Asheville History: The Legendary E.W. Grove," Explore Asheville, November 4, 2020, https://www .exploreasheville.com/stories/post/the-legendary-ew-grove/.

121 **In Nebraska, the *Omaha Daily Bee*** "Omaha Doctors Coining Money Off People's Misery," *Omaha Daily Bee,* December 13, 1918.

121 **"We are advised that fruit retailers"** *Tampa Times,* October 28, 1918.

121 **Many of the nation's grocers** *San Francisco Examiner,* December 17, 1918.

122 **By December 1919** Ibid.

122 **In West Haven, Connecticut** Dorothy Ann Pettit, "A Cruel Wind: America Experiences Pandemic Influenza, 1918–1920: A Social History" (PhD diss., University of New Hampshire, 1976), https://scholars.unh.edu/dissertation/1145.

122 **As Dorothy Ann Pettit wrote** Ibid.

122 **At one point** Bill Hogan, "The Plague," December 1, 1982, https://www .billhogan.com/1982/12/the-plague-2/.

123 **To secure coffins** Ibid.

123 **City leaders protected their people** Ibid.

123 **In both times** Becky Little, "When Mask-Wearing Rules in the 1918 Pandemic Faced Resistance," History.com, May 6, 2020, https://www.history .com/news/1918-spanish-flu-mask-wearing-resistance.

123 **people were shot and killed** Jemima McEvoy, "Killing of Georgia Cashier Is Latest in a String of Fatal Shootings over Mask-Wearing—Here Are the Rest," *Forbes,* June 15, 2021, https://www.forbes.com/sites/jemimamcevoy /2021/06/15/killing-of-georgia-cashier-is-latest-in-a-string-of-fatal-shootings -over-mask-wearing-here-are-the-rest/?sh=4601e72b764e.

123 **local officials fought with state governors** J. Alex Navarro, *The American Influenza Epidemic of 1918: A Digital Encyclopedia,* September 19, 2016, https://www .influenzaarchive.org/about.html.

123 **Theaters and restaurants** Ibid.

123 **It is remarkable that hydroxychloroquine** "Fact Check: Hydroxychloroquine Is Not the Same as Quinine and Can't Be Made at Home," Reuters, May 31,

2020, https://www.reuters.com/article/uk-factcheck-quinine/fact-check
-hydroxychloroquine-is-not-the-same-as-quinine-and-cant-be-made-at-home
-idUSKBN2370R9.

11. "Juanita Ramos Is Either a Stripper in Atlanta or a Native American Medicine Woman"

126 **"It's like stumbling into the drug business"** J. David McSwane, "The Secret, Absurd World of Coronavirus Mask Traders and Middlemen Trying to Get Rich off Government Money," ProPublica, June 1, 2020, https://www.propublica.org /article/the-secret-absurd-world-of-coronavirus-mask-traders-and-middlemen -trying-to-get-rich-off-government-money.

12. How to Make Millions Selling Masks, in Three Easy Steps!

129 **A few hours earlier** J. David McSwane, "The Secret, Absurd World of Coronavirus Mask Traders and Middlemen Trying to Get Rich off Government Money," ProPublica, June 1, 2020, https://www.propublica.org/article/the-secret-absurd -world-of-coronavirus-mask-traders-and-middlemen-trying-to-get-rich-off-govern ment-money.

130 **Just four days after the company** Ibid.

131 **VPL was incorporated by Bobby Bedi** Ibid.

131 **The N95 mask they advertised** Ibid.

132 **Long story short** Ibid.

136 **working for a company called** Ibid.

138 **The trade commission accused Cardiff** Ibid.

141 **Cardiff was, in fact, the shadow** J. David McSwane, "One Federal Agency Was Suing Him for Fraud. Another Paid His Company Millions for Masks," ProPublica, July 8, 2020, https://www.propublica.org/article/one-federal-agency -was-suing-him-for-fraud-another-paid-his-company-millions-for-masks.

141 **obtained emails that showed Cardiff** Ibid.

142 **VPL paid a Chinese manufacturer** J. David McSwane, "You Can Make Millions Selling Masks to the Government in Three Easy Steps," ProPublica, July 11, 2020, https://www.propublica.org/article/you-can-make-millions-selling -masks-to-the-government-in-three-easy-steps.

143 **His ticket to riches** Ibid.

13. "I'm Not Going to Take Any of This"

146 **Bright's complaint described egregious and destructive efforts** Rick Bright, *Complaint of Prohibited Personnel Practice and Other Prohibited Activity by the Department of Health and Human Services Submitted by Dr. Rick Bright* (Washington, DC: Katz, Marshall & Banks LLP, 2020).

146 **Bright leaked information and emails** Ibid.

146 **The 1918 influenza** Eric Adler, "A Coronavirus Lesson? How KC's Response to 1918 Flu Pandemic Caused Needless Death," *Kansas City Star,* March 17, 2020, https://www.kansascity.com/news/business/health-care/article241058181.html.

147 **The first COVID-19 death** Harriet Blair Rowan and Emily DeRuy, "Exclusive: How Did a Kansas Grandmother Just Become the First U.S. Covid Death? Not Even Her Family Knew Until This Week," *Mercury News,* September 4, 2021, https://www.mercurynews.com/2021/09/02/exclusive-how-did-a-kansas -grandmother-just-become-the-first-u-s-covid-death-not-even-her-family-knew -until-this-week/.

147 **The morning of May 14** Nicholas Florko, "Trump's HHS Fires Back at Ousted Vaccine Expert Rick Bright," *STAT,* May 14, 2020, https://www.statnews.com /2020/05/14/trump-fires-back-rick-bright/.

148 **After Eshoo called the hearing** "Rick Bright and Mike Bowen Testimony on Coronavirus Pandemic Response," C-SPAN, May 14, 2020, https://www.c-span .org/video/?471986-1/vaccine-official-rick-bright-testifies-coronavirus-pandemic -response.

148 **"I am Dr. Rick Bright"** Ibid.

150 **"I can confirm that the emails"** Ibid.

150 **Navarro in turn would tell the press** Aaron C. Davis, "In the Early Days of the Pandemic, the U.S. Government Turned Down an Offer to Manufacture Millions of N95 Masks in America," *Washington Post,* May 11, 2020, https://www .washingtonpost.com/investigations/in-the-early-days-of-the-pandemic-the -us-government-turned-down-an-offer-to-manufacture-millions-of-n95-masks -in-america/2020/05/09/f76a821e-908a-11ea-a9c0-73b93422d691_story.html.

153 **As of that day** Zamira Rahim and Adam Renton, "May 14, 2020 Coronavirus News," CNN, May 15, 2020, https://www.cnn.com/world/live-news/coronavirus -pandemic-05-14-20-intl/index.html.

14. "It Works as Hand Sanitizer, Too!"

159 **Having failed to catch the action** J. David McSwane, "He Removed Labels That Said 'Medical Use Prohibited,' Then Tried to Sell Thousands of Masks to Officials Who Distribute to Hospitals," ProPublica, June 25, 2020, https: //www.propublica.org/article/he-removed-labels-that-said-medical-use -prohibited-then-tried-to-sell-thousands-of-masks-to-officials-who-distribute -to-hospitals.

161 **He also detailed what he had paid** Ibid.

164 **The wallet was Brennan Mulligan** Ibid.

165 **Comparing Rivera's photo and TDEM's** Ibid.

166 **FEMA had agreed to pay him** J. David McSwane and Ryan Gabrielson, "The Trump Administration Paid Millions for Test Tubes—and Got Unusable Mini Soda Bottles," ProPublica, June 18, 2020, https://www.propublica.org /article/the-trump-administration-paid-millions-for-test-tubes-and-got -unusable-mini-soda-bottles.

168 **Mulligan said he was** McSwane, "He Removed Labels That Said 'Medical Use Prohibited,' Then Tried to Sell Thousands of Masks to Officials Who Distribute to Hospitals."

15. "Greg Abbott Cares About Greg Abbott"

172 **state revenues of more than $250 billion** Glenn Hegar, *State of Texas Sources of Revenue: A History of State Taxes and Fees 1972–2020* (Austin: Texas Comptroller of Public Accounts, 2020).

174 **He ordered the Texas State Guard** Greg Abbott, letter to General Gerald "Jake" Betty, April 28, 2015.

174 **attracted troubling responses from Texans** Sam Biddle, " 'I Do Not Trust Barak Obama': The Paranoid Emails of Jade Helm 15," *Gawker,* June 16, 2015, https://www.gawker.com/i-do-not-trust-barak-obama-the-paranoid-emails -of-ja-1711669400.

174 **But even the most conservative businesspeople** Christopher Hooks, "Greg Abbott's Penchant for the Path of Least Resistance Has Led Texas to the Brink of Disaster," *Texas Monthly,* July 17, 2020, https://www.texasmonthly.com /news-politics/greg-abbott-coronavirus-disaster/.

175 **He chose instead to leave** Lauren McGaughy, "Bathroom Showdown: Legislative Leaders Square Off over 'Bathroom Bill,' Threaten Special Session," *Dallas News,* August 25, 2019, https://www.dallasnews.com/news/politics/2017/05/26 /bathroom-showdown-legislative-leaders-square-off-over-bathroom-bill -threaten-special-session/.

176 **"Those of us who are seventy-plus"** Jamie Knodel, "Texas Lt. Gov. Dan Patrick Suggests He, Other Seniors Willing to Die to Get Economy Going Again," NBC News, March 24, 2020, https://www.nbcnews.com/news/us-news /texas-lt-gov-dan-patrick-suggests-he-other-seniors-willing-n1167341.

177 **His order superseded any local ordinance** Philip Jankowski, "Abbott's Coronavirus Order Nixes Austin's Enforcement of Face Mask Mandate," *Austin American-Statesman,* April 27, 2020, https://www.statesman.com/story/news /local/flash-briefing/2020/04/27/abbotts-coronavirus-order-nixes-austins -enforcement-of-face-mask-mandate/1280470007/.

178 **In late April, Patrick used the Fox News bullhorn** Alex Samuels, "Dan Patrick Says 'There Are More Important Things than Living and That's Saving This Country,' " *Texas Tribune,* April 21, 2020, https://www.texastribune.org /2020/04/21/texas-dan-patrick-economy-coronavirus/.

178 **reporters at the *Daily Beast*** Olivia Messer, "Texas Governor Admits Dangers of Reopening State on Private Call with Lawmakers," *Daily Beast,* May 6, 2020, https://www.thedailybeast.com/texas-governor-greg-abbott-admits-dangers -of-reopening-state-on-private-call-with-lawmakers.

178 **The same day Abbott's eyes-open analysis** LaVendrick Smith, "Dallas Salon Owner Jailed for Reopening in Violation of Court Order," *Dallas News,* May 6, 2020, https://www.dallasnews.com/news/courts/2020/05/05/dallas-salon -owner-ordered-to-spend-a-week-in-jail-for-keeping-salon-open/.

178 **Patrick paid her fine** Ross Ramsey, "Analysis: With a Wingman like Dan Patrick, Who Needs Critics?" *Texas Tribune,* July 2, 2020, https://www.texastribune .org/2020/07/02/dan-patrick-greg-abbott-texas-coronavirus/.

179 **Luther, by now a famous and formidable critic** Catherine Marfin, "Salon

Owner Shelley Luther Announces Run for Texas Senate Seat," *Dallas News,* August 22, 2020, https://www.dallasnews.com/news/politics/2020/08/22 /dallas-salon-owner-shelley-luther-announces-run-for-texas-senate/.

180   **Abbott opened the state ahead of infection** Julián Aguilar and Anna Novak, "Texas Attributes Record-High Coronavirus Cases to Bars, Beaches and a Data Backlog in Harris County," *Texas Tribune,* June 21, 2020, https://www .texastribune.org/2020/06/20/coronavirus-texas-cases-daily-record/.

16. "What's Your Problem, Man?"

183   **That job was yet more important** Marshall Allen, Caroline Chen, Lexi Churchill, and Isaac Arnsdorf, "Key Missteps at the CDC Have Set Back Its Ability to Detect the Potential Spread of Coronavirus," ProPublica, February 28, 2020, https://www.propublica.org/article/cdc-coronavirus-covid-19-test.

183   **Adding to our concern** J. David McSwane and Ryan Gabrielson, "The Trump Administration Paid Millions for Test Tubes—and Got Unusable Mini Soda Bottles," ProPublica, June 18, 2020, https://www.propublica.org/article/the -trump-administration-paid-millions-for-test-tubes-and-got-unusable-mini-soda -bottles.

183   **In business filings** Lydia DePillis, Ryan Gabrielson, J. David McSwane, Derek Willis, and Connor Sheets, "A Closer Look at Federal Covid Contractors Re-veals Inexperience, Fraud Accusations and a Weapons Dealer Operating out of Someone's House," ProPublica, May 27, 2020, https://www.propublica.org /article/a-closer-look-at-federal-covid-contractors-reveals-inexperience-fraud -accusations-and-a-weapons-dealer-operating-out-of-someones-house.

184   **From 2005 to 2012** Ibid.

188   **Behind him, I could see** McSwane and Gabrielson, "The Trump Administra-tion Paid Millions for Test Tubes—and Got Unusable Mini Soda Bottles."

189   **After this encounter** Ibid.

191   **As the Fillakit story gained momentum** J. David McSwane and Ryan Gabriel-son, "FEMA Ordered $10.2 Million in COVID-19 Testing Kits It's Now Warn-ing States Not to Use," ProPublica, June 26, 2020, https://www.propublica.org /article/fema-ordered-10-2-million-in-covid-19-testing-kits-its-now-warning -states-not-to-use.

17. Money for Nothing, Checks for Free

194   **that's what federal investigators say** "Seminole County Man Charged with Covid Relief Fraud," U.S. Department of Justice, February 8, 2021, https: //www.justice.gov/usao-mdfl/pr/seminole-county-man-charged-covid-relief -fraud.

194   **opened a bank account** *United States of America v. Don V. Cisternino,* U.S. Dis-trict Court, Middle District of Florida, Orlando Division, February 3, 2021.

194   **He also submitted fake payroll records** Ibid.

195   **Two days after the money was wired** Ibid.

195   **he paid $175,000 to GoDaddy.com** Gabrielle Russon, "Couple Buys Mansion

in Seminole County with Fraudulent $7.2 Million PPP Loan, Feds Say," *Orlando Sentinel,* December 23, 2020, https://www.orlandosentinel.com/business /os-bz-ppp-fraud-house-seminole-20201223-cswwnoyx4jedhbcntbpamqleb4 -story.html.

195 **news outlets reported that 3,778 Floridians had died** Dan DeLuca, "Coronavirus in Florida: What You Need to Know Monday, July 6," *Fort Myers News-Press,* July 6, 2020, http17s://www.news-press.com/story/news/coronavirus /2020/07/06/florida-coronavirus-cases-deaths-hospitalizations/5382351002/.

195 **After his indictment** HINA, "American Film Producer Don Victor Cisternino Ends Up in Remetinic Jail," *Total Croatia News,* April 14, 2021, https://www.total -croatia-news.com/news/52132-american-film-producer-ends-up-in-remetinec -jail-jutarnji-list-daily-reports.

196 **On the Gulf Coast of Florida** "Fort Myers Businessman Sentenced to Three Years in Federal Prison for Covid Relief Fraud and Mortgage Fraud," U.S. Department of Justice, July 1, 2021, https://www.justice.gov/usao-mdfl/pr /fort-myers-businessman-sentenced-three-years-federal-prison-covid-relief -fraud-and.

196 **A network of nine people** "NFL Player Charged for Role in $24 Million Covid-Relief Fraud Scheme," U.S. Department of Justice, September 10, 2020, https: //www.justice.gov/opa/pr/nfl-player-charged-role-24-million-covid-relief -fraud-scheme.

197 **Dinesh Sah sought more** "Texas Man Sentenced for $24 Million COVID-19 Relief Fraud Scheme," U.S. Department of Justice, July 28, 2021, https: //www.justice.gov/opa/pr/texas-man-sentenced-24-million-covid-19-relief -fraud-scheme.

197 **In Georgia, a reality TV personality** "Reality TV Star Sentenced for PPP Fraud and for Operating a Multimillion-Dollar Ponzi Scheme," U.S. Department of Justice, September 15, 2021, https://www.justice.gov/usao-ndga/pr /reality-tv-star-sentenced-ppp-fraud-and-operating-multimillion-dollar -ponzi-scheme.

197 **more than 120 people** "CARES Act Fraud Tracker," Arnold & Porter, October 28, 2021, https://www.arnoldporter.com/en/general/cares-act-fraud-tracker.

197 **the Justice Department had charged** "DOJ Continues to Combat COVID-19 Fraud with 'Historic' Levels of Enforcement: Enforcement Edge: Blogs," Arnold & Porter, April 2, 2021, https://www.arnoldporter.com/en/perspectives /blogs/enforcement-edge/2021/04/doj-continues-to-combat-covid-fraud.

197 **Banks focused on providing fewer big loans** Emily Flitter and Stacy Cowley, "Banks Gave Richest Clients 'Concierge Treatment' for Pandemic Aid," *New York Times,* April 23, 2020, https://www.nytimes.com/2020/04/22/business /sba-loans-ppp-coronavirus.html?action=click&module=Top+Stories&amp ;pgtype=Homepage.

198 **The nation's largest bank** Ibid.

198 **By mid-April 2020** Danielle Kurtzleben, "Small Business Emergency Relief Program Hits $349 Billion Cap in Less than 2 Weeks," NPR, April 16, 2020, https:

//www.npr.org/sections/coronavirus-live-updates/2020/04/16/835958069/small
-business-emergency-relief-program-hits-349-billion-cap-in-less-than-2-week.

198 **Yet the smallest and neediest companies** Stacy Cowley and Ella Koeze, "1
Percent of P.P.P. Borrowers Got over One-Quarter of the Loan Money," *New
York Times,* December 2, 2020, https://www.nytimes.com/2020/12/02
/business/paycheck-protection-program-coronavirus.html.

198 **The parent company** of Ruth's Chris Steak House Charity L. Scott, "Ruth's
Chris Steak House Gets $20 Million from Coronavirus Aid Program," *Wall
Street Journal,* April 17, 2020, https://www.wsj.com/articles/ruths-chris-steak
-house-gets-20-million-from-coronavirus-aid-program-11586895864.

198 **Shake Shack** "Shake Shack Provides First Quarter 2020 Preliminary Results,"
U.S. Securities and Exchange Commission, 2020.

199 **the National Community Reinvestment Coalition** Emily Flitter, "Black Business Owners Had a Harder Time Getting Federal Aid, a Study Finds," *New
York Times,* July 15, 2020, https://www.nytimes.com/2020/07/15/business
/paycheck-protection-program-bias.html.

199 **75 percent of loans** Ibid.

199 **As ProPublica reported** Lydia DePillis, "How the Pandemic Economy Could
Wipe Out a Generation of Black-Owned Businesses," ProPublica, March 4, 2021,
https://www.propublica.org/article/the-pandemics-existential-threat-to-black
-owned-businesses.

200 **businesses owned by Black people** Silvia Foster-Frau, "Racial Bias Affected
Black-Owned Small Businesses Seeking Pandemic Relief Loans, Study
Finds," *Washington Post,* October 15, 2021, https://www.washingtonpost.com
/national/ppp-bias-black-businesses/2021/10/15/b53e0822-2c4f-11ec-baf4
-d7a4e075eb90_story.html.

200 **Two companies, Blueacorn and Womply** Stacy Cowley and Ella Koeze, "How
Two Start-Ups Reaped Billions in Fees on Small Business Relief Loans," *New
York Times,* June 27, 2021, https://www.nytimes.com/2021/06/27/business/ppp
-relief-loans-blueacorn-womply.html.

200 **So, ProPublica and four other** Paul Kiel, "ProPublica Joins News Organizations in Suing for Small Business Program Loan Info," ProPublica, May 12,
2020, https://www.propublica.org/article/propublica-joins-news-organizations
-in-suing-for-small-business-program-loan-info.

201 **one fintech company had awarded** Lydia DePillis and Derek Willis, "Hundreds
of PPP Loans Went to Fake Farms in Absurd Places," ProPublica, May 18, 2021,
https://www.propublica.org/article/ppp-farms.

201 **Ocean County, New Jersey** Ibid.

202 **In New Jersey, several people** Ibid.

202 **Kabbage had processed nearly 300,000 loans** Ibid.

202 **By August 2020, the company had completed $7 billion** Ibid.

203 **According to the inspector general** Ibid.

203 **The Center for Public Integrity** Alexia Fernández Campbell, Joe Yerardi, and
Taylor Johnston, "These Companies Took $1.8 Billion in Federal Aid to Save

Jobs. They Laid off 90,000 Workers Anyway," Center for Public Integrity, December 18, 2020, https://publicintegrity.org/inequality-poverty-opportunity/covid-divide/companies-took-covid-19-aid-they-laid-off-90000-workers-anyway/.

203 **Still, more than $395 billion** Moiz Syed and Derek Willis, "Tracking PPP: Search Every Company Approved for Federal Loans," ProPublica, July 7, 2020, https://projects.propublica.org/coronavirus/bailouts/.

203 **The company popped up** Ibid.

18. Dazed and Confused

206 **She had spent years ambling about** Kristen Gould Case, "Local Color," *Park City Magazine,* October 25, 2016, https://www.parkcitymag.com/news-and-profiles/2013/06/local-color.

208 **This friend had launched a family business** "Introducing Pro Vibe Life," Pro-Vibe Life, August 3, 2020, https://provibelife.com/introducing-pro-vibe-life/.

209 **"I told my daughter"** J. David McSwane, "Cannabis, Lies and Foreign Cash: A Mother and Daughter's Journey through the Underground Mask Trade," ProPublica, August 3, 2020, https://www.propublica.org/article/cannabis-lies-and-foreign-cash-a-mother-and-daughters-journey-through-the-underground-mask-trade.

210 **The VA and FEMA deals had come** Ibid.

211 **Emails show that various representatives** Ibid.

212 **Not to mention that 3M's deal** "3M Awarded Department of Defense Contracts to Further Expand U.S. Production of N95 Respirators," 3M News Center, May 7, 2020, https://news.3m.com/3M-Awarded-Department-of-Defense-Contracts-to-Further-Expand-U-S-Production-of-N95-Respirators.

213 **Massachusetts business filings show** McSwane, "Cannabis, Lies and Foreign Cash."

19. Lucrative Lies

217 **In a faint and rusty vibrato** Fifth International Public Conference on Vaccination—Video Briefs, National Vaccine Information Center, 2020, https://www.nvic.org/nvic-video-briefs/2020-conference.aspx.

219 **As a recent study out of Europe** Paul Bertin, Kenzo Nera, and Sylvain Delouvée, "Conspiracy Beliefs, Rejection of Vaccination, and Support for Hydroxychloroquine: A Conceptual Replication-Extension in the COVID-19 Pandemic Context," *Frontiers in Psychology* 11 (September 18, 2020), https://doi.org/10.3389/fpsyg.2020.565128.

220 **he is also the founder and chairman** Keziah Weir, "How Robert F. Kennedy Jr. Became the Anti-Vaxxer Icon of America's Nightmares," *Vanity Fair,* May 13, 2021, https://www.vanityfair.com/news/2021/05/how-robert-f-kennedy-jr-became-anti-vaxxer-icon-nightmare.

220 **Kennedy collects a $255,000 a year salary** "Children's Health Defense—Form 990 for Period Ending Dec 2019," ProPublica, December 31, 2019,

https://projects.propublica.org/nonprofits/display_990/260388604
/03_2021_prefixes_23-26%2F260388604_201912_990_2021030117770223.

220 **With millions a year in donations** Will Stone, "An Anti-Vaccine Film Targeted to Black Americans Spreads False Information," Georgia Public Broad-
casting, June 8, 2021, https://www.gpb.org/news/shots-health-news/2021
/06/08/anti-vaccine-film-targeted-black-americans-spreads-false.

220 **according to an analysis** *Pandemic Profiteers: The Business of Anti-vaxx* (London: Center for Countering Digital Hate, 2021).

220 **"the flu shot is 2.4x more deadly"** Marisha Goldhamer, "Seasonal Flu Vaccines Are Safe, Needed during Covid-19 Pandemic," Fact Check, September
25, 2020, https://factcheck.afp.com/seasonal-flu-vaccines-are-safe-needed
-during-covid-19-pandemic.

221 **an osteopath named Joseph Mercola** Ibid.

221 **He oversees about 159 employees** Sheera Frenkel, "The Most Influential
Spreader of Coronavirus Misinformation Online," *New York Times,* July 24,
2021, https://www.nytimes.com/2021/07/24/technology/joseph-mercola
-coronavirus-misinformation-online.html.

221 **This network of private companies** Neena Satija and Lena H. Sun, "A Major
Funder of the Anti-Vaccine Movement Has Made Millions Selling Natural
Health Products," *Washington Post,* December 23, 2019, https://www
.washingtonpost.com/investigations/2019/10/15/fdc01078-c29c-11e9-b5e4
-54aa56d5b7ce_story.html.

221 **In the fifteen years leading up** Kim Janssen, "Accused by Feds, Sun Bed–
Selling Doctor Settles for up to $5.3 Million," *Chicago Tribune,* June 11, 2018,
http://www.chicagotribune.com/business/ct-sunbed-doc-settles-0415-biz
-20160414-story.html.

221 **He set up StopCovidCold.com** Sheera Frenkel, "Joseph Mercola Is the Most Influential Spreader of COVID-19 Misinformation Online, Researchers Say," *Balti-
more Sun,* July 25, 2021, https://www.baltimoresun.com/coronavirus/ct-aud-nw-nyt
-coronavirus-misinformation-mercola-20210725-amteliewy5dihmi6ntjnc3b4sa
-story.html.

221 **marketed and sold expensive tanning beds** Janssen, "Accused by Feds, Sun
Bed–Selling Doctor Settles for up to $5.3 Million."

221 **In 2016, Mercola settled the case** "FTC Providing Full Refunds to Mercola
Brand Tanning System Purchasers," Federal Trade Commission, April 25,
2019, https://www.ftc.gov/news-events/press-releases/2017/02/ftc-providing
-full-refunds-mercola-brand-tanning-system.

222 **In April 2020, Mercola promoted** *Pandemic Profiteers.*

222 **meme-oriented social media campaign** AAFA Community Services, "Dan-
ger! Don't Nebulize Hydrogen Peroxide and Breathe It to Try to Treat or
Prevent Covid-19," Asthma and Allergy Foundation of America, September
21, 2021, https://community.aafa.org/blog/danger-don-t-nebulize-hydrogen
-peroxide-and-breathe-it-to-try-to-treat-or-prevent-covid-19.

222 **he directly reached about 4 million people** *Pandemic Profiteers.*

222 **his empire brought in about $7 million** Ibid.

222 **would become a bestseller** Joseph Mercola, Ronnie Cummins, and Robert Francis Kennedy, *The Truth about COVID-19* (London: Somerset House, 2021).

222 **Mercola also spoke** Fifth International Public Conference on Vaccination, Video Briefs, National Vaccine Information Center, 2020, https://www.nvic .org/nvic-video-briefs/2020-conference.aspx.

222 **Erin Elizabeth** *The Disinformation Dozen: Why Platforms Must Act on Twelve Leading Online Anti-Vaxxers* (London: Center for Countering Digital Hate, 2021).

222 **"Hydroxychloroquine was more thoroughly tested"** Ibid.

222 **Married couple Ty and Charlene Bollinger** Michelle R. Smith, "Inside One Network Cashing In on Vaccine Disinformation," Associated Press, May 13, 2021, https://apnews.com/article/anti-vaccine-bollinger-coronavirus-disinformation -a7b8e1f33990670563b4c469b462c9bf.

223 **The couple claims to have sold** Ibid.

223 **Sayer Ji and Kelly Brogan** *Pandemic Profiteers.*

223 **Brogan claims to be a practitioner** Dean Sterling Jones, "Gwyneth Paltrow Doc Pushes Wacky Coronavirus Conspiracies," *Daily Beast,* March 25, 2020, https://www.thedailybeast.com/the-gwyneth-paltrow-approved-goop-doctor -pushing-wacky-coronavirus-conspiracies.

223 **In the first weeks of the pandemic** Ibid.

223 **She was among the first** Ibid.

224 **Kennedy's Children's Health Defense** Moiz Syed and Derek Willis, "Tracking PPP: Search Every Company Approved for Federal Loans," ProPublica, July 7, 2020, https://projects.propublica.org/coronavirus/bailouts/.

224 **The Bollingers applied for loans** Ibid.

224 **Brogan and her husband** Ibid.

20. Underlying Conditions

225 **Colorado State University asked me** "Webinar Series: CSU Grads on the Political Frontlines," College of Liberal Arts, Colorado State University, October 16, 2020, https://www.libarts.colostate.edu/events/webinar-series-csu-grads -on-the-political-frontlines/.

227 **A vast majority were white** Keven Ruby and Robert A. Pape, "The Capitol Rioters Aren't like Other Extremists," *The Atlantic,* February 2, 2021, https://www .theatlantic.com/ideas/archive/2021/02/the-capitol-rioters-arent-like-other -extremists/617895/.

227 **They were CEOs, salon owners, lawyers** Ibid.

227 **Many who perpetuated the "Stop the Steal" movement** Curt Devine and Drew Griffin, "How Two Anti-Government Conspiracy Theories Converged," CNN, February 5, 2021, https://www.cnn.com/2021/02/04/politics/anti-vaxxers -stop-the-steal-invs/index.html.

21. "Capitalism, Baby"

230 **By emulating spike proteins** "Understanding mRNA COVID-19 Vaccines,"
Centers for Disease Control and Prevention, November 3, 2021, https:
//www.cdc.gov/coronavirus/2019-ncov/vaccines/different-vaccines/mrna
.html.

231 **If scientists could tell cells** Damian Garde, Jonathan Saltzman, Robert J.
Walczak, Arlete A. M. Coelho-Castelo, László Dézsi, Hildur Blythman, William Belsom, Jawed Iqbal, and Ray Freebury, "The Story of mRNA: From a
Loose Idea to a Tool That May Help Curb Covid," *STAT*, January 7, 2021, https:
//www.statnews.com/2020/11/10/the-story-of-mrna-how-a-once-dismissed
-idea-became-a-leading-technology-in-the-covid-vaccine-race/.

231 **Dr. Katalin Karikó** Gina Kolata, "Kati Kariko Helped Shield the World from
the Coronavirus," *New York Times*, April 8, 2021, https://www.nytimes.com/2021
/04/08/health/coronavirus-mrna-kariko.html.

231 **By the mid-1990s** Ibid.

231 **Their immune systems were sensing treachery** Garde et al., "The Story of
mRNA."

231 **Karikó's many appeals for grant funding** Ibid.

231 **She pressed on** Elie Dolgin, "The Tangled History of mRNA Vaccines," *Nature
News*, September 14, 2021, https://www.nature.com/articles/d41586-021
-02483-w.

232 **Together the two secured about $2.3 million** Hussain S. Lalani, Jerry Avorn,
and Aaron S. Kesselheim, "US Taxpayers Heavily Funded the Discovery of
COVID-19 Vaccines," *Clinical Pharmacology & Therapeutics*, 2021, https://doi
.org/10.1002/cpt.2344.

232 **They realized that their synthetic mRNA** Ibid.

232 **Eventually they proved they could induce** Kolata, "Kati Kariko Helped
Shield the World from the Coronavirus."

232 **Could the same process be used** Ibid.

232 **They patented their method** Mario Gaviria and Burcu Kilic, "A Network
Analysis of COVID-19 mRNA Vaccine Patents," *Nature News*, May 12, 2021,
https://www.nature.com/articles/s41587-021-00912-9?sa=X&ved=2ahUKEwj5
1v7ZsJfxAhXUV3wKHQhNCHgQ9QF6BAgFEAI.

232 **That pioneering 2005 paper** Garde et al., "The Story of mRNA."

232 **In 2007, working as an assistant** Ibid.

233 **Langer's résumé boasts** Robert Langer, curriculum vitae, Langer Lab, Department of Biological Engineering, Massachusetts Institute of Technology.

233 **The three ambitious scientists managed** Arthur Allen, "For Billion-Dollar
COVID Vaccines, Basic Government-Funded Science Laid the Groundwork,"
Scientific American, November 18, 2020, https://www.scientificamerican.com
/article/for-billion-dollar-covid-vaccines-basic-government-funded-science
-laid-the-groundwork/.

233 **the founders' wealth grew by billions** Robert Frank, "New Vaccine Billionaires
Gain Wealth as Moderna and BioNTech Shares Soar," CNBC, December 9,

2020, https://www.cnbc.com/2020/12/09/new-vaccine-billionaires-gain
-wealth-as-moderna-pfizer-shares-soar-.html.

233 **scientist couple in Germany** David Gelles, "The Husband-and-Wife Team
Behind the Leading Vaccine to Solve Covid-19," *New York Times,* November 10,
2020, https://www.nytimes.com/2020/11/10/business/biontech-covid-vaccine
.html.

233 **In 2013, the company hired Karikó** Allen, "For Billion-Dollar COVID Vaccines,
Basic Government-Funded Science Laid the Groundwork."

233 **In 2016, the University of Pennsylvania** Gaviria and Kilic, "A Network Analysis of COVID-19 mRNA Vaccine Patents."

233 **that Wisconsin company would make easy money** *Patent Sublicense Agreement*
(Madison, WI: U.S. Securities and Exchange Commission, 2020).

233 **After raising more than $2 billion** Damian Garde, "Moderna's Record-Setting
IPO Dives in Its Debut," *STAT,* December 7, 2018, https://www.statnews.com
/2018/12/07/modernas-record-setting-ipo-slumps-in-its-debut/.

233 **the company was worth around $6 billion** Tom Dreisbach, "'Bad Optics' or
Something More? Moderna Executives' Stock Sales Raise Concerns," NPR,
September 4, 2020, https://www.npr.org/2020/09/04/908305074/bad-optics
-or-something-more-moderna-executives-stock-sales-raise-concerns.

233 **BioNtech also went public** "BioNTech's IPO Values It at $3.4 Billion in One
of the Largest Biotech Listings of All Time," NASDAQ, October 10, 2019,
https://www.nasdaq.com/articles/biontechs-ipo-values-it-at-%243.4-billion
-in-one-of-the-largest-biotech-listings-of-all-time.

233 **a more modest $150 million** Garde et al., "The Story of mRNA."

233 **As soon as scientists in China** "China Delayed Releasing Coronavirus Info,
Frustrating WHO," Associated Press, June 2, 2020, https://apnews.com
/article/united-nations-health-ap-top-news-virus-outbreak-public-health
-3c061794970661042b18d5aeaaed9fae.

234 **Unlike other companies** Facts First searchable database, CNN, November 9,
2020, https://www.cnn.com/factsfirst/politics/factcheck_565aa63a-4c46
-4eea-9586-093253d1bdf3.

234 **Moderna managed to design its vaccine** "Moderna Ships mRNA Vaccine Against
Novel Coronavirus (mRNA-1273) for Phase 1 Study," Moderna press release, February 24, 2020, https://investors.modernatx.com/news-releases/news-release
-details/moderna-ships-mrna-vaccine-against-novel-coronavirus-mrna-1273.

234 **it would become one of the top beneficiaries** Miriam Valverde, "How Pfizer's
and Moderna's COVID-19 Vaccines Are Tied to Operation Warp Speed,"
PolitiFact, November 19, 2020, https://www.politifact.com/article/2020
/nov/19/pfizer-moderna-covid-19-vaccines-and-operation-war/.

234 **After Congress approved the CARES Act** Stephanie Baker and Cynthia
Koons, "Inside Operation Warp Speed's $18 Billion Sprint for a Vaccine,"
Bloomberg, October 29, 2020, https://www.bloomberg.com/news/features
/2020-10-29/inside-operation-warp-speed-s-18-billion-sprint-for-a-vaccine.

234 **Moderna was given about $483 million** Kevin Stank, "Moderna Soars after Get-

ting $483 Million in Federal Funding for Coronavirus Vaccine Development,"
CNBC, April 17, 2020, https://www.cnbc.com/2020/04/17/moderna-soars-on
-483-million-in-funding-for-coronavirus-vaccine.html.

234 **the company awarded board member** *Statement of Changes in Beneficial Ownership c/o Moderna, Inc.* (Cambridge, MA: U.S. Securities and Exchange Commission, 2020).

235 **That day, Slaoui's Moderna portfolio** Rachana Pradhan, "How Pharma Money
Colors Operation Warp Speed's Quest to Defeat Covid," Kaiser Health News,
November 30, 2020, https://khn.org/news/article/how-pharma-money-colors
-operation-warp-speeds-quest-to-defeat-covid/.

235 **In that time, Moderna executives made a mint** Damian Garde, "Moderna
Executives Have Cashed Out $89M in Shares This Year," *STAT,* May 27, 2020,
https://www.statnews.com/2020/05/27/moderna-executives-cashed-out-shares
-stock-price-soared/.

235 **In July, BARDA gave Moderna another $472 million** "Moderna Announces
Expansion of BARDA Agreement to Support Larger Phase 3 Program for
Vaccine (mRNA-1273) against COVID-19," Moderna press release, July 26,
2020, https://investors.modernatx.com/news-releases/news-release-details
/moderna-announces-expansion-barda-agreement-support-larger-phase.

235 **By October 2020** Damian Garde, "Selling Stock at a Clip, Top Moderna Doctor Gets $1 Million Richer Each Week," *STAT,* January 8, 2021, https://www
.statnews.com/2020/10/13/selling-stock-like-clockwork-modernas-top-doctor
-gets-1-million-richer-every-week/.

235 **On December 18** "Moderna Announces FDA Authorization of Moderna
Covid-19 Vaccine in U.S.," Moderna press release, December 18, 2020,
https://investors.modernatx.com/news-releases/news-release-details/moderna
-announces-fda-authorization-moderna-covid-19-vaccine-us.

235 **The federal government would order 300 million doses** Operation Warp
Speed Contracts for COVID-19 Vaccines and Ancillary Vaccination Materials, 2021.

235 **By February 2021, roughly a year** Inti Pacheco, "Insiders at Covid-19 Vaccine
Makers Sold Nearly $500 Million of Stock Last Year," *Wall Street Journal,* Feb-
ruary 17, 2021, https://www.wsj.com/articles/insiders-at-covid-19-vaccine
-makers-sold-nearly-500-million-of-stock-last-year-11613557801.

235 **the company's valuation ballooned** Matthew Frankel, "Could Moderna Jus-
tify Its $129 Billion Valuation?" NASDAQ, October 16, 2021, https://www
.nasdaq.com/articles/could-moderna-justify-its-%24129-billion-valuation
-2021-10-16.

235 **Just before the stock peaked** Samanth Subramanian, "Moderna Is Buying
Back $1 Billion of Its Stock after Another Bumper Quarter," *Quartz,* August
5, 2021, https://qz.com/2043038/moderna-is-buying-back-1-billion-of-its
-stock-after-another-bumper-quarter/.

235 **cashing investors out** Nicholas Reimann, "Moderna Crash Wipes Out over
$20 Billion in Market Value after Concerns Stock Is Overhyped," *Forbes,*

August 11, 2021, https://www.forbes.com/sites/nicholasreimann/2021/08/11
/moderna-crash-wipes-out-over-20-billion-in-market-value-after-concerns
-stock-is-overhyped/?sh=6cb94d257df7.

236 **the National Institutes of Health has claimed** Bob Herman, "The NIH
Claims Joint Ownership of Moderna's Coronavirus Vaccine," *Axios,* June 25,
2020, https://www.axios.com/moderna-nih-coronavirus-vaccine-ownership
-agreements-22051c42-2dee-4b19-938d-099afd71f6a0.html.

236 **Moderna would have owed taxpayers** Samanth Subramanian, "In the Push
for New Vaccines, Taxpayers Keep Paying and Paying," *Quartz,* May 12, 2021,
https://qz.com/2006390/taxpayers-are-paying-twice-or-more-for-the-covid
-19-vaccine/.

236 **Moderna isn't the only company** Operation Warp Speed Contracts for
COVID-19 Vaccines and Ancillary Vaccination Materials, 2021.

236 **It did help that the government promised** Valverde, "How Pfizer's and
Moderna's COVID-19 Vaccines Are Tied to Operation Warp Speed."

236 **The boom in biotech and healthcare stocks** Giacomo Tognini, "Meet the 40
New Billionaires Who Got Rich Fighting Covid-19," *Forbes,* April 7, 2021,
https://www.forbes.com/sites/giacomotognini/2021/04/06/meet-the
-40-new-billionaires-who-got-rich-fighting-covid-19/?sh=25efda0f17e5.

22. The Death Pits

240 **More than 80 of his fellow residents** COVID-19 Long-Term Care Facilities
Data for Pennsylvania, Pennsylvania Department of Health, https://www
.health.pa.gov/topics/disease/coronavirus/Pages/LTCF-Data.aspx, accessed
December 2, 2021.

240 **More than 400 of them, including Gill** Ibid.

240 **Almost one in every three Americans** "State Covid-19 Data and Policy Actions," KFF, December 2, 2021, https://www.kff.org/coronavirus-covid-19
/issue-brief/state-covid-19-data-and-policy-actions/#longtermcare.

240 **"death pits"** Farah Stockman, Matt Richtel, Danielle Ivory, and Mitch Smith,
"'They're Death Pits': Virus Claims at Least 7,000 Lives in U.S. Nursing
Homes," *New York Times,* April 17, 2020, https://www.nytimes.com/2020/04/17
/us/coronavirus-nursing-homes.html.

240 **Nursing homes are a highly profitable business** Dylan Scott, "Private Equity
Ownership Is Killing People at Nursing Homes," *Vox,* February 22, 2021,
https://www.vox.com/policy-and-politics/22295461/nursing-home-deaths
-private-equity-firms.

241 **Numerous studies have shown** Joshua M. Wiener and Charlene Harrington,
"Key Issues in Long-Term Services and Supports Quality," KFF, October 28,
2017, https://www.kff.org/medicaid/issue-brief/key-issues-in-long-term-services
-and-supports-quality/.

241 **About 70 percent of all U.S. nursing homes** Atul Gupta, Sabrina Howell,
Constantine Yannelis, and Abhinav Gupta, "Does Private Equity Investment

in Healthcare Benefit Patients? Evidence from Nursing Homes," working paper, National Bureau of Economic Research, February 2021, https://doi .org/10.3386/w28474.

241 **One 2020 study examined** Atul Gupta, Sabrina Howell, Constantine Yannelis, and Abhinav Gupta, "Does Private Equity Investment in Healthcare Benefit Patients? Evidence from Nursing Homes," *SSRN Electronic Journal,* 2020, https://doi.org/10.2139/ssrn.3537612.

241 **That study, commissioned by the federal government** Atul Gupta, Sabrina Howell, Constantine Yannelis, and Abhinav Gupta, "Does Private Equity Investment in Healthcare Benefit Patients? Evidence from Nursing Homes," working paper, National Bureau of Economic Research, February 2021, https://doi.org/10.3386/w28474.

242 **In early 2019** Beaver, PA: Centers for Medicare & Medicaid Services, 2019.

242 **CMS cited the facility** Lena V. Groeger and Charles Orenstein, "Nursing Home Inspect," ProPublica, March 17, 2017, https://projects.propublica.org /nursing-homes.

243 **In December 2019, the Pennsylvania Department of Health** COVID-19 Long-Term Care Facilities Data for Pennsylvania, Pennsylvania Department of Health, https://www.health.pa.gov/topics/disease/coronavirus/Pages/LTCF -Data.aspx, accessed December 2, 2021.

243 **On March 22** Daveen Rae Kurutz, "Brighton Rehab Medical Director Sounded Alarm on PPE, Testing Needs in Late March," *Beaver County Times,* April 1, 2020, https://www.timesonline.com/story/news/coronavirus/2020 /04/01/brighton-rehab-medical-director-sounded/1419409007/.

244 **hydroxychloroquine, which the president had been touting** Sean D. Hamill, "State Report: Brighton Knew It Didn't Have State OK to Use Experimental Drug on Residents," *Pittsburgh Post-Gazette,* November 25, 2021, https://www .post-gazette.com/news/health/2020/07/28/Brighton-Rehab-Wellness-knew -didnt-have-Pennsylvania-OK-experimental-drug-residents-hydroxychloroquine -inspection/stories/202007280157.

245 **On April 16, local news outlets reported** Nicole Ford, "Beaver County Ice Rink Refrozen for Contingency Morgue but Officials Say That Would Be 'Worst -Case Scenario,' " CBS Pittsburgh, April 16, 2020, https://pittsburgh.cbslocal .com/2020/04/16/bradys-run-park-ice-arena-refrozen-coronavirus-bodies/.

245 **By the second week of May** Sean D. Hamill, "National Guard Arrives to Help Beaver County Nursing Home Battling Covid-19 Outbreak," *Pittsburgh Post-Gazette,* May 10, 2020, https://www.post-gazette.com/news/health/2020/05/10 /National-Guard-help-Beaver-County-nursing-home-Brighton-Wellness -COVID-19/stories/202005100104.

246 **She and a dozen other families** *Jodi Gill et. al v. Comprehensive Healthcare Management Services LLC,* U.S. District Court for the Western District of Pennsylvania, November 12, 2020.

246 **the facility's management was slow** Ibid.

246 **Even after burying his mother** Ibid.

247 **A five-month investigation** Sean D. Hamill, "Brighton's Plight," *Pittsburgh Post-Gazette,* November 15, 2020, https://newsinteractive.post-gazette.com /brighton/.

247 **the company had significantly cut** Ibid.

247 **the company made upgrades** Ibid.

247 **By 2018, the company had increased** Ibid.

247 **The company pockets yet more money** Ibid.

248 **The Brighton facility alone** Ibid.

248 **When the Trump administration set up** Jonathan D. Silver and Joel Jacobs, "How a Federal Program Created to Reward Nursing Homes for Saving Lives Doled Out Millions To Some of Pa.'s Most Troubled Facilities," *Pittsburgh Post-Gazette,* February 14, 2021, https://www.post-gazette.com/news/covid-19 /2021/02/14/COVID-19-pandemic-Pennsylvania-nursing-homes/stories /202102140060.

23. A Pirate Walks the Plank

250 **The first count** J. David McSwane, "Contractor Who Was Awarded $34.5 Million in Government Money and Provided Zero Masks Pleads Guilty to Fraud," ProPublica, February 3, 2021, https://www.propublica.org/article /contractor-masks-guilty-plea.

250 **The second count** *United States of America v. Robert S. Stewart Jr.,* U.S. District Court for the Eastern District of Virginia, Alexandria Division, February 2021.

252 **Longtime friends of Stewart** Ibid.

Epilogue

257 **70 percent of eligible Americans** Shannon Pettypiece, "Biden Pushes Americans to Reach Goal of 70 Percent Vaccinated Adults by July 4," NBCNews.com, June 3, 2021, https://www.nbcnews.com/politics/white-house/biden-pushes -americans-reach-goal-70-percent-vaccinated-adults-july-n1269397.

257 **"Post-pandemic rise in sexually transmitted diseases"** Lauren Dunn, "Post-Pandemic Rise in Sexually Transmitted Diseases Imminent, Experts Warn," NBCNews.com, July 6, 2021, https://www.nbcnews.com/health/sexual-health /post-pandemic-rise-sexually-transmitted-diseases-imminent-experts-warn -n1271996.

259 **the Delta variant was first identified** Kathy Katella, "5 Things to Know about the Delta Variant," Yale Medicine, Yale University, December 10, 2021. https://www.yalemedicine.org/news/5-things-to-know-delta-variant-covid.

259 **40 percent of Texans** Texas Tribune Staff, "40% Of Texans Are Fully Vaccinated as Daily Covid Deaths Drop to Lowest Point in More than a Year," ABC13 Houston, KTRK-TV, June 26, 2021. https://abc13.com/covid19-vaccine -coronavirus-numbers-texas-how-many-texans-are-vaccinated-hospitalizations /10834845/.

259 **ripping through a Texas prison** Katie Camero, "Covid Outbreak in Texas Prison Reveals Delta Variant's Wrath. Did Vaccines Help?," *Fort Worth Star Telegram*, September 22, 2021, https://www.star-telegram.com/news/corona virus/article254435113.html.

260 **Kansans of the year** "2020 Distinguished Kansans Worked to Help Others in Difficult Year," *Topeka Capital-Journal*, December 31, 2020, https://www.cj online.com/story/news/2020/12/30/many-helped-others-2020-here-our -distinguished-kansans/4056091001/.

INDEX

FEMA (Federal Emergency
Management Agency) (cont.)
  Prestige Ameritech contract with,
  151
  Project Airbridge and, 60
  Stewart, Robert Jr. and, 211
Fillakit LLC, 182–183. See also Wexler,
  Paul
  FEMA's acceptance of test kits,
  190–191
  inquiries into, 191
  ownership, 183
  profits, 191
  sterilization of vials, 188
  testing media rejected by labs, 190
  test tubes of, 185–186
  unsanitary conditions and, 189
  visit to warehouse of, 181–182,
  186–189
  working conditions at, 189–190
Financial Crimes and Public
  Corruption, 251
fintech, Paycheck Protection Program
  (PPP) loans and, 199–200,
  201–203
Fitzpatrick, William, 253–254
5G conspiracy, 219, 220
Flagship Pioneering, 237
Florida
  Cisternino's mansion in, 193–194
  Fillakit LLC and, 183, 184
  Global Medical Supply Group LLC
  in, 77
  PPP fraud schemes, 196, 201
flu shot, 220
Food and Drug Administration. See
  FDA (Food and Drug
  Administration)
food pirates, during the Great
  Influenza, 121–122
food supply chain, Tyson Foods and,
  10
Forbes magazine, 236
Ford (company), 59, 152

forgivable loans, 194, 196, 201, 224. See
  also loans; Paycheck Protection
  Program (PPP) loans
for-profit nursing homes, 241
Fowler, William, 123
Freedom of Information Act, 8, 41, 46,
  191, 200
free school lunch program, 17
Fruman, Igor, 209
Fuentes, Zach, 92
funeral costs, 122

G

Gabrielson, Ryan, 182, 184, 186, 190
Garde, Damien, 235
Gates, Bill, 219, 220
General Motors, 59, 67, 152
Georgia, 103, 107, 114, 197
Gilead Sciences, 82
Gill, Glenn Oscar, 239–240, 243,
  244–246
Gill, Jodi, 239–240, 242, 243–246
Gingrich, Newt, 80
Giuliani, Rudy, 209
Global Medical Supply Group LLC, 77
Government Accountability Office, 19
Granger, Kay, 25
Great Influenza (Spanish flu), 119–123,
  146–147
Green, Teresa, 189, 190
Grove, Edwin Wiley, 120–121
Guthrie, Brett, 152–153

H

H1N1 "swine flu" epidemic (2009), 17,
  20, 30, 51, 119
hand sanitizer, price gouging, 3–4
Harris, Kamala, 234
Harvard Business Review, 96
Hasan, Bassam "Sam," 167–168
Hassel, Christian, 51
Hatfill, Steven, 35, 82, 84, 88–89
Health and Human Services
  Commission, 172

counterfeits, 69

counterfeits/fraudulent, 69

design on, 68–69

found at Home Depot, 33

Kadlec entertaining solicitation
about, 47

price of, 42

proof of life videos and, 110, 125–126

Romano, Ronald and, 66–68, 70

Stewart, Robert Jr. and, 3, 4, 5, 211

Three Percenters, 227

Three Seconds Until Midnight (Hatfill),
35, 82

Tokarz, Bernie, 76–77

transgender students, Texas "bathroom
bill" and, 174

Treasury Department, 198

treatment
anthrax, 7, 18–19

during the Great Influenza, 120–121

hydrogen peroxide, 221–222

of Trump, 225–226

Trump, Donald/Trump administration
Abbott, Greg and, 174

Bannon, Steve and, 32

belated action by, 8

Bowen, Mike on, 32

CARES Act and, 86

conference call with governors, 50

conspiracist ideologies during, 219

downplaying threat of coronavirus,
39, 41

hydroxychloroquine and, 123

January 6th insurrection and,
227–228

misleading the public, 42

Navarro, Peter and, 31, 80

Navarro's memo to, March 1, 2020,
81–82

receiving treatment for COVID,
225–226

Slaoui, Moncef and, 234–235

spending to address the Covid
pandemic, 2

on testing, 47

on war against COVID-19, 65–66

The Truth About COVID-19 (Mercola),
222

"The Truth About Vaccines 2020,"
222–223

TTAC Publishing, 224

Tukay, Joseph M.G., 120

Türeci, Özlem, 233

Twitter, 125, 126, 128, 223

Tyson Foods, 10

U

UDECM, 214

unemployment, 11, 59, 258

University of Pennsylvania, 231–232,
233

unvaccinated people, 261. *See also* anti-
vaccination industry/propaganda

U.S. Department of Health and
Human Services (HHS), 15. *See
also* BARDA (Biomedical
Advanced Research and
Development Authority); Centers
for Disease Control and
Prevention (CDC); Kadlec, Robert;
Strategic National Stockpile
about, 15

Bright, Rick and, 27, 28

Bright's complaints about, 146, 150

COVID spending by, 87

Department of Defense and, 49–51

Disaster Leadership Group and, 28

hydroxychloroquine and, 146

Indian Health Service, 92

on mask supply, 31, 33–34

media message about masks, 34, 42

Navarro requesting increased
funding for, 82

Obama administration budget
request for, 17

Obamacare and, 14

PPE supplies to China and, 40–41

VPL Medical and, 130, 140, 143

ABOUT THE AUTHOR

J. DAVID McSWANE is a reporter in ProPublica's Washington, D.C., office. Previously, he was an investigative reporter for the *Dallas Morning News* and the *Austin-American Statesman*. McSwane's reporting has spurred new laws and state and federal criminal investigations; forced belt-tightening lawmakers to invest in social programs; and won awards including Harvard's Goldsmith Prize for Investigative Reporting, the Worth Bingham Prize, a Scripps Howard award, an IRE award, and the Peabody.